PRAY WITH US

PRAY WITH US

A SAINT FOR EVERY DAY

BELINDA TERRO MOONEY

Our Sunday Visitor
Huntington, Indiana

Nihil Obstat
Msgr. Michael Heintz, Ph.D.
Censor Librorum

Imprimatur
✠ Kevin C. Rhoades
Bishop of Fort Wayne-South Bend
June 18, 2024

The *Nihil Obstat* and *Imprimatur* are official declarations that a book is free from doctrinal or moral error. It is not implied that those who have granted the *Nihil Obstat* and *Imprimatur* agree with the contents, opinions, or statements expressed.

Our Sunday Visitor Publishing Division
Our Sunday Visitor, Inc.
200 Noll Plaza
Huntington, IN 46750
www.osv.com
1-800-348-2440

ISBN: 978-1-63966-210-4 (Inventory No. T2901)
1. RELIGION—Christianity—Saints & Sainthood.
2. RELIGION—Christian Living—Prayer.
3. RELIGION—Christianity—Catholic.
eISBN: 978-1-63966-211-1
LCCN: 2024943847

Cover design: Tyler Ottinger
Interior design: Amanda Falk
Cover and interior art: AdobeStock

PRINTED IN THE UNITED STATES OF AMERICA

This book is dedicated to all the saints throughout history who inspire and encourage us with their witness and courage, and to all my children.

And those who are wise shall shine like the brightness
of the sky above; and those who turn many to
righteousness, like the stars forever and ever.

— Daniel 12:3

Cling to the saints, for those who cling
to them will be sanctified.

— Pope Clement I, Epistle to the Corinthians

Contents

Foreword *by Mike Aquilina*   9

Introduction   11

January: The Month of the Holy Name of Jesus   17

February: The Month of the Passion of Our Lord   51

March: The Month of Saint Joseph   83

April: The Month of the Resurrection of Jesus   117

May: The Month of the Blessed Virgin Mary   149

June: The Month of the Sacred Heart of Jesus   183

July: The Month of the Precious Blood of Jesus   215

August: The Month of the Assumption of Mary   249

September: The Month of the Seven Sorrows of Mary   283

October: The Month of the Holy Rosary   315

November: The Month of the Souls in Purgatory   349

December: The Month of the Immaculate Conception   381

Epilogue   413

Acknowledgments   415

Calendar of Saints   417

Works Cited   423

Foreword

The Church forms us in many different ways, and the calendar is one of the most important.

Think about it. Most people, through most of history, couldn't read. So they didn't learn the Faith from catechisms. There were no catechisms, and there was no technology to mass-produce such books. And again, very few people could read anyway. But they learned the Faith, and they passed it along to their children, through the celebration of the feasts. They did what this book asks all of us to do.

I remember reading that, in antiquity, when a Jewish boy read from the Torah for the first time, his rabbi would stick a spoonful of honey in his mouth — so the Law would always be a sweet memory. Well, that's what the feasts do for us. They make the Faith memorable, and they make it sweet.

We see the beginnings of a Christian calendar emerging already in the New Testament, and the Church was already observing the "birthdays" of the martyrs in the second century. We want to be like those early Christians. Theirs were the generations that converted the world, in spite of intense persecutions.

Still today, the liturgy adds another dimension to life, and it does this by enhancing otherwise ordinary days. The Christian calendar gives a certain momentum to spiritual life, and you can feel the difference it makes. One season presses us to the next; each season resolves the dramatic suspense of the last; and every season is steeped in the mysteries of Jesus Christ and the lives of His saints. There are no dull days when you're walking in their company and meditating on their accomplishments.

If you stay tuned to the calendar, you're growing deeper in your knowledge of history, theology, and culture. If you pay attention to the feasts, you'll open yourself up to treasures of art, music, and poetry. Life in this world is so much richer when lived in light of eternity.

I am grateful to Belinda Mooney for helping us all as we hand on the Faith to our children and grandchildren. May we succeed, with the prayerful support of the saints, as our most ancient ancestors did.

Mike Aquilina
April 2024

Introduction

Jesus encouraged us to be united in prayer when He said, "For where two or three are gathered in my name, there am I among them" (Mt 18:20). He invited us to pray with one other in His name and promised that He would be with us when we do.

The *Catechism of the Catholic Church* defines the communion of saints as "the unity in Christ of all the redeemed, those on earth and those who have died." This beautiful doctrine teaches that we can pray with those here on earth in the Church Militant, we pray for those in purgatory in the Church Suffering, and we receive the support of prayer from those in heaven in the Church Triumphant. It is a good and holy thing to ask people to pray *for* us and to pray *with* us — both those with us here on earth and those in heaven.

Following Jesus' example, our brothers and sisters in heaven pray for us continually. Before the face of God, they make intercession for us with Jesus, who "lives to make intercession for [us]" (Heb 7:25). Jesus' whole mission on earth was to bring us to His Father. He made reparation for our sins and thus restored our relationship to our Father. Everything He did was His Father's work. Jesus still intercedes for us in heaven, and the saints follow Him in this prayer. Indeed, the power of their prayers is inestimable and unfathomable.

The saints in heaven are particularly powerful in their prayers because they have completed their time on earth and are already enjoying eternity with God in heaven. The Church teaches, "Being more closely united to Christ, those who dwell in heaven fix the whole Church more firmly in holiness. ... [T]hey do not cease to intercede with the Father for us, as they proffer the merits which they acquired on earth through the one mediator between God and men, Christ Jesus. ... So by their fraternal concern is our weakness greatly helped" (CCC 956).

We celebrate many saints every single day of the year, and each feast day is an opportunity to spend time with the saint, joining in prayer and interceding with and praising God together. As Catholics, we should regularly ask the saints to pray for our intentions — for us, our families, and the needs of others. In this book, we will also focus on developing the habit of asking the saints to pray *with* us, much as we might grab the hands of a friend here and pray to God together. In this book, during the prayers for each day, we will be spiritually holding the saints' hands, asking them to enter into our prayer and to let us enter their pure prayer before God. This way of praying has borne incredible fruit in my life, and I have experienced firsthand the power of this unified intercessory prayer. I hope that, through this book, you will too!

Several years ago, I was privileged to visit the incorrupt body of Saint Bernadette in Nevers, France. I had loved Saint Bernadette since I was a child and watched the movie *The Song of Bernadette*. I always wanted to see her incorrupt body, and now at last there I was at her glass coffin. I was so excited to kneel there and give her all the things I needed her to ask God for on my behalf. Yet when I started saying, "Saint Bernadette please pray for my family, friends, etc.," I heard very clearly in my heart, "Tell Him." Startled, I looked around, not knowing what she meant. Then I realized that the tabernacle containing the Blessed Sacrament was close by, and I understood that she was asking me to speak directly to God and that *she would be praying with me*. I cannot express how wonderful it was to talk to Jesus and know that my dear sister was praying alongside me as I prayed, and I was praying with her as she prayed. Jesus' promise, "Where two or three are gathered in my name ..." became absolutely real for me at that moment.

As we enter into prayer with the saints before the Holy Face of Jesus, we grow closer to the Most Holy Trinity. It is also a daily opportunity to grow in friendship with the different saints and to ask them to help us grow deeper in our relationship with the Father, Son, and Holy Spirit. The *Catechism* encourages this kind of union with the saints, saying:

> It is not merely by the title of example that we cherish the memory of those in heaven; we seek, rather, that by this devotion to the exercise of fraternal charity the union of the whole Church in the Spirit may be strengthened. Exactly as Christian communion among our fellow pilgrims brings us closer to Christ, so our communion with the saints joins us to Christ, from whom as from its fountain and head issues all grace, and the life of the People of God itself. (957)

After uniting our prayers here on earth with the saints' pure prayers before our Father in heaven, we can surrender the outcome to God, knowing that the saints will always help us to intercede effectively for ourselves and others. Indeed, Mother Mary, Saint Joseph, and all the saints in heaven are incredibly powerful prayer warriors. Whether God answers our prayer in the way we hope or in a different way, when the saints pray with us, we are better able to accept His will, knowing He always does what is most loving for us. With the help of the saints and the support of their prayers, even when the outcome is different than what we prayed for, we can say, "Yes, His will is best," and we can rest in it.

I pray that this book will help you develop a consistent prayer life with the saints on their feast days. Its simple format can be used by families, individual laypeople, priests, and religious. The book contains stories of 365 people whom the Church has designated Saint, Blessed, Venerable, or Servant of God — one for each day of the year. Some are the same as those featured on the Church calendar. Some are other, less well-known saints who share that feast day. At the end of this book, I have also included a Calendar of the Saints for quick reference.

I hope you will love the saints contained in this book. I surely do. Please know that I have prayed and will continue to pray with the saints on their feast days for all who use this book. May the witness, the prayers, and the love of the saints bring us ever closer to God.

JANUARY

THE MONTH OF
THE HOLY NAME OF JESUS

JANUARY 1

Mary, Mother of God

From the moment Mary gave her *fiat*, "let it be to me according to your word" (Lk 1:38), she became the *Theotokos*, or "God-bearer." Her title as the Mother of God, which was officially proclaimed and confirmed by the Church at the Council of Ephesus in 431, declares that all her graces proceed from her divine maternity. As Saint Thomas Aquinas said, "The Blessed Virgin, from the fact that she is the Mother of God ... has a certain infinite dignity from the Infinite Good, which is God." Because she is mother of the Head of the Church, she is also the mother of the Church (the Body of Christ) and queen of all the saints.

PRAYER

Mary, you are the mother of God and, by His grace, our mother too. Pray for us and with us on this feast day, teaching us to pray with a generous trust like yours: Dear Father, give us the virtues Mary exemplified so perfectly. Inspire us to imitate her in every way possible to become your holy children and strong witnesses. Fill us with the Holy Spirit, her divine spouse. Conform our thoughts, words, and lives to Jesus, her Son, in total surrender to you. Purify our hearts and minds. Grant us the grace to live an ordered life with an undivided heart, consenting to all you ask of us, as modeled by your holy mother. Guide us to find and fulfill our vocations and the work you set before us. Confirm us in love and make us saints. We ask this in the name of Jesus. Amen.

JANUARY 2

Saints Basil the Great (329–379) and Gregory of Nazianzus (329–390)

Saints Basil and Gregory were great friends who encouraged and challenged each other in striving to be holy. Saint Basil wrote many letters and works and is known as the Father of Eastern Monasticism. The monastic Rule he wrote structures prayer, study, and work. Saint Gregory, also a prolific writer, composed poems and many theological works, earning him the honorific "The Theologian." He once wrote, "It is necessary to remember God more often than one breathes." Both men were monks who became bishops and fought the Arian heresy (which taught that Jesus was not divine). These Doctors of the Church, together with Saint Gregory of Nyssa, are called the Cappadocian Fathers. Saint Basil is a patron saint of Russia, and Gregory of poets and theologians.

PRAYER

Saints Basil and Gregory, your lives and work show us what it means to seek true wisdom. On your feast day, we pray with you in confidence: Loving Father, grant us the virtue of charity and move us to strive to grow in all virtues. Inspire us to learn the Faith through study. Teach us how to seek out holy, faith-filled friendships, and bless our families, making them true domestic churches. Make us great communicators and encouragers. Bless our bishops, making them true shepherds and virtuous leaders. Bless all who follow the Rule of Saint Basil and keep them faithful to you. We ask this in the name of Jesus. Amen.

JANUARY 3

Saint Genevieve (c. 422–512)

Saint Genevieve grew up near Paris, and, as a little girl of seven, she longed to give herself to God. She was encouraged by the bishop Saint Germain of Auxerre to practice virtue, and, when she was fifteen, she finally consecrated herself to God. She had the gifts of prophecy and visions and was persecuted by people who thought she was a fraud. Yet in 451, she confidently prophesied that Attila the Hun would not attack Paris, and the people followed her leadership and did not flee. The Huns did not attack. Another time, the people asked her intercession to save the city from an epidemic, and it was saved. Her Christian witness was so strong that it impacted even pagan kings. Saint Genevieve is the patron saint of Paris, France.

PRAYER

Saint Genevieve, you loved the Lord with an undivided heart, and you show us how we should love and trust in God. On your feast day, we ask you to pray for us and with us: Gracious Father, help us to hear your voice in our daily prayer time and to be conscious of your presence as we go about our daily duties. Assist us in striving for virtue, especially the virtues Saint Genevieve exemplified — piety, leadership, courage, and confidence in you. Grant that we might be strong witnesses of our faith to others who do not yet know you. Fortify us to endure persecution for love of you and the work you ask us to do. We ask this in the name of Jesus. Amen.

JANUARY 4

Saint Elizabeth Ann Seton (1774–1821)

Born into a wealthy Episcopalian family in New York, Saint Elizabeth married well but was widowed at a young age. After her husband's death, she converted to Catholicism and was abandoned by her family, leaving her to raise her five children alone. She was devoted to Jesus in the Blessed Sacrament and tried hard to follow His will, founding Catholic schools, orphanages, and even a religious order: the Daughters of Charity of Saint Joseph. She once said, "The first end I propose in our daily work is to do the will of God; secondly, to do it in the manner he wills it; and thirdly, to do it because it is his will." She is the first natural-born citizen of the United States to be declared a saint and is the patron of converts, Catholic schools, widows, and persons whose parents have died.

PRAYER

Saint Elizabeth Ann Seton, your trust in God even in the most difficult trials inspires us. United with you, we turn in confidence to God, praying: Merciful Father, through the intercession of Saint Elizabeth, inspire us to surrender to your will as she did. Help us to remain steadfast in the face of loss, rejection, and seemingly impossible challenges. Increase our love for and trust in the Blessed Sacrament. Guide mothers and fathers to be loving and patient with their children. Assist all Catholic schools, homeschools, and universities in teaching the truth, and guide children to a deep love of learning. Bless the Daughters of Charity, keeping them faithful to you. We ask this in the name of Jesus. Amen.

JANUARY 5

Saint John Neumann (1811–1860)

Saint John Neumann came to America from Bohemia (Czech Republic) to become the first priest in the United States ordained as a Redemptorist priest. As fourth bishop of Philadelphia, he worked with focus and diligence to build fifty churches while increasing the number of Catholic schools in his diocese to over one hundred. He also brought the Forty Hours Devotion to America. Neumann established fruitful ministries to German immigrants and the poor. He is the patron of Catholic education, immigrants, and sick children. Pope Saint Paul VI said of him, "He was close to the sick, he loved to be with the poor, he was a friend of sinners, and now he is the glory of all immigrants."

PRAYER

Saint John Neumann, pray for us to give our lives to the service of God, as you did. On your feast day, we pray with you: Dear Father, through the intercession of Saint John Neumann, give us the virtues we need to carry out your work with zeal. Inspire us to adore you in adoration with faith and confidence. Guide all Catholic educators, including parents, as they teach the Faith to your littlest ones, that they may serve Christ. Teach us how to encourage and assist immigrants. Make bishops, priests, and deacons virtuous leaders with holy, fruitful ministries. Bless all children who are sick. We ask this in the name of Jesus. Amen.

JANUARY 6

Saint André Bessette (1845–1937)

Saint André had a hard time as a child, but he did not give up! He lost both parents and was sick much of the time, but he found strength in following God's will. He joined the Congregation of the Holy Cross in Montreal, Canada, serving as doorkeeper at the College of Notre Dame. He once quipped, "When I joined this community, the superiors showed me the door, and I remained forty years." Known as the miracle-worker of Montreal, André had the gift of healing through the intercession of Saint Joseph, of whom he said, "It is Saint Joseph who cures. I am just his little dog." For fifty years, he worked to build Saint Joseph's Oratory on Mount Royal, which is now a place of pilgrimage.

PRAYER

Saint André Bessette, you were a model of humility and faithfulness. We ask you to pray for us and with us on your feast day: Loving Father, through the intercession of Saint Andre, enable us to grow in the virtues of humility, humor, and determination. May we find our strength in doing your will. Heal us and allow us to help you heal others. Grant us the determination to finish what you ask us to do without discouragement. Bless the Congregation of the Holy Cross, keeping it faithful to you. We ask this in the name of Jesus. Amen.

Saint Raymond of Peñyafort (1175–1275)

Saint Raymond seemed to get a late start in life, joining the Order of Preachers (Dominicans) at the age of forty-seven. Yet God's timing is perfect, and Raymond spent many productive years in His service (before his death at the age of one hundred). He was a professor and friend of Saint Thomas Aquinas, whom he encouraged to write the *Summa Contra Gentiles*. Eventually he became Archbishop of Tarragona, Spain, and he also served as third prior general of the order, instituting reforms. He wrote a canon law for Pope Gregory IX and a treatise about the Sacrament of Reconciliation. In addition, he assisted Saint Peter Nolasco in founding the Order of Mercedarians. Saint Raymond is the patron saint of attorneys.

PRAYER

Saint Raymond of Peñyafort, thank you for showing us through your life that God's timing is perfect. United with you on your feast, we pray: Gracious Father, through the intercession of Saint Raymond, help us to give our lives to you, trusting in your perfect plan. Help us to grow in the virtues of perseverance, leadership, and diligence. May we always use our gifts in your service, conducting ourselves with honor. Help attorneys to be honest and to work for justice. Bless the Dominican order, keeping it faithful to you. We ask this in the name of Jesus. Amen.

JANUARY 8

Saint Severinus of Noricum (d. 482)

Saint Severinus was a hermit, monk, and founder of many monasteries along the Danube around the time of the fall of the Roman Empire. He was also a preacher, evangelist, and miracle worker. He had the gift of prophecy, correctly foretelling that the Huns would destroy Asturis, where he had been preaching. When King Odovakar asked him for his blessing before he marched against Rome, Severinus prophesied that he would conquer, telling him: "Go forward, my son. Today thou art still clad in the worthless skins of animals, but soon shalt thou make gifts from the treasures of Italy." It is even said that he knew the day he would die. His austerities were extreme, and he refused to sleep in a bed. Six years after his death, his body was found to be incorrupt. He is the patron saint of Austria and Bavaria.

PRAYER

Saint Severinus, you generously used your spiritual gifts in service to the Church. Pray for us to be generous enough to put our gifts at God's disposal, and pray with us today: Merciful Father, give us steadfastness and generosity to serve you as Saint Severinus did. Inspire us to repent. Grant us the grace to deny ourselves so as to be detached from worldly things and attached only to you. Help us to use our gifts, no matter what is going on in the world around us, for your glory and the salvation of souls. We ask this in the name of Jesus. Amen.

JANUARY 9

Saint Epictetus (d. 250)

Little is known of Saint Epictetus, an African bishop and martyr of the early Church. We do know that he held fast to his faith and endured a brutal death along with the other martyrs in Africa under the Roman Emperor Decius. He, Vitalis, Jucundus, Felix, Secundus, and seven other people were tortured by the Romans when they would not renounce their faith. He joyfully entered his time of trial, prepared to go to his death for love of the Lord. He had "run the good race" and won.

PRAYER

Saint Epictetus, pray for us to be able to imitate your courage and generosity in giving your life for love of God, and pray with us today: Dear Father, help us to imitate the courage, constancy, and joy of Saint Epictetus and all the other martyrs of Africa. Like them, may we have unwavering hope and trust in your mercy. Grant us the grace to cling to our faith to the very end, even if we are called to witness to the Faith with our very lives. Deliver us from fear and timidity. We ask this in the name of Jesus. Amen.

JANUARY 10

Saint Agatho (d. 681)

Saint Agatho became pope when he was over one hundred years old, just over two years before he died. As pope, he assisted with the Third Council of Constantinople (680–681), which condemned the heresy of Monothelitism — the false teaching that Jesus did not have a human will. It is believed that Agatho was a Benedictine monk before he ascended to the papacy. This foundation in a life of prayer allowed him to become a contemplative in action. He is credited with working many miracles, earning him the title *Thaumaturgus* ("Miracle Worker").

PRAYER

Saint Agatho, you continued to serve God generously even in your old age, reminding us that our whole life should be at God's disposal. Pray for us and with us on your feast: Loving Father, inspire us to pray always, and form us into instruments of healing and unity as contemplatives in action. Grant us the virtue of faith, and increase our faith each day. Keep us grounded in the true Faith and do not let us be led astray by false teachings and ideologies. Bless our Holy Father and guide him in all his actions, making him and all bishops strong pastors and virtuous leaders. Bless the Benedictine order, keeping it faithful to you. We ask this in the name of Jesus. Amen.

Saint Theodosius the Cenobiarch (423–529)

Saint Theodosius was a hermit and founder of a monastic community in the Holy Land. He lived in silence, praying, doing penance, and fasting. During his prayers, he often wept. He helped his monks focus on preparing for death by dying to themselves in every way possible. He was known to have the gift of hospitality, providing food and shelter to those in need, and God worked many miracles through him. Byzantine Emperor Anastasius tried to win him over to heretical teachings, even attempting to bribe him, but Theodosius gave the bribe money away to the poor. Saint Theodosius was 105 years old when he died, still faithful to the true teachings of the Church.

PRAYER

Saint Theodosius, pray for us to cultivate a deep life of prayer and sacrifice, and pray with us today: Gracious Father, like Saint Theodosius, make us virtuous leaders. Grant us wisdom, tenacity, and courage. Inspire us to develop a strong prayer life and teach us to listen for your Spirit's gentle voice in the silence of our hearts. Grant us the gift of contemplation and confirm us in love. Make us saints. We ask this in the name of Jesus. Amen.

JANUARY 12

Saint Marguerite Bourgeoys (1620–1700)

Born in France, Saint Marguerite Bourgeoys heard God calling her to go to the Jesuit mission territory of Montreal, Canada, to teach the native Iroquois children. She obeyed, eventually founding an order of teaching sisters, the Congregation of Notre Dame de Montreal. She was called "Mother of the Colony" in Montreal due to her tireless work there. She wrote, "It seems to me that we do not pay enough attention to prayer, for unless it arises from the heart which ought to be its center it is no more than a fruitless dream." Saint Marguerite Bourgeoys is the patron saint of people in poverty, those who have lost a parent, and those who have been rejected by religious orders.

PRAYER

Saint Marguerite, your obedience to God's call sprang from your life of prayer, which drew you into deep union with him. Pray for us to love God as you did, and pray with us on your feast: Merciful Father, inspire us to truly trust in your providence as Saint Marguerite did. May we learn our faith first and then teach others and bring them into your holy Catholic Church. Assist all Catholic teachers and keep them faithful to the Church. Bless the Congregation of Notre Dame, keeping it faithful to you. We ask this in the name of Jesus. Amen.

JANUARY 13

Saint Hilary of Poitiers (315–368)

Saint Hilary was raised a pagan and converted to Christianity as an adult. After he was made bishop of Poitiers (in what is now France), Hilary fought hard against the Arian heresy, which taught that Jesus was not divine. He was exiled for his commitment to orthodoxy, and during his exile he wrote one of his most important theological works: *De Trinitate* (*On the Trinity*). Because of his important teachings and writings in defense of the Faith, he is a Doctor of the Church.

PRAYER

Saint Hilary, pray for us to grow in wisdom and to seek constantly to know God more deeply. On your feast day, pray with us: Dear Father, through the intercession and teaching of Saint Hilary, help us to know and understand the mysteries of our Catholic Faith. Guard our speech and grant us simplicity of heart so that we will desire you alone and seek to do your will in everything. Keep us from falling into confusion and heresy. We ask this in the name of Jesus. Amen.

JANUARY 14

Blessed Odoric of Pordenone (d. 1331)

Blessed Odoric was an engaging preacher, missionary, and miracle worker. He was born in Italy, and almost nothing is known of his early life before he joined the Franciscan order. He eventually became a missionary, bringing the Gospel to many places, including India, the Philippines, Japan, and China. He wrote of his journeys: "According to my wish, I crossed the sea and visited the countries of the unbelievers in order to win some harvest of souls." God allowed him to perform many miracles on his journeys, thus helping people believe his preaching.

PRAYER
Blessed Odoric, like you, we want to love and serve God and "win some harvest of souls" through our prayers and example. Pray for and with us: Loving Father, inspire us to seek out those who do not yet know you. Form in us missionary hearts, and enable us to bring souls to you through our intercessory prayer. Give us wisdom and courage to serve and proclaim you always. Help us to use all our talents and gifts for your service without reserve. Grant eloquence and monetary assistance to those engaged in missionary work throughout the world. Bless the Franciscan order, keeping it faithful to you. We ask this in the name of Jesus. Amen.

JANUARY 15

Saint Maurus (d. 584)

Saint Maurus was a young boy when his father entrusted him to the care of Saint Benedict for his formation. He was known for his obedience and his love of prayer. God gave him extraordinary gifts, including healing people of diseases and injuries, and walking on water to save another monk from drowning. Eventually, Saint Benedict appointed him as coadjutor in the care and administration of the monastery in Subiaco, Italy. Many of his healing miracles have been recorded, and he often performed miracles by blessing people in need of healing with a relic of the true cross. The Blessing of Saint Maurus over the Sick continues to be offered today, either with a relic of the true cross or (if not available) a medal of Saint Benedict.

PRAYER

Saint Maurus, your faith in God allowed you to work miracles in his name when people sought your prayers. Pray for us and with us today: Gracious Father, instill in us a love of prayer and obedience. Guide us to listen to you and follow your will for our lives. Like Saint Maurus, may we be strengthened by our time alone with you in contemplation to be active and fruitful in doing good works. May we reach out in love to serve anyone who needs us, for love of you. Bless the Benedictine order, keeping it faithful to you. We ask this in the name of Jesus. Amen.

JANUARY 16

Saint Marcellus I (d. 309)

Saint Marcellus inherited a difficult job when he became pope after the persecution of Christians under Emperor Diocletian. He ascended to the papacy in 308, four years after the martyrdom of his predecessor, Pope Saint Marcellinus, and during his short pontificate he strove to bring order and peace back to the Church. While he welcomed back those Christians who had apostatized during the persecutions, he required that they perform penance before they could be received back into full communion with the Church. This angered many people, including the Emperor Maxentius, who eventually banished Marcellus from Rome. After reigning for only one year, the pope died in exile. He is now buried under the altar of San Marcello al Corso in Rome.

PRAYER

Saint Marcellus, you led the Church in a difficult time of confusion, and you showed how important repentance and conversion are in our life of faith. Pray with us on your feast: Merciful Father, give us the virtues of constancy and determination. Teach us how to work with our pastors in building up the Church, bringing back Catholics who have stopped practicing their faith and evangelizing everyone we encounter. Heal our wounds and trauma. Make us steadfast in doing what we know is right, even when it makes us unpopular. Bless the pope and all cardinals and bishops, making them strong pastors and virtuous leaders. We ask this in the name of Jesus. Amen.

JANUARY 17

Saint Anthony of the Desert (251–356)

Saint Anthony was born into a wealthy family in Egypt. From a young age he craved a deeper relationship with God in silence. After his parents died, he left all his wealth behind to become a hermit in the desert of Egypt, where he prayed, fasted, and did penance. Over time, other people followed him into the desert, seeking to live as he did, and a community of men seeking a structured life of prayer and asceticism grew up around him. He is known as one of the founders of monasticism, because he was one of the first people to create a schedule of worship, work, and penance for a community. Throughout his life, many people sought him out for advice and prayers, and he even worked miracles. He is also said to have fought with demons. He assisted Saint Athanasius in combating the Arian heresy (which denied the divinity of Christ), and Saint Athanasius later wrote a biography of him. Saint Anthony is the patron saint of butchers, gravediggers, and persons with skin diseases.

PRAYER

Saint Anthony, you longed only for God, and you left the world behind to seek Him in prayerful solitude. On your feast day, pray for and with us: Dear Father, through the intercession of Saint Anthony of the Desert, help us to live a life of prayer, silence, and penance, according to our state in life. Form us to be intercessory prayer warriors. Guide us to follow a rule of life based on the Gospels. Make us contemplatives in action. Grant us the grace to be modest, kind, courteous, and hospitable to all, caring for the poor and sick, and helping with their healing in every way possible. We ask this in the name of Jesus. Amen.

JANUARY 18

Blessed Juan Barrera
Méndez (1967–1980)

Blessed Juan ("Juanito" as he was called) was only twelve years old when he died a martyr for his Catholic Faith. Growing up in Quiche, Guatemala, he was very active in the Church. He faithfully attended Mass and helped teach younger children the Faith, preparing them to receive their first Communion. He was also a member of a Catholic Action group. Because of his strong faith and leadership in the Catholic Church, Juanito was kidnapped and murdered by the communist government, which persecuted and killed Catholics. As his captors tortured him, he said: "I am dying because I am working on the Word of God. I will give my soul in the name of the Lord."

PRAYER

Blessed Juan, you show us by your witness that we can give God our all no matter how young we are. Pray for us to have your courage and pray with us on your feast: Loving Father, make us such strong witnesses of your love and faithfulness that people will be drawn to you because they see you in us. Inspire us to be willing to give our lives for our faith. Grant us the grace to pray consistently and work for peace in our communities. Let us study our faith and teach it to others. Show all children that, like Blessed Juan, they can be your faithful disciples, no matter how young. Protect those who are being persecuted for their faith in you. We ask this in the name of Jesus. Amen.

JANUARY 19

Saint Wulfstan (1008–1095)

Saint Wulfstan was a Benedictine bishop and reformer in England whose life remains a shining example of humble, pious leadership. After studying at Evesham and Peterborough, he was ordained and became a Benedictine monk at Worcester, eventually becoming prior. He became bishop of Worcester in 1062, and he performed his duties so excellently that even William the Conqueror — who deposed all other Saxon bishops after the Battle of Hastings — left him alone. Wulfstan loved to help the poor and was known to wash their feet every day, and he died while carrying out this labor of love.

PRAYER

Saint Wulfstan, you showed by your daily example how we should strive to grow in humility and generosity. Pray for us on your feast day, that we may become saints, and pray with us: Gracious Father, grant us the grace to reform our lives, our families, and the Church. Enable us to become virtuous leaders who excel in everything that you ask us to accomplish. Make us faithful to our duties and inspiring witnesses of a true Christian life. Bless the Benedictine order and keep it faithful to you. We ask this in the name of Jesus. Amen.

Blessed Cyprian Michael Iwene Tansi (1903–1964)

Blessed Cyprian, born in Nigeria, was a pious, studious, and responsible child. He was baptized when he was nine years old and began teaching when he was sixteen. Later, he entered seminary and was ordained a priest of the Diocese of Onitsha at age thirty-four. A zealous and compassionate priest, he labored to support and build up Christianity, traveling from village to village to serve his people. His bishop requested that he travel to England to study to be a Trappist monk, then return home to begin monastic life in Nigeria. Cyprian obeyed, moving to England in 1950, and he pursued his religious formation with zeal. Sadly, he died of an aneurysm before he could return to Africa.

PRAYER

Blessed Cyprian, pray for us to grow in the virtues you exemplified, especially piety and obedience. On your feast day, pray with us: Merciful Father, help us to be responsible and faithful to our duties. Calm our minds and quiet our hearts so that we may hear your voice and follow the vocation you have for us. Nurture our prayer life and make us contemplatives in action. Bless your priests and all Trappist monks, keeping them faithful to you. We ask this in the name of Jesus. Amen.

JANUARY 21

Saint Agnes (d. 304)

Saint Agnes was very young — about twelve years old — when she was martyred for refusing to give up her faith and sacrifice to the Roman gods. She had consecrated herself to Jesus, so when a wealthy young man wanted to marry her, she refused, saying, "I will be His who first chose me for himself." The rejected suitor reported her to the authorities for being a Christian, and she was sentenced to death. Agnes was strong and trusted God with her life, speaking boldly about her faith. They tried to kill her by fire, but the flames went out when she prayed. At last, she died by the sword. Among other things, Saint Agnes is the patron saint of girls and chastity. Her name means "lamb" (a symbol of purity).

PRAYER

Saint Agnes, you held fast to your faith and your consecration to Jesus, even though it meant certain death. We want to imitate your purity, and we ask you to pray with us: Dear Father, help us to be pure as Agnes was, and wholeheartedly dedicated to you. Inspire us to imitate the purity of all the saints so that we, like them, may one day see you face to face. Grant us the grace to trust your holy will for our lives and to fearlessly obey you in everything. Teach us how to boldly proclaim and stand fast in our faith and lead others to it. We ask this in the name of Jesus. Amen.

JANUARY 22

Blessed Laura Vicuña (1891–1904)

Blessed Laura was a young Chilean girl who became very close to God through visits to the Blessed Sacrament while she was at boarding school. When she prayed, she spoke to God as a friend. She longed to become a religious sister like her teachers. But even more than that, she longed for heaven and for the conversion of her mother, who was living a sinful life, trapped in a relationship with a cruel man. This man had designs on Laura, and when she continually refused him, he beat her. Laura died of injuries she sustained from the abuse, offering her life for her mother. Moved by her sacrifice, her mother came back to the Faith and courageously left her abuser. Blessed Laura Vicuña is the patron saint of abuse victims.

PRAYER

Blessed Laura, you saw the evil in the world all too clearly, yet you knew that God's grace and love are stronger than any sin. On your feast, pray with us: Loving Father, help us to live chastely, modestly, and generously, and inspire us to pray and to offer sacrifices for love of you. Instill in us the patience and meekness we need to be gentle with ourselves and others. Give us hearts of mercy toward those who suffer any kind of abuse. Protect the vulnerable and free all children and adults who are in abusive situations. Show us our dignity as your sons and daughters. Teach us how to care for our bodies as temples of your Holy Spirit. Grant us the courage to seek help if we are being or have been abused. We ask this in the name of Jesus. Amen.

JANUARY 23

Saint Marianne Cope (1838–1918)

Mother Marianne bravely answered the call to move to the Hawaiian Islands to help Saint Damien of Molokai care for people with Hansen's disease (leprosy). She was a Franciscan sister from Syracuse, New York, where she helped found and run hospitals. When she was asked to minister to the outcast victims of leprosy and their families, she said, "I am hungry for the work … I am not afraid of any disease." She took six sisters to Hawaii, promising them that they would not contract the disease if they joined her. God honored her promise: None of the sisters became sick. Together they built and ran a medical center to help the people heal. Marianne courageously served the sick, including Father Damien when he fell ill with the fatal disease. Saint Marianne is the patron saint of those with leprosy and HIV/AIDS.

PRAYER

Saint Marianne, pray for us to be hungry for the work God gives us, as you were. On your feast, pray with us: Gracious Father, inspire us to assist those who are suffering, whether physically or spiritually. Grant us the grace to hear your call and respond with generosity. Guide us to serve you in exactly the place you need us, using all our gifts and talents. Teach us how to have your understanding and empathy for others instead of judging them. Bless the Franciscan order, keeping it faithful to you. We ask this in the name of Jesus. Amen.

JANUARY 24

Saint Francis de Sales (1567–1622)

Saint Francis was a nobleman who heard God's call to become a priest and followed it. Eventually he became bishop of Geneva, which at that time was under the control of Calvinist reformers, who hated the Catholic Church. He was forced to live outside of his diocese, but his kindness, gentleness, humility, and excellent writings helped many people return to Catholicism. His famous book *Introduction to the Devout Life* shows that holiness is God's will for all of us, no matter our state in life. We are called to be saints, and Saint Francis's practical suggestions help us do just that. He and Saint Jane Frances de Chantal founded the Order of the Visitation. Saint Francis is a Doctor of the Church and the patron saint of authors, spiritual writers, journalists, teachers, and people with deafness.

PRAYER

Saint Francis de Sales, your spiritual guidance continues to transform minds and hearts today. Pray for us to grow in holiness, and pray with us: Merciful Father, show each of us the unique path to sainthood you have planned for us. Inspire us to live holy lives so that we can attract and serve those who do not believe in you or your Church. Dispel confusion regarding truths of the Faith, and teach us to study our faith for the sake of our conversion and the conversion of others. Assist authors to use their writing to uphold and promote the truth. Heal people with deafness. Bless the Order of the Visitation, keeping it faithful to you. We ask this in the name of Jesus. Amen.

JANUARY 25

The Conversion of Saint Paul

A devout and zealous Jewish pharisee, Paul (whose name was Saul before he became a Christian) persecuted Christians. Then, while he was on a journey to Damascus to arrest the Christians there, we read in the Acts of the Apostles: "Suddenly a light from heaven shone around him. And falling to the ground, he heard a voice saying to him, 'Saul, Saul, why are you persecuting me?' And he said, 'Who are you, Lord?' And he said, 'I am Jesus, whom you are persecuting. But rise and enter the city, and you will be told what you are to do'" (9:3–6). He obeyed Jesus and became a great Christian apostle. He made many missionary journeys and wrote many of the letters in the New Testament. Saint Paul is the patron saint of missionaries, evangelists, writers, and tentmakers.

PRAYER

Saint Paul, pray for us to be filled with apostolic zeal, as you were, and to share the Gospel with courage. Pray with us on your feast: Dear Father, you have made each of us with a unique and specific purpose in mind; help us to follow your will and carry out your plan for us to give you glory. Grant us the grace to grow in spiritual maturity and teach us to share our faith with others, following Saint Paul's example. Protect missionaries, evangelists, and writers and grant them success in leading others to you. Bless our bishops and make them true shepherds and virtuous leaders. We ask this in the name of Jesus. Amen.

JANUARY 26

Saints Timothy (d. 97) and Titus (d. 96)

Saints Timothy and Titus were privileged to be companions of Saint Paul on his missionary journeys. Determined to spread the Good News of Jesus Christ, they faithfully went where they were needed and followed Paul's direction. Their assistance was crucial, and Saint Paul wrote three pastoral letters to them (two to Timothy and one to Titus), which are part of the New Testament. Interestingly, these are the only letters we have from him that were addressed to individuals, not whole communities. Saint Timothy became the bishop of Ephesus, while Saint Titus became the bishop of Crete. They are patron saints of people with stomach disorders.

PRAYER

Saints Timothy and Titus, just as you assisted Paul in his mission-ary journeys, assist us by your prayers in our journey to heaven, and pray with us on this feast day: Loving Father, make us con-stant and diligent in your service. Inspire us to pray and perform works of mercy. Teach us to be obedient to your will in all things, and to boldly spread the Faith in all we do. Bless our bishops, making them true shepherds and virtuous leaders. We ask this in the name of Jesus. Amen.

JANUARY 27

Saint Angela Merici (1470–1540)

Saint Angela knew loss at an early age, as she was only ten years old when her parents died. She and her older sister went to live with an uncle, and then her sister also died. She became a lay Franciscan and started educating young girls in her home. Over time, other women joined her in her work. She then sensed God calling her to begin the first teaching order, the Ursuline order, to sustain her work in teaching young women. Obedient to God, she established the order when she was sixty-one years old. The Ursulines were the first religious order of women to come to the New World, building a mission in Canada. Saint Angela is the patron saint of disabled people, people grieving the loss of their parents, and women's education.

PRAYER

Saint Angela, despite loss and grief, you were faithful to God's call, and you served the Church with great charity. Pray for us and with us on your feast: Gracious Father, may we never tire of seeking and doing your will, even in difficult circumstances. Instill in us a love of helping others, and make us fearless in learning about the Faith and teaching it to others. Guide teachers to know how best to help students. Turn our grief into blessings and comfort those suffering from loss and trauma. Bless the Ursuline order and keep it faithful to you. We ask this in the name of Jesus. Amen.

JANUARY 28

Saint Thomas Aquinas (1225–1274)

Thomas Aquinas came from a noble family in Italy, and, against their wishes, he joined the newly formed Dominican order, devoting himself to a life of poverty and study. He became a professor of theology and a prolific writer. He had a rare gift of being able to dictate many books at once, and he wrote many theological works. His *Summa Theologiae* remains one of the most studied works of theology. He also wrote beautiful hymns to the Eucharist, which we still sing today. His deep spirituality shines through in this prayer that he wrote: "Grant me, O Lord my God, a mind to know you, heart to seek you, wisdom to find you, conduct pleasing to you, faithful perseverance in waiting for you, and a hope of finally embracing you." Saint Thomas is a Doctor of the Church and the patron saint of students, Catholic schools and universities, doctors, theologians, and the virtue of chastity.

PRAYER

Saint Thomas, your wisdom continues to bless and teach the Church. Pray for us to love God above all else, and pray with us: Heavenly Father, grant us true wisdom to know and seek you in all that we do. Increase faith, hope, and love in us, and help us to grow in all virtues with the help of your grace. Give us profound reverence for the Blessed Sacrament. Grant us the grace to love and study the truths of our Faith. Bless all who teach and write about the Faith, and give them clarity, eloquence, and commitment to the truth. Bless the Dominican order, keeping it faithful to you. We ask this in the name of Jesus. Amen.

JANUARY 29

Saint Sabinian of Troyes (d. 275)

Saint Sabinian (sometimes called Savinian) and his sister Saint Sabina (whose feast is celebrated on August 29) were natives of Samos and converts to the Christian faith. Sabinian had a gift for preaching and evangelization, and he used this gift for God's glory. The fruitfulness of his preaching in Gaul was so great that he came to the attention of the Romans and suffered martyrdom under Emperor Aurelian. He is known as the apostle of Troyes.

PRAYER

Saint Sabinian, just as you preached the Gospel with zeal, pray for us to share the Good News even when it is dangerous. And pray with us on your feast: Merciful Father, grant us the virtue of holy boldness, especially in the face of danger. Inspire us to imitate the martyrs in their unflinching testimony. By your grace, may we overcome any obstacle to living and proclaiming the Gospel. Strengthen us to bear witness to the truth of our Catholic Faith even unto death. Bless our siblings and give us gracious, loving, and forgiving relationships with them. Reconcile our families. Protect all who are being persecuted for their faith. Bless preachers, evangelists, and missionaries with eloquence to powerfully proclaim your truth. We ask this in the name of Jesus. Amen.

JANUARY 30

Saint David Galván-Bermúdez (1881–1915)

David Galván-Bermúdez was a young, faithful priest in Jalisco, Mexico, who would not renounce his faith when the communist government arrested him. He is one of the martyrs of the Mexican Revolution, who were targeted for their faith, hunted down, tortured, and murdered by the communists. While in prison, Father David heard the confessions of other condemned people and helped them prepare for death. He was fearless in the face of persecution, saying, "What greater glory is there than to die saving a soul?" A true priest who loved his people, he served them faithfully to the end.

PRAYER
Saint David, your love for God overflowed in your love for the souls in your care. Pray for us to love as you did, and pray with us: Dear Father, strengthen our faith and inspire us to encourage and lift up others in their faith. Make us so courageous and filled with love of your Church that we would never renounce our faith. Preserve us from secular, atheistic ideologies that seek to replace you and your Church. Protect those who are being persecuted for their faith in you. We ask this in the name of Jesus. Amen.

JANUARY 31

Saint John Bosco (1815–1888)

Saint John Bosco grew up in a poor family in Italy. He followed God's call to study for the priesthood, and after ordination, he discovered his mission to serve the street boys of Turin. Possessed of a charismatic personality, he used magic tricks to entertain and teach young people the truths of the Faith. He gave the boys the sacraments, encouraged them to be holy, and worked to prevent problems before they arose. By teaching the boys trades such as shoemaking, publishing, and tailoring, he enabled them to earn a living. He founded the Oratory of Saint Francis de Sales and a priestly order, the Salesians. Later, he founded the Salesian Sisters. Saint John Bosco is the patron saint of boys, schoolchildren, young apprentices, editors, and Catholic publishers.

PRAYER

Saint John Bosco, you won the hearts of even the most difficult boys in Turin, and you inspired them to live virtuous lives. Pray with us today: Loving Father, may we always use our gifts to serve those who are most in need. Inspire us to always be good examples to others. Help us to find and fulfill the unique missions you have for us, using the gifts you have given us. May we work to prevent problems and illnesses in children. Teach all parents how to form their children in virtue and love. Bless the Salesian order, keeping it faithful to you. We ask this in the name of Jesus. Amen.

FEBRUARY

THE MONTH OF
THE PASSION OF OUR LORD

FEBRUARY 1

Blessed Benedict Daswa (d. 1990)

Blessed Benedict was a catechist who worked perseveringly to teach others the Faith. A member of the Lemba Tribe, he followed traditional Jewish customs and laws until he converted to Catholicism at age seventeen. A husband and father of eight children, he served as principal and teacher of Nweli Primary School at his parish. He was martyred by a group of men from his village because he refused to have anything to do with witchcraft. He is the first person who was born in South Africa to be beatified.

PRAYER

Blessed Benedict, your firm example of faith inspired all who knew you, and you held fast even though it meant a violent death. Pray for us and with us today: Dear Father, grant us the grace to resist and be detached from worldly and pagan practices and to be faithful and constant in the practice of our faith. Inspire us to help others to see the harm that comes from not living in line with your commandments. Free and heal those who are engaged or entrapped in the occult. Bless all teachers and catechists. We ask this in the name of Jesus. Amen.

FEBRUARY 2

The Presentation of the
Lord (Saints Simeon and Anna)

We read in the Gospel of Luke that Simeon had waited years for God's promise of a messiah to be fulfilled. Finally, forty days after Jesus' birth, Simeon witnessed the fulfillment of God's promise. When Mary and Joseph brought Jesus to the Temple to present Him according to Jewish Law, the elderly Simeon recognized Him as the messiah. He praised God, saying, "Lord, now you are letting your servant depart in peace, according to your word; for my eyes have seen your salvation that you have prepared in the presence of all peoples, a light for revelation to the Gentiles, and for glory to your people Israel" (2:29–32). Anna, an elderly widow who prayed and spent most of her time in the Temple, also recognized Jesus and thanked God. We celebrate the feast of the Presentation (also known as Candlemas) with the blessing of candles and processions, signifying our love for Jesus who is the Light of the world.

PRAYER

Saints Simeon and Anna, you waited with hopeful expectation for the fulfillment of God's promise, and you were not disappointed. Pray for us and with us: Loving Father, through the intercession of Saints Simeon and Anna, inspire us to see you as the Light of our lives. Grant us the grace to keep your commandments faithfully, that we may always walk in your light. Teach us how to be faithful as you are faithful and trust in the truth of your promises. Thank you for the many gifts you have given us and for all the blessings you have prepared for us. We ask this in the name of Jesus. Amen.

FEBRUARY 3

Saint Blaise (d. 316)

Little is known about the life of Saint Blaise, who was a physician and bishop in Armenia. He is said to have saved a boy who was choking on something lodged in his throat. Because of this incident, the blessing of throats became a yearly occurrence in the Church on his feast day. The blessing states, "Through the intercession of Saint Blaise, Bishop and martyr, may God deliver you from every disease of the throat and from every other illness." Blaise was martyred under the Roman Emperor Licinius. He is the patron of people with throat ailments.

PRAYER

Saint Blaise, you were a fearless shepherd of your people, and you willingly gave your life for your faith. Pray for us to witness to our faith even to death, and pray with us: Gracious Father, grant us the virtues of courage and constancy, that we may never waver in our service to you. Inspire us to care for our bodies, which are temples of the Holy Spirit, and thus honor you. Free us from all illnesses, especially those of the throat. Bless doctors, nurses, paramedics, policeman, firemen, and all others who serve, protect, and help people in need. Bless all bishops in the Church and make them wise and faithful leaders. We ask this in the name of Jesus. Amen.

FEBRUARY 4

Saint Isidore of Pelusium (d. c. 450)

Saint Isidore was an Egyptian abbot who did not shy away from controversy, but steadfastly and moderately took it on, especially in the many letters he wrote — according to one estimate, more than ten thousand of them. His written works and preaching emphasized detachment from material things and living by what we profess to believe. He strenuously defended veneration of relics and fought the Nestorian heresy, which claimed there are two persons in Jesus Christ, one human and one divine. After the Council of Ephesus, Isidore continued to defend the Church's teaching that Jesus is one divine Person with two natures, pushing back on the Eutychian heresy, which claimed Jesus had only one (divine) nature.

PRAYER

Saint Isidore, you show us by your example that we need not fear controversy, but that we can rely on the Holy Spirit to teach us all truth. Pray with us today: Heavenly Father, we ask for simplicity and integrity to love you with our whole hearts and serve you in all that we do. Draw us into a strong, consistent prayer life. Grant us the gift of contemplation and make us contemplatives in action. Strengthen us to stand firm in the midst of controversy, give us clarity in the face of error, and always help us speak the truth in charity. We ask this in the name of Jesus. Amen.

FEBRUARY 5

Saint Agatha (d. 251)

Saint Agatha was born to a noble family in Sicily. Her heroic martyrdom inspired the early Church to such a degree that she is one of seven women listed in the Roman Canon (the oldest Eucharistic prayer in the Roman rite). Determined to protect her purity against the advances of the pagan proconsul Quintian, Agatha was martyred during the persecutions under the Roman Emperor Decius. An ancient homily praises her, saying, "*Agatha*, the name of our saint, means 'good.' Agatha, her goodness, coincides with her name and way of life. She won a good name by her noble deeds, and by her name she points to the nobility of those deeds. Agatha, her mere name wins all men over to her company. She teaches them by her example to hasten with her to the true Good, God alone." Saint Agatha is the patron saint of nurses, miners, jewelers, Alpine guides, Palermo, and Catania, and she is invoked for protection against fire, earthquake, thunderstorms, famine, and volcanic eruptions.

PRAYER

Saint Agatha, you willingly died for love of Jesus. Pray for us to have that same spirit of courage and self-sacrifice, and pray with us on your feast: Merciful Father, grant us chastity, modesty, and the strength and courage to protect both, in ourselves and others, at all costs. Inspire us to seek purity of mind, heart, intention, and action. Guide us to follow the saints in their beautiful examples of purity. May we willingly and patiently suffer trials and obstacles without giving in to discouragement. Make us strong witnesses to our faith for your greater glory. We ask this in the name of Jesus. Amen.

FEBRUARY 6

Saint Paul Miki and Companions (d. 1597)

Saint Paul Miki was only a few months away from being ordained a Jesuit priest when he was arrested, along with twenty-five companions, for his Christian faith. The men were tortured and forced to walk six hundred miles before they were crucified on a hill outside of Nagasaki in Japan. The martyrs included Fathers Pasio, Rodriguez, and Bursar, and Brothers Martin, Francis Branco, and Gonsalvo. There were also some boys with them: Louis (ten), Anthony (thirteen), Thomas (sixteen), and Gabriel (nineteen). All were crucified for their faith, encouraging one another and singing hymns. Paul preached from the cross, urging the bystanders, "Ask Christ to help you become happy. I obey Christ. After Christ's example, I forgive my persecutors. I do not hate them. I ask God to have pity on all, and I hope my blood will fall on my fellow men as a fruitful rain." Their martyrdom was indeed fruitful. When Catholic missionaries returned to Japan two hundred years later, they found the Catholic Faith still alive there.

PRAYER

Saint Paul Miki and companions, your martyrdom sowed seeds of faith in Japan. Pray for us and with us: Heavenly Father, inspire us to speak and act faithfully and boldly about our Christian faith. Strengthen in us the virtues of faith, courage, and perseverance. Teach us the way to true happiness and make us fearless in clinging to our faith no matter what it may cost us. Bless the Jesuit order and keep it faithful to you. We ask this in the name of Jesus. Amen.

FEBRUARY 7
Saint Mél of Ireland (d. c. 490)

Saint Mél followed his uncle, Saint Patrick, in his missionary journeys throughout Ireland. He and his brothers Rioch, Munis, and Melchu, sons of Saint Patrick's sister Saint Darerca, helped Patrick to catechize the Irish. Ordained bishop of Ardagh, Mél was determined to do everything he could to help the Irish people come to Christ, and he spent his life in this work. Saint Brigid of Kildare professed her religious vows before Saint Mél. He is the patron saint of the Diocese of Ardagh and Clonmacnoise.

PRAYER

Saint Mél, you were faithful and tireless in bringing the Gospel to the Irish people. On your feast day, pray for us and with us: Dear Father, make us true evangelizers and strong witnesses of our faith, sharing the Gospel with everyone we meet. Give us wisdom and prudence and a deep sense of compassion for the lost and the least. Guide catechists in teaching the Faith. Teach us the most effective ways to lovingly help people into the Church. Bless all bishops and make them true shepherds and virtuous leaders. We ask this in the name of Jesus. Amen.

FEBRUARY 8

Saint Josephine Bakhita (1869–1947)

Saint Josephine Bakhita was only nine years old when she was kidnapped from her home in Sudan and sold as a slave. The trauma of what she went through was so extreme that she forgot her name, and her captors named her Bakhita, which means "fortunate." She saw and went through many terrible things that no child should have to live through. Eventually, she was sold to an Italian family, and in 1890 she was baptized Catholic, taking the name Josephine. She obtained her freedom and, in 1896, became a Canossian Sister. After all that she experienced, she would say, "What a grace it is to know God!" She died in 1947 and is buried in the Canossian Convent in Schio, Italy. Saint Josephine is the patron saint of those enslaved.

PRAYER

Saint Josephine, pray for us to love and trust God so that we, like you, may praise and thank Him even for the sufferings He allows us. On your feast day, pray with us: Loving Father, free us from slavery to sin and make us long to know you better, and to make you known. Support the vulnerable and enslaved, and give us the means and opportunity to help them. Give strength and courage to those who rescue people who are enslaved. Return the innocence of children and adults who have been abused. Free and heal us from all the trauma we have endured. Bring us peace and give us the grace to forgive our enemies. May we use all our talents and gifts for your service without reserve. Bless the Canossian Daughters of Charity and keep them faithful to you. We ask this in the name of Jesus. Amen.

FEBRUARY 9

Blessed Anne Catherine Emmerich (1774–1824)

Blessed Anne Catherine Emmerich was a German Augustinian nun who experienced many visions of the life, passion, and death of Jesus, as well as visions of the life of Mary. Despite poor health, she dictated all her visions to Father Clemens Brentano. She bore the stigmata and suffered for sinners and the holy souls in purgatory. Although she was very sickly, she still sought to serve and help others, saying: "Every pious desire, every good thought, every charitable work inspired by the love of Jesus, contributes to the perfection of the whole body of the faithful. A person who does nothing more than lovingly pray to God for his brethren participates in the great work of saving souls." About six weeks after her death, her body was found to be still incorrupt.

PRAYER

Blessed Anne Catherine, your love for Jesus led you to such close union with Him that you were able to share in His passion. Pray for us to love the Lord as you did, and pray with us: Gracious Father, we want to seek you in all things. Inspire us to pray with perseverance and to study the lives of Jesus and Mary, always striving to imitate them. Increase in us the virtues of charity, humility, and trust, and help us to offer up our sufferings in union with the sufferings of Jesus. Give us a profound love for Jesus and all that He suffered for our sake. Teach us to be obedient to the promptings of the Holy Spirit. Bless the Augustinian order, keeping it faithful to you. We ask this in the name of Jesus. Amen.

Saint José Luis Sánchez del Rio (1913–1926)

Saint José became part of the Cristero movement in Mexico when he was only thirteen years old. The Cristeros were fighting the tyrannical communist government, which ruthlessly worked to eradicate the Catholic Faith in Mexico. Joselito, as he was affectionately called, served as a flagbearer, and when he was fourteen, he was captured, tortured, and ultimately killed for his faith. Through it all, he proclaimed his belief in Jesus and His holy Catholic Church. His last words as he was shot to death on February 10, 1928, were *"Vivo Cristo Rey y Santa Maria de Guadalupe!"* ("Long live Christ the King and Holy Mary of Guadalupe!").

PRAYER

Saint José, you knew no fear in the face of injustice, and you boldly gave your life in witness to the Faith. Pray with us on your feast: Merciful Father, help us, like Saint José, to be courageous and steadfast in trials. No matter how young we are, give us the strength to hold fast to the truth you have taught us through your holy Catholic Church. Embolden children to do your will and stand firm in their faith. Grant us the grace to listen to you and to tell others about you. Fill us with the Holy Spirit. Guide us to live pure and holy lives that we might shine in the darkness. Protect those who are being persecuted for their faith in you. We ask this in the name of Jesus. Amen.

FEBRUARY 11

Saint Saturninus and Companions (d. 304)

Saint Saturninus was a priest in Abitina (in what is now Tunisia) who was arrested with his congregation while saying Mass. The persecutions under Emperor Diocletian were raging at this time, and Saturninus was taken, along with forty-eight other people — four of whom were his own children — to Carthage to stand trial. Of those who accompanied him, we know the names of ten: Dativus, Felix, Hilarion, Mary, Felix, Ampelius, Emeritus, Rogatian, Thelica, and Victoria. In the face of severe torture, these courageous African martyrs held fast to their faith and died for it.

PRAYER

Saint Saturninus and companions, you courageously laid down your lives for the Faith, and we want to follow your heroic example. Pray with us today: Heavenly Father, inspire us to imitate the martyrs in their integrity, character, and firmness of faith. No matter how young we are, may we hold fast to you, even in the face of ridicule and danger. Make us so firm in our faith that we would rather die than forsake it. Help us to grow in all virtues, especially faith, fortitude, and piety. We ask this in the name of Jesus. Amen.

FEBRUARY 12

Saint Julian the Hospitaller
(date unknown)

As a young man, Julian the Hospitaller (also called Julian the Poor) mistakenly killed his own parents while in a jealous rage. Horrified at what he had done, he went to confession and then spent the rest of his life doing penance. He took care of the poor and people with leprosy, building an inn and a hospital for them near a river, where he also helped ferry people back and forth. Saint Julian is the patron saint of boatmen, innkeepers, travelers, carnival and circus workers, clowns, and fiddle players.

PRAYER
Saint Julian, pray for us to have the grace to trust in God's will for our lives, and to do penance for our sins. On your feast, pray with us: Dear Father, give us forgiving and compassionate hearts. Inspire us to think about the good, the true, and the beautiful and put away angry thoughts. Calm and convert our minds and hearts, taking away all anger and vengeance. Grant us the grace to care for the poor and the sick, and give us the virtues of charity, humility, and hospitality. Inspire us to do penance for our sins. We ask this in the name of Jesus. Amen.

FEBRUARY 13

Blessed Jordan of Saxony (1190–1237)

Jordan was a German nobleman and student at the University of Paris when he was inspired by the Dominican preacher Reginald of Orleans to become a Dominican himself. He succeeded Saint Dominic as Master General of the Order of Preachers in 1222. Jordan was a tremendously gifted preacher, captivating audiences and bringing many young men into the Dominican order, including Saint Albert the Great. He helped start universities and was a superb spiritual director. Under his leadership, the new Dominican order expanded greatly. He wrote many books, including a biography of Saint Dominic. He died in a shipwreck on the way home from the Holy Land when he was only forty-seven years old. Blessed Jordan is the patron saint of Dominican vocations.

PRAYER

Blessed Jordan, your preaching and witness won many souls for Christ and helped the new Dominican order to grow. Pray for us and with us on your feast: Loving Father, make us zealous in preaching the Gospel and winning souls for you. May we, like Blessed Jordan, have a love of friendship with Jesus that compels us to make Him known to others. Grant us eloquence in speech, and guide us to respect youth and encourage them to achieve the purpose for which you created them. Make us magnanimous, virtuous leaders. Bless the Dominican order and keep it faithful to you. We ask this in the name of Jesus. Amen.

FEBRUARY 14

Saints Cyril and Methodius
(d. 869 and 885)

Cyril and Methodius were brothers from Thessalonica who both became priests. They shared the Faith with the Slavic people. They were so eager for them to understand the Faith that they created an alphabet and translated the Bible and liturgical texts into Slavonic. Following God's will, the brothers faithfully used all the gifts He had given them to serve the Slavic people while encouraging each other to be holy. Both were ordained bishops. Cyril died in Rome in 869, and Methodius carried on their work in Moravia until his death in 885. They are called the apostles to the Slavs.

PRAYER

Saints Cyril and Methodius, you were generous in sharing the Faith and using your great gifts to lead souls to God. Pray for us and with us: Gracious Father, grant us the apostolic zeal that motivated Cyril and Methodius. May we seek only to do your will, so we may help as many people as possible come to know you. Grant us growth in all virtues, especially prudence and fortitude. Guide us to love Sacred Scripture, and encourage us to use all our talents and gifts for your service, without reserve. Make us saints. We ask this in the name of Jesus. Amen.

FEBRUARY 15

Saint Claude de la Colombière (1641–1682)

Saint Claude, a Jesuit missionary preacher, was privileged to be the spiritual director of Saint Margaret Mary Alacoque, who championed devotion to the Sacred Heart of Jesus. During his time as rector of the Jesuit college in Paray-le-Monial, France, he assisted Saint Margaret in promoting devotion to the Sacred Heart. Through his sermons, he encouraged people to be confident in God's love and mercy. He wrote: "May the Heart of Jesus Christ be our school! Let us make our abode there. Let us study its movements and attempt to conform ours to them." Sent to England to be a chaplain to a duchess, he was falsely accused of treason and imprisoned. After a month he was released and returned, gravely ill, to France, where he died a few years later at the age of forty-one.

PRAYER

Saint Claude, pray for us to love the Sacred Heart of Jesus and to follow your example of fidelity and trust in all things. Pray with us today: Merciful Father, grant us unwavering trust in your love. May we grow in confidence and devotion to the Sacred Heart of Jesus and share this devotion with others. Grant us purity of heart to love you fully and live according to your will. May we grow strong in all virtues, especially charity and trust. Enable us to bear trials and obstacles patiently and forgive those who falsely accuse and hurt us. Make us saints. We ask this in the name of Jesus. Amen.

FEBRUARY 16

Saint Gilbert of Sempringham
(1083–c. 1189)

Saint Gilbert, the son of an English knight, was educated in Paris and then became a priest. He founded a religious order for young women, later adding lay brothers, lay sisters, and canons regular (priests). He composed the Rule and governed the order, which came to be known as the Gilbertine order. Later in his life, Gilbert patiently bore the pain of being falsely accused and imprisoned by King Henry II. He also suffered from calumny and rebellion by the lay brothers, and eventually blindness, which forced him to retire. He was over one hundred years old when he died. The Gilbertines had expanded to twenty-two houses in England before King Henry VIII suppressed them in the sixteenth century.

PRAYER

Saint Gilbert, your life of dedication to God and servant leadership, even in difficult trials, shows us what fidelity looks like. On your feast, pray for us and with us: Heavenly Father, help us not to be afraid of any suffering you may allow us, but let us accept all things for your glory. Inspire us to carry out the duties of our state in life faithfully and conscientiously. Grant us growth in the virtues of constancy and prudence, and give us the grace to forgive those who gossip, lie about us, and accuse us falsely. Bless priests and religious, and give them the grace to live out their vocations faithfully. We ask this in the name of Jesus. Amen.

Seven Holy Founders of the Servite Order (founded 1233)

These seven men from Florence, Italy, took action to change the culture by first changing themselves. They were merchants who were troubled by the political and religious upheaval around them, so they joined together and left everything to live in poverty, penance, and prayer. Saints Binfilius Monaldi, John Bonagiunta, Gerard Sostegni, Bartholomew Amidei, Benedict dell'Antella, Ricoverus Uguccione, and Alexis Falconieri shared a strong devotion to the Blessed Mother, calling their order the Servants of Mary. All but one of the founders were ordained priests; Alexis chose to remain a lay brother. He is the only one who lived to see the order receive official approval in 1304.

PRAYER

Holy Founders, you chose to combat the evils of your day through penance and prayer, under Mary's protection. Pray with us today: Righteous Father, through the intercession of the Seven Holy Founders, inspire us to truly live our faith in righteousness, no matter what evils may surround us. Allow us to change the culture by first changing ourselves so that we will be credible witnesses. May we leave our place of comfort to follow you. Teach us to live humbly and charitably in our communities. Give us a firm devotion to Mary, so she can lead us to you. We ask this in the name of Jesus. Amen.

FEBRUARY 18

Saint Theotonius (c. 1082–1162)

Saint Theotonius, the first Portuguese saint, was famous for his preaching. He was a founder and prior of the Augustinian monastery of the Holy Cross at Coimbra, and a trusted advisor to King Alfonso Henriques. His special love for the holy souls in purgatory and people in poverty led him to offer Friday Mass for them, and he also took up weekly collections to assist the poor. He was not afraid to speak the truth, even correcting the queen for being in an adulterous relationship. He humbly refused when offered the bishopric and died as a hermit at the age of eighty.

PRAYER

Saint Theotonius, you exercised prudent leadership in the Church and shunned worldly honor. Pray with us on your feast: Dear Father, make us bold in proclaiming the Faith and generous in serving those in need. Grant us growth in humility and prudence. Inspire us to serve the holy souls through consistent prayer and works of mercy. Free us from worldly ambition and make us willing to speak the truth even when it is unpopular. Bless the Augustinian order, keeping it faithful to you. We ask this in the name of Jesus. Amen.

FEBRUARY 19

Saint Lucy Yi Zhenmei (1815–1865)

Saint Lucy was a very pious Chinese girl who committed herself to a life of chastity when she was only twelve years old. After a sickness that almost took her life when she was twenty, she committed herself to a life of deep prayer study, which she loved. Because of her love for her faith, she was asked to be a catechist for children in one parish, then later a catechist for women in another. While she was assisting the missionary priest Father Jean-Pierre Neel, a persecution of Catholics arose. Lucy and Father Neel were killed, along with Martin Wu Xuesheng, John Chen Xianheng, and John Zhang Tianshen. Together, these five are called the martyrs of Guizhou, part of the larger group known as the martyrs of China.

PRAYER

Saint Lucy, pray for us to love God with everything that we are, as you did, and to work tirelessly to share His love with others. Pray with us now: Loving Father, grant us the virtues of piety and chastity that Saint Lucy had. Guide us to love and be faithful to our Catholic Faith, boldly proclaiming it even in the face of persecution. Bless catechists and parents who teach the Faith. Protect all who suffer persecution for their faith in you. We ask this in the name of Jesus. Amen.

FEBRUARY 20

Saints Jacinta (1910–1920) and Francisco Marto (1908–1919)

Saints Jacinta and Francisco Marto were seven and nine years old, respectively, when Mother Mary appeared to them and their cousin, Venerable Lucia dos Santos, in Fatima, Portugal, in 1917. Over the course of five apparitions, the Blessed Mother asked the children to do penance for sinners and pray for the conversion of Russia. On October 13, the date of the last apparition, thousands watched as the sun danced in the sky — a miracle to assure the world that the message these children received was authentic. All three children remained faithful to prayer and penance, offering up their sufferings for sinners. Jacinta and Francisco both died very young, soon after the apparitions took place. They were canonized October 13, 2017. Together with Lucia, who died in 2005, they are buried in the basilica at the Cova da Iria, built where Our Lady appeared.

PRAYER

Saints Jacinta and Francisco, pray for us to willingly offer sacrifices in reparation for sin, as you did, and pray with us on this feast: Loving Father, give us all a childlike faith and a fervent longing for the salvation of souls and the conversion of sinners. Inspire us, especially children, whose prayers are so powerful, to pray, fast, give alms, and do penance. Teach us to honor our Blessed Mother and to do what she asks of us, so that she can lead us to you. We ask this in the name of Jesus. Amen.

FEBRUARY 21

Saint Peter Damian (1007–1072)

Peter Damian suffered neglect as a child, particularly at the hands of one of his older brothers. In spite of this, he developed a deep life of prayer, and eventually, with the support of another brother, he became a university professor. Desiring to give his whole life to God, he became a Benedictine monk and later was made abbot. He wrote many documents and letters, many of which still exist today. He stressed the importance of virtue, yet also understood human weakness, once writing in a letter: "Do not be depressed. Do not let your weakness make you impatient. Instead, let the serenity of your spirit shine through your face." In 1057, he was appointed Cardinal-Bishop of Ostia and served in this office for several years before retiring again to the monastery. Pope Leo XII proclaimed him a Doctor of the Church in 1828.

PRAYER

Saint Peter, you possessed the gift of wisdom, and you shared it through your writing and leadership in the Church. Pray with us today: Gracious Father, inspire us to persevere in developing virtue and reform anything in our character that is displeasing to you. Guide us to study and learn our faith. Teach us how to use our gifts and talents for your glory and our neighbor's good. Fill us with joy in your goodness and help us never to despair of our weaknesses. Make us saints. We ask this in the name of Jesus. Amen.

FEBRUARY 22

Saint Margaret of Cortona (1247–1297)

Saint Margaret of Cortona, abused as a child by her stepmother, later had an illicit relationship with a nobleman and gave birth to a son. After the boy's father died, Margaret experienced a deep conversion, confessed her sins, and began a new life. She became a committed lay Franciscan, and her son eventually became a friar. Living simply, Margaret practiced penance and served the sick. God granted her many mystical gifts. She founded a hospital in Cortona and the lay Confraternity of Our Lady of Mercy to help run it. Her incorrupt body lies in the church of Saint Basil in Cortona, Italy. Margaret is the patron saint of single mothers.

PRAYER

Saint Margaret, you turned from a life of sin to dedicated, loving service. On your feast, pray for us to experience lasting conversion, and pray with us: Merciful Father, never let us doubt your mercy and forgiveness. Draw us back to you when we go astray, and give us a steadfast love for our neighbor. Make us zealous in serving the poor, sick, and vulnerable. Fill us with the Holy Spirit. Assist us in making perfect penance for our sins. Bless the Franciscan order, keeping it faithful to you. We ask this in the name of Jesus. Amen.

FEBRUARY 23

Saint Polycarp (d. 156)

Saint Polycarp, bishop of Smyrna (today Izmir in Turkey) was so holy that, in his old age, people vied for the opportunity to help him take off his shoes. He learned the Faith from Saint John the Apostle, and he himself taught Saint Irenaeus. Polycarp had a reputation for wisdom, inspiring others by the maturity of his faith. When a persecution broke out, Polycarp was arrested and sentenced to death for his faith. His captors tried to convince him to apostatize, but he famously replied: "Eighty-six years have I served Him, and He has done me no harm. How then can I curse my King that saved me?" They tried to burn him at the stake, but the fire did not touch him, so at last they stabbed him to death. Saint Polycarp is the patron saint of earaches.

PRAYER

Saint Polycarp, even in your old age, you loved God above all things and willingly gave your life for your faith. Pray with us now: Loving Father, inspire us to stand fast, firm in our faith, constantly working for unity within ourselves, our families, and the Church. May we always encourage and support others, holding fast to our faith no matter what it may cost. Grant us the virtues of fortitude and fidelity. Have mercy on those who are persecuted for their faith in you. Bless all bishops and make them true shepherds and virtuous leaders. We ask this in the name of Jesus. Amen.

FEBRUARY 24

Blessed Josefa Naval Girbés (1820–1893)

Blessed Josefa, a pious, responsible child from the Valencia region of Spain, was only thirteen when her mother died, and she began to take care of her younger siblings. With guidance from her spiritual director, she made a vow of perpetual chastity at the age of eighteen. Later she became a Secular Carmelite and brought young women into her home to teach them the art of embroidery and help deepen their prayer. Near the end of her life, she worked tirelessly to care for victims of a cholera epidemic. When she died from heart failure at the age of seventy-two, she was buried in the Carmelite habit.

PRAYER

Blessed Josefa, you generously served God and your neighbors throughout your life. Pray for us to be able to do the same, and pray with us: Heavenly Father, make us completely devoted to you in all that we do, no matter our state in life. Lead us into a deep friendship with you and teach us to pray always, and to make you known. May we recognize the gifts you have given us and use them joyfully in your service. Increase in us the virtues of charity and generosity, and fill us with determination to be faithful in all the duties of our state in life. We ask this in the name of Jesus. Amen.

FEBRUARY 25

Blessed Rani Maria (1954–1995)

Blessed Rani Maria became a sister with the Franciscan Clarists in India. She loved the poor and helped them in every way possible. She wanted to help improve their position in life and free them from the bonded labor that enslaved them. Unfortunately, this angered the people making money from their labor, and they had her murdered. She was stabbed to death, martyred for following Jesus' admonition to help the poor. She died saying the name of Jesus. Similar to Saint Maria Goretti, her family later forgave her murderer, and in a marvelous turn of events, after he was released from prison, he attended her beatification.

PRAYER

Blessed Rani Maria, you served the poor with compassion and courage, giving your life for doing what was right. Pray for us and with us today: Gentle Father, help us to follow the commandments, which show us how to love one another with unselfish concern and self-sacrifice. Give us wisdom to know how to help the poor that we encounter, recognizing that we are all brothers and sisters. Free all people in slavery of any kind and convert those who abuse them. Bless the congregation of Franciscan Clarists and keep them faithful to you. We ask this in the name of Jesus. Amen.

FEBRUARY 26

Saint Alexander of Alexandria (250–328)

Saint Alexander, bishop of Alexandria, was known for his strong leadership against the Arian heresy, which taught that Jesus was not divine. He excommunicated Arius, the leading proponent of this false teaching. Revered by those who knew him, Alexander was just, virtuous, mild, and eloquent in speech. He helped lead the First Council of Nicaea (325), which declared that Jesus Christ is truly God. Before dying, he handpicked Saint Athanasius to be his successor.

PRAYER

Saint Alexander, you provided leadership and clarity in the Church in confusing times. Pray for us to recognize the truth always, and pray with us now: Loving Father, give us the wisdom to see the truth, the humility to accept it, and the courage to proclaim it. Bless our pope and all bishops, and make them strong pastors, true shepherds, and virtuous leaders, ready to correct those who cause scandal. Bring back those who have fallen away from the Faith and keep us faithful to the Church. May we always be ready to defend our faith when necessary. We ask this in the name of Jesus. Amen.

FEBRUARY 27

Saint Gregory of Narek (950–1003)

Saint Gregory of Narek, an Armenian monk, was a gifted theologian, poet, and writer who spoke about the Holy Trinity and the healing power of prayer. He emphasized the great benefit of the sacraments as instruments of grace in building a life of holiness. At the same time, he had a profound understanding of the ways in which sin works to destroy us, and what we must do to recover from sinful habits to stop the effects of sin in our lives. He relied on the goodness and mercy of God, writing, "In the face of my darkness, you are light. In the face of my mortality, you are life." His lengthy *Book of Lamentations*, which was his last written work, is considered a spiritual masterpiece. Pope Francis declared him a Doctor of the Church in 2015.

PRAYER

Saint Gregory, in your beautiful writing, you taught us about God's goodness and our own need to turn away from sin and toward God. Pray with us on your feast: Gracious Father, increase our desire to know you, to praise you, and to live united with you, Jesus, and the Holy Spirit. Put an end to invasions, unjust war, and genocide throughout the world. Heal and restore all who are victims of war, especially those suffering from loss of loved ones, property, and home. Bless Catholic poets and theologians who write and teach your truth. We ask this in the name of Jesus. Amen.

FEBRUARY 28

Blessed Daniel Bottier (1876–1936)

Blessed Daniel was a French missionary priest in the Congregation of the Holy Spirit. He served in West Africa, later raising money to build a cathedral to honor Africans who gave their lives for France and vice versa. He returned to France because of poor health, and then served as a military chaplain in World War I. Devoted to Saint Thérèse, he asked her intercession for protection during the war, and he survived. He won awards for his bravery, including the Croix de Guerre and the Legion of Honor. After the war, he built and administered an orphanage for children who had been orphaned or abandoned.

PRAYER

Blessed Daniel, your life of service bore witness to God's great love. Pray for us to love God generously, and pray with us: Heavenly Father, give us courage to face our fears and assist others in their time of need. Grant us your protection in difficult and dangerous times. Give us the virtues of fortitude, prudence, and generosity. Guide us to ask the intercession of the saints in our time of need. Bless and protect all soldiers and chaplains. We ask this in the name of Jesus. Amen.

FEBRUARY 29

Saint Oswald of Worcester (d. 992)

Saint Oswald lived surrounded by saints, and his life stands as a beautiful reminder that holiness begets holiness. He studied under his uncle, Saint Odo of Canterbury, before becoming a Benedictine monk in France. Later, Oswald returned to England at the encouragement of Saint Dunstan, who appointed him bishop of Worcester. The saintly king Edgar the Peaceful assisted him in becoming bishop. As bishop, Oswald worked with Saints Dunstan and Ethelwold to enact monastic and ecclesial reforms. Named archbishop of York in 972, he was devoted to serving the poor and died while washing their feet according to his customary Lenten practice.

PRAYER

Saint Oswald, pray for us to grow in holiness ourselves and to encourage our family and friends to grow in holiness as well. Pray with us today: Righteous Father, make us tireless and fearless in carrying out your will. Grant us holy friendships, and help us to spur one another on to greater love for you and your Church. Strengthen us in all virtues, especially humility and charity. Bless the Benedictine order and keep it faithful to you. We ask this in the name of Jesus. Amen.

MARCH

THE MONTH OF
SAINT JOSEPH

MARCH 1

Saint David of Wales (d. c. 600)

Very little is known about Saint David, but there are many stories and legends about his life. His mother was Saint Non, and it is said that his father was royal. David became bishop of Menevia, and he helped lead two local synods. He worked hard to erect monasteries and to end the heresy of Pelagianism (a heresy that denied original sin and the necessity of grace). He lived an ascetic life and is said to have survived for years solely on leeks and water. He taught that holiness can be found in doing our ordinary duties, and in his last words to his followers he said, "Be joyful, keep the faith and do the little things that you have heard and seen me do." Saint David is the patron saint of poets and of Wales.

PRAYER

Saint David, you exemplified growing in holiness by carrying out our daily duties with fidelity. Pray for us to grow in holiness through faithfulness to little things, and pray with us today: Heavenly Father, make us holy in our ordinary life. Help us to carefully carry out all the duties in our state of life. Help us to grow in the virtues of fidelity, simplicity, and, above all, love. Bless all bishops, making them true shepherds and virtuous leaders. We ask this in the name of Jesus. Amen.

MARCH 2

Saint Agnes of Bohemia (1200–1282)

Saint Agnes of Bohemia was a princess. Her father was King Ottocar of Bohemia, and her mother was Queen Constance of Hungary, who was a relative of Saint Elizabeth of Hungary. Agnes gave up the chance to become queen, refusing to marry Frederick II of Germany because she wanted to consecrate her life to God. She asked the pope to intervene on her behalf with Frederick, who reportedly answered, "If she had left me for a mortal man, I would have taken vengeance with the sword, but I cannot take offense because in preference to me she has chosen the King of Heaven." Agnes founded and then joined the monastery of Saint Savior of Poor Clares in Prague. Saint Clare herself supported Agnes's foundation and sent her letters, four of which still exist. Agnes had the gifts of prophecy and working miracles.

PRAYER

Saint Agnes, you preferred to live in union with God even more than worldly honors. On your feast day, pray for us to have that same humility, and pray with us: Loving Father, bless us with saintly friends who will encourage and urge us on to love and follow you more faithfully. Give us the courage to follow your will for our lives, and grant us growth in the virtues of humility and simplicity. Bless the Franciscan order and all Poor Clare sisters, keeping them faithful to you. We ask this in the name of Jesus. Amen.

MARCH 3

Saint Katharine Drexel (1858–1955)

Saint Katharine, an heiress from Philadelphia, Pennsylvania, had a life-changing meeting with Pope Leo XIII, becoming a missionary at his request. She founded a religious order, the Sisters of the Blessed Sacrament, to serve the impoverished Native American and African American people in the United States. Her generosity knew no bounds, and she gave everything — her gifts, talents, and tremendous wealth of more than 12 million dollars — to serve God, establishing missions, Catholic schools, and Xavier University in New Orleans. She even turned her family summer home in Pennsylvania into the first convent for her religious sisters. She once remarked, "The patient and humble endurance of the cross — whatever nature it may be — is the highest work we have to do."

PRAYER

Saint Katharine, pray for us to serve God and our neighbor with generosity as you did. Pray with us today: Gracious Father, give us generous hearts, and show us how you want us to use our gifts in your service. Never let us forget our responsibility to live out the social teaching of the Church, and make us sensitive to the needs of vulnerable populations. In your goodness, raise up virtuous leaders in the Church and society. Strengthen us in all the virtues, especially generosity and charity. Convert hearts from prejudice and racism to love and compassion. Conform our thoughts, actions, and lives to Jesus. Make us saints. We ask this in the name of Jesus. Amen.

MARCH 4

Saint Casimir of Poland (1458-1483)

From a very young age, Prince Casimir immersed himself in prayer, study, fasting, mortifications, and true devotion to Mother Mary. Son of King Casimir IV, Casimir was called "the Peacemaker" because he refused to engage in an unjust war to take the throne of Hungary when he was a young teenager. Later, Casimir ruled Poland as regent while his father was away for a time in Lithuania. He refused to marry, choosing instead to embrace chastity in the single state. He died of a lung disease when he was twenty-five and is buried in the Church of Saint Stanislaus, where miracles were reported. Saint Casimir is the patron saint of Lithuania, Poland, and the Knights of Saint John.

PRAYER

Saint Casimir, you sought to make peace in your life and leadership, always mindful of your duty to God. Pray for us and with us today: Righteous Father, fill the world with your peace, beginning with our hearts. Help us to set aside ambition, pride, and greed, and to seek only to do your will in all things. Draw us into prayer. Teach us how to fast and do penance according to our age and state in life. Make us strong in character, form our conscience, and strengthen us to live our convictions even when it is difficult. Give us the virtues of compassion, fortitude, and chastity. Bless our civil leaders and give them the grace and the courage to govern in accord with your law. We ask this in the name of Jesus. Amen.

MARCH 5

Saint John Joseph of the Cross (1654–1734)

Saint John Joseph grew up on Ischia Island near Naples, Italy, and from an early age he showed a deep love for God and for the poor. At the age of sixteen, he joined the Franciscan order, choosing to follow the reforms enacted by Saint Peter of Alcantara. At the urging of his superiors, he became a priest. When he was only twenty-four years old, he became novice master, and he worked to teach his novices the value of self-discipline, austerity, and recreation. He became guardian of his monastery and then provincial of the Alcantarine Reform in Italy. God gave him many gifts, including levitation during ecstasies, bilocation, supplying and multiplying food, mysticism, prophesy, healing touch, healing of hearts (especially when hearing confessions), and spiritual direction.

PRAYER

Saint John Joseph, God showered you with spiritual gifts, and you freely offered them in His service. Pray for us to be open to God's work in and through us. Pray with us today: Merciful Father, grant us determination and purity of heart to seek you in all things and to die to ourselves. Help us to persevere in prayer and fasting. May we see your goodness and miracles in our lives and give thanks in all circumstances. Give us the grace we need to fulfill our duties according to our state in life, while not neglecting rest and recreation. Make us saints. Bless the Franciscan order, keeping it faithful to you. We ask this in the name of Jesus. Amen.

MARCH 6

Saint Colette (d. 1447)

Saint Colette was born in Corbie, France, and was orphaned at seventeen. Desiring rigor in the spiritual life, she joined different religious communities, eventually becoming a Third Order Franciscan and living as a hermit. Then Saint Francis appeared to her in a vision, asking her to reform the Poor Clares, restoring the original austerity that the order had lost. Colette was obedient. Over time, despite opposition, she founded many convents and reformed many existing convents. She was a virtuous, trusted leader, and God granted her mystical gifts and allowed her to work miracles, including bringing a stillborn child back to life. She also helped her friend, Saint Vincent Ferrer, in the work of healing the Great Western Schism.

PRAYER

Saint Colette, you followed God's call for reform, and you led your sisters with wisdom and grace. Pray with us on your feast: Loving Father, fill us with determination to love you without reserve, and make us unafraid of sacrifice. Inspire us to practice silence and listen carefully to your voice. May we seek your will in all things and follow it with obedience. Strengthen in us the virtues of self-control, prudence, and obedience. Grant us a deep, abiding love for our neighbor and fill us with joy in serving you. Bless the Poor Clare nuns and all members of the Franciscan order, keeping them faithful to you. We ask this in the name of Jesus. Amen.

MARCH 7

Saints Perpetua, Felicity, and Companions (d. 203)

Perpetua and Felicity were among a group of Christians who were arrested and condemned in Carthage, during the persecutions under Roman Emperor Septimius Severus. Perpetua was a noblewoman with an infant son, and Felicity a slave, who delivered her baby girl in prison. Perpetua's father begged her to apostatize and return home, but she refused, even though it meant being separated from her son. Both Perpetua and Felicity remained faithful to the bitter end. They were martyred in the arena along with their catechumen companions Revocatus, Saturninus, and Secundis. Thrown to a wild beast, the women were not killed instantly and finally had to be killed by gladiators. Saint Perpetua kept a diary — known now as the *Passion of Perpetua and Felicity* — which is one of the oldest written accounts by a Christian woman.

PRAYER

Saints Perpetua and Felicity, you willingly gave your lives for love of God, and you never wavered even though you faced bitter suffering. Pray with us now: Gracious Father, fill us with the courage to hold fast to our faith, no matter what it may cost us. Inspire us to imitate the zeal of the martyrs. Make us great saints, willing to face opposition and even death for love of you, standing firm in our convictions. Grant us holy friendships, so that we can support one another in loving and serving you. Protect all who are persecuted for their faith. We ask this in the name of Jesus. Amen.

MARCH 8

Saint John of God (1495–1550)

Saint John of God was born in Portugal, but he was abducted when he was eight years old and taken to Spain. He served as a soldier in the Spanish army for many years. Later, he sold religious goods in Granada, until the preaching of Saint John of Ávila inspired him to perform public penance for his past sins. His penances were so extreme that people thought he had gone mad. At last, John of Ávila encouraged him to devote himself to caring for the sick and the poor. He obeyed and humbly threw himself into this work. At one point, he was accused of keeping unsavory people in his hospitals. He told the archbishop, "I know of no bad person in my hospital except myself, who am unworthy to eat the bread of the poor." Over time others joined him in his work, eventually forming a religious order, the Brothers Hospitallers. Saint John is the patron saint of booksellers, firefighters, heart patients, hospitals, nurses, printers, the sick, and skin diseases.

PRAYER

Saint John, you wanted only to serve God after your conversion, and you did so by serving the poor. Pray for us to love our neighbors, and pray with us today: Dear Father, give us generosity to serve the poor and the sick without counting the cost. Fill us with your Holy Spirit. Conform our thoughts, actions, and lives to Jesus in total surrender to you. May we use all our talents and gifts for your service, without reserve. Bless the order of the Brothers Hospitallers, keeping it faithful to you. We ask this in the name of Jesus. Amen.

MARCH 9

Saint Dominic Savio (1842–1857)

Saint Dominic Savio, a student of Saint John Bosco, was determined to stay pure in mind, heart, and body. He once asked God to take his life rather than allow him to commit a sin against his purity, for he knew that only the pure shall see the face of God. He was an altar server with a deep love for the Eucharist and a profound prayer life. He was known to say, "I cannot do big things. But I want all I do, even the smallest thing, to be for the greater glory of God." Dominic died when he was only fourteen years old, and, according to John Bosco, he never committed a mortal sin. Saint Dominic is the patron saint of choirboys.

PRAYER

Saint Dominic Savio, pray for us to have pure and undivided hearts like yours, focused on God alone, and pray with us: Loving Father, give us pure and open hearts, and make us desire nothing more than to serve you in our littleness. Grant us purity in mind and heart. Lead us to spiritual directors who can help us to discern your will for our lives. Bless all children and draw them to yourself. We ask this in the name of Jesus. Amen.

MARCH 10

Saint John Ogilvie (c. 1579–1615)

Saint John Ogilvie was born in Scotland and raised as a Calvinist. He converted to Catholicism when he was seventeen and went on to become a Jesuit priest in Paris. He longed to return to Scotland as a missionary, and after a time his superiors finally permitted it, although they knew the mission would be dangerous, for Catholicism was against the law in Britain. After only eleven months of ministry to the distressed Catholics in Scotland, John was betrayed by someone who pretended to be interested in converting. Arrested, tortured, and deprived of sleep for eight days, he held fast to his faith. At last, he was convicted of treason and publicly hanged in Glasgow. He was only thirty-six years old.

PRAYER
Saint John Ogilvie, you courageously brought the Faith to your native land despite the dangers, and you gave your life for it. Pray with us on your feast: Heavenly Father, grant us the courage to share our faith no matter what it may cost us. Instill in us such a strong faith that we would rather die than abandon you. Teach us how to forgive those who betray or abandon us. Bless and protect all who are persecuted for their faith in you. We ask this in the name of Jesus. Amen.

MARCH 11

Saint Eulogius of Cordoba (d. 859)

Saint Eulogius was born to a noble Christian family in Cordoba, Spain, which at that time was ruled by Muslims. He became a priest and was known for his humility and kindness. He was also a voracious reader and writer. Many of his writings still exist today, including his *Exhortation to Martyrdom*, which he wrote while imprisoned during the Christian persecution that broke out in Cordoba in 850. In 858, he was named archbishop of Toledo, but he was arrested before he could be consecrated. He had given sanctuary to a young woman named Leocritia, who had become a Christian, and when he refused to give up his faith, he was beheaded. He is buried in the Cathedral of Oviedo.

PRAYER

Saint Eulogius, pray for us to be kind and courageous as we live our faith, and pray with us today: Gracious Father, grant us the courage to live and die for love of you. Instill in us a love of learning our faith and sharing it with others. May we use our gifts and creativity for your glory. Keep us humble and help us always to be kind, just as you are kind. We ask this in the name of Jesus. Amen.

MARCH 12

Blessed Manuel Solórzano (1905–1977)

Blessed Manuel Solórzano, a Salvadorian layman, was married to Eleuteria Guillen and had ten children. He was a good father and Catholic, active in evangelization in his parish, and he served as a catechist. He was traveling with his parish priest, Father Rutilio Grande, SJ, and Nelson Lemus, a sixteen-year-old boy, when they were attacked and martyred in 1977. Father Rutilio, who was a friend of Saint Oscar Romero, had received death threats because of his work on behalf of the poor. The three men were beatified together in 2022.

PRAYER
Blessed Manuel, you served the Church faithfully throughout your life and willingly accepted death for standing firm in the face of injustice. Pray for us and with us on your feast day: Merciful Father, help us to live our faith through works of mercy and assist others whenever possible. Help us to evangelize those who do not know you. Free us from fear and make us ready to do your will no matter the cost. Give us the virtues of fortitude and justice, and uphold the dignity of all the oppressed throughout the world. Bless those who are persecuted and threatened for their faith. Bless the Jesuit order and keep it faithful to you. We ask this in the name of Jesus. Amen.

MARCH 13

Blessed Agnellus of Pisa (1195–1236)

Blessed Agnellus, born of the noble Agnelli family in Pisa, gave up his inheritance, and was received into the Franciscan order by Saint Francis himself. Later, Francis sent him to establish friaries in France and then England. He is known as the first minister provincial of the English Province. He worked to establish a school for the friars at Oxford and brought in Robert Grosseteste to teach them, turning the school into a center for learning. Agnellus died at Oxford and was buried there, and his body was incorrupt for three hundred years until Henry VIII destroyed the monasteries and relics in England. Blessed Agnello of Pisa is the patron saint of the sick, the poor, and hospitals.

PRAYER

Blessed Agnellus, you were a wise and prudent leader, and your fidelity paved the way for many friars to learn theology at Oxford. Pray for us to be faithful to the duties of our state in life, both big and small, and pray with us: Loving Father, keep us faithful in doing your will. Inspire us with a love of learning, and teach us how to apply what we learn through consistent prayer, work, study, and action. Give us the virtues of prudence and tenacity, and help us to be wise leaders in the areas that you have placed under our stewardship. Bless the Franciscan order, keeping it faithful to you. We ask this in the name of Jesus. Amen.

MARCH 14

Saint Matilda (895–968)

Saint Matilda was a faithful queen and mother. She was also a Benedictine Oblate and gave generously from her wealth. The daughter of Count Dietrich of Westphalia, she married King Henry the Fowler of Germany, and they had three sons: German Emperor Otto the Great, Henry the Duke of Bavaria, and Saint Bruno, archbishop of Cologne. They also had two daughters, Gerberga and Hedwig. She encouraged her sons to be just and moderate rulers. Throughout her life, she founded churches and monasteries, including the monastery at Quedlinburg, Germany, where she died and was buried next to her husband, who preceded her in death. She is a patron saint of widows and large families.

PRAYER

Saint Matilda, you lived a holy life and inspired your children to serve the Lord faithfully. Pray for us and with us on your feast: Heavenly Father, make us generous in our service of you and your Church. Guard our minds and hearts from worldly ambition. Grant us detachment from material wealth, and strengthen in us the virtues of wisdom, justice, and charity. Bless married couples and help them to be good to one another, and help all parents to raise their children to love you and serve you. Protect all widows. Bless the Benedictine order, keeping it faithful to you. We ask this in the name of Jesus. Amen.

MARCH 15

Saint Louise de Marillac (1591–1660)

Louise was only a little girl when her mother died, and her father died while she was still a teenager. She wanted to be a religious sister, but she was discouraged from this vocation. Instead, she married Antoine LeGras and had a son, Michel. After Antoine's death, Louise helped Saint Vincent de Paul found the Daughters of Charity. She wrote a Rule of Life and trained and directed the sisters, whose mission was to support the sick, elderly, and orphaned. She once wrote, "What a good thing it is to persevere in the love and service of God … it is very difficult for us to carry out our responsibilities well, but God who has given them to us will not deny us His grace." Louise and Saint Vincent died within six months of each other and are buried a few blocks apart in Paris. Saint Louise is the patron saint of Christian social workers.

PRAYER
Saint Louise de Marillac, you generously gave your life to the Lord, both as a wife and mother and as a religious sister and founder. Pray with us now: Loving Father, help us to trust you and your plan for our lives, even when all seems dark. Help us to grow in all the virtues, especially charity, humility, and fidelity. Inspire us to combine prayer with action in caring for our neighbors. Comfort and provide for all widows. Bless the Daughters of Charity, keeping them faithful to you. We ask this in the name of Jesus. Amen.

MARCH 16

Saint Dentlin (d. seventh century)

Saint Dentlin, a holy child born into a family of saints, died when he was only seven years old. His father, Saint Vincent, was the abbot of a Benedictine monastery, and his mother, Saint Waldetrudis, founded a convent. His brother, Saint Landericus, was bishop of Paris. His sisters were Saint Madalbarta, a Benedictine nun, and Saint Aldetrudis, a Benedictine abbess. His aunt, Saint Aldegund (Waldetrudis's sister), was an abbess. Even his maternal grandparents, Walbert and Bertila, were saints! Even though he was very young, Dentlin loved to live and proclaim his faith. For this reason, he is considered a confessor of the Faith.

PRAYER

Saint Dentlin, your holy life reminds us that we can be holy at any age, because God calls us all, young and old. Pray for us and with us: Gentle Father, thank you for the gift of our faith. Grant us the graces we need to live it joyfully and to share it with everyone we meet. Make us contemplatives in action. Build our families into holy domestic churches full of saints. Inspire children to follow the examples of all the child saints and to seek holiness no matter how young they are. Bless the Benedictine order, keeping it faithful to you. We ask this in the name of Jesus. Amen.

MARCH 17

Saint Patrick (385–461)

Saint Patrick was only sixteen when he was kidnapped from his home in Britain, taken to Ireland, and sold as a slave to do shepherd's work. For six years he worked and prayed during the long, lonely nights, and he became close to God and learned to love Him deeply. After he escaped and returned to his home, he followed God's call to become a priest. Following his ordination, he returned to Ireland as a bishop, and he worked tirelessly to convert the whole island to Christianity. He had the gifts of healing and miracles, and the Irish people revered him. He wrote the "Confessio" and a beautiful prayer called "The Breastplate of Saint Patrick." Saint Patrick is the patron saint of Ireland.

PRAYER

Saint Patrick, you turned the trauma of your kidnapping and slavery into an opportunity for abundant grace for you and for Ireland. Pray for us to be open to God's work in us through our suffering, and pray with us: Dear Father, inspire us to proclaim the truth of your Gospel with love, accepting any suffering you allow. Give us a heart of compassion for all people, and free those who are enslaved in any way. Strengthen and increase in us the virtues of faith, hope, and charity. Bless all bishops, making them true shepherds and virtuous leaders. We ask this in the name of Jesus. Amen.

MARCH 18

Saint Cyril of Jerusalem (315–386)

Saint Cyril was not afraid to tackle the Arian heresy head on, even though it meant facing controversy, false accusation, and exile. He was ordained bishop of Jerusalem and spent many years combating heresy and false accusations. He was known for his tender care for the poor and for his clear teaching of the Faith. Among his writings, his *Catecheses* helped to teach the people the correct truths of the Catholic Faith amidst confusion caused by heresy. Cyril was present at the Council of Constantinople in 381, which condemned Arianism. Pope Leo XIII named Cyril a Doctor of the Church in 1883.

PRAYER

Saint Cyril, your wisdom and leadership helped guide the Church in confusing times. Pray for the Church today, and pray with us on your feast: Loving Father, inspire us to learn about and defend our faith even when it is unpopular. Be with us and give us the grace we need to carry on when we are falsely accused or misunderstood. Grant us the virtues of wisdom and courage. Bless all who are preparing to enter the Church. We ask this in the name of Jesus. Amen.

MARCH 19

Saint Joseph (d. first century)

The Bible describes Saint Joseph as "a just man" (Mt 1:19) who took his job as provider for the Holy Family seriously. Although he did not understand what was going on, after the Annunciation, he took Mary as his wife and raised Jesus as his own. He lovingly, faithfully, and obediently protected his family, taking them to Egypt at the angel's warning to protect the infant Jesus from King Herod. As Jesus grew up, Joseph taught Him how to pray, took Him to Synagogue, and trained Him in carpentry. Saint Joseph is the patron saint of the Universal Church, fathers, working men, married couples, and a happy death.

PRAYER

Saint Joseph, pray for us to be just as you were and to respond with fidelity to all God asks of us, even when we don't understand. Pray with us on your feast: Merciful Father, thank you for your providence and constant care for all our needs. Like Saint Joseph, may we always trust in your goodness and do as you ask, even when we do not understand it. Bless our work, and help us to do everything we do humbly and for your greater glory. Grant us all virtues, and help us always to strive to grow in holiness. Teach us to live out our commitment to family life, and grant us unity and stability in our families. We ask this in the name of Jesus. Amen.

MARCH 20

Saint Jozef Bilczewski (1860–1923)

Saint Jozef Bilczewski was the oldest of nine children in a Polish peasant family. He was ordained a priest in 1884. His great intellectual ability led him to obtain a doctorate degree in theology, and in 1891, he became professor at the University of Lviv. He quickly became dean and then rector at the university before he was appointed archbishop of Lviv. As archbishop, he focused on aiding the poor and homeless, and he wrote "On the Social Matters," a pastoral letter on Catholic social justice. He encouraged devotion to the Eucharist and the Sacred Heart, and he worked for peace, especially throughout the upheavals of World War I. He is buried in the cathedral in Lviv, Ukraine.

PRAYER
Saint Jozef Bilczewski, you worked tirelessly for justice and led the Church with fidelity. Pray for us and with us today: Heavenly Father, may we always use our gifts to serve you and bring others to you. Give us tender compassion for the poor and zeal for justice. May we always strive for peace in our world, in the Church, and in our own hearts. We ask this in the name of Jesus. Amen.

MARCH 21

Saint Nicholas von Flüe (1417–1487)

Saint Nicholas von Flüe was a husband, father of ten children, and later a hermit in Switzerland. After raising his family, serving in the military, and working in the Swiss government, when he was fifty years old, he followed God's call to become a hermit. His wife and children gave their blessing, and he moved into a hermit's cell not far from his family's home. Miraculously, he lived only on the Eucharist for nineteen years. This prayer that he wrote encapsulates his spirituality: "My Lord and my God, take from me everything that distances me from you. My Lord and my God, give me everything that brings me closer to you. My Lord and my God, detach me from myself to give my all to you" (quoted in CCC 226). Saint Nicholas von Flüe is the patron saint of Switzerland and those who are separated from a spouse.

PRAYER
Saint Nicholas, you always sought God first, putting Him ahead of everything in your life. Pray for us to do the same, and pray with us: Righteous Father, inspire us to lovingly care for our families while still putting you first. Give us the virtues of diligence and justice, and make us wise and caring leaders. Comfort us, especially when those we love are absent or distant from us. May we serve you faithfully through consistent prayer while carrying out the duties of our state in life. We ask this in the name of Jesus. Amen.

MARCH 22

Saint Darerca of Ireland (d. fifth century)

Although Saint Darerca, the sister of Saint Patrick, was the mother of many saints, she herself is hardly known. At least four of her sons became bishops of Ireland and saints, accompanying Saint Patrick on his missionary journeys. She had two daughters who are also saints. While little is known of her life, we know from her legacy that she lived up to her Irish name, *Diar-Sheare*, which means constant and firm love. She is the patron saint of Valencia Island.

PRAYER

Saint Darerca, you lived a hidden life, yet your children are a shining testament to your holiness. Pray for us and with us on your feast: Gentle Father, bless our families, and grant us the grace to spiritually lift others up and help them grow in holiness. Guide mothers and fathers to raise holy children and share the Faith with the world. Help us all to grow in virtue, especially the virtues of charity, humility, and kindness. Grant us the ability to be constant and firm in our love for you and others. We ask this in the name of Jesus. Amen.

MARCH 23

Saint Turibius de Mogrovejo (1538–1606)

Saint Turibius, born into a noble family in Spain, became archbishop of Lima, Peru. He was so holy that he impacted and influenced many other saints, including Rose of Lima (whom he confirmed) and Martin de Porres. Turibius urged people to use the time God gives us wisely because we will have to account for it. A true reformer, he worked for twenty-six years to help the native people in his diocese in every way possible, building schools and hospitals to care for them. He held the Spanish colonists accountable, and he refused to let anyone try to justify or excuse unjust behavior toward the native people. He is justly called their defender.

PRAYER

Saint Turibius, you led the Church in the New Word, modeling justice and charity in all you did. Pray for us and with us: Loving Father, make us generous in serving you and sharing your love with the world. Fill us with all virtues, especially justice and charity. May we use our time wisely and fulfill the unique mission you have entrusted to each one of us. Help us to see the truth and accept no justification of bad behavior or injustice from ourselves or others. Bless and protect the vulnerable, especially the unborn. Guide all bishops, making them faithful shepherds and virtuous leaders. We ask this in the name of Jesus. Amen.

MARCH 24

Saint Oscar Romero (1917–1980)

Saint Oscar Romero was born into a large family in El Salvador in 1917. When he was fourteen years old, he entered seminary, and he was ordained to the priesthood in 1942. Shortly after he was ordained, he wrote in his journal: "In recent days the Lord has inspired in me a great desire for holiness. I have been thinking of how far a soul can ascend if it lets itself be possessed entirely by God." Many years later, in 1970, he became the archbishop of San Salvador in a time of great political turmoil. After the murder of his friend Blessed Rutilio Grande Garcia, Romero zealously began to denounce the violence and injustice that were rampant in the country. His outspoken stance angered powerful people in the government and military. After many threats against his life, he was shot to death while saying Mass on March 23, 1980. Saint Oscar Romero is the patron saint of persecuted Christians.

PRAYER

Saint Oscar, pray for us to have the courage to strive for justice, especially for the most vulnerable, and pray with us today: Gracious Father, make us bold and determined in serving you and upholding the dignity of all people. Strengthen in us the virtues of justice and fortitude, and guide us to see clearly where and when you call us to act, giving us the courage to respond. May we always uphold the Church's teachings on social justice. Make us holy saints. We ask this in the name of Jesus. Amen.

MARCH 25

The Annunciation of the Lord

Jesus, the second Person of the Most Holy Trinity, came to pay a debt we owed that we could never repay. He fulfilled the prophesy in Isaiah 7:14, "Therefore, the Lord himself will give you a sign. Behold, the virgin shall conceive and bear a son, and shall call his name Immanuel." At the Annunciation, the Angel Gabriel appeared to the Virgin Mary and asked her if she would be the mother of God. She said yes, and God the Son became incarnate in her womb. Mary cooperated with God's plan, trusting that He would do what He said no matter how bleak the situation looked. Her simple "yes" gave Jesus to the world.

PRAYER

Mother Mary, your trust and openness to God's will opened the way for God to do His saving work in the world. Pray for us and with us today: Merciful Father, thank you for your great love, which caused you to send your Son to earth to redeem us from our sin. Through Mary's intercession, grant us the grace to trust in Jesus' saving power in our lives and in the world. May we reach out to you in prayer and gratitude in all circumstances of our lives. Show us how you want us to develop and give back all the gifts and talents you have given to us, for your glory and the salvation of souls. We ask this in the name of Jesus. Amen.

MARCH 26

Saint Margaret Clitherow (1555–1586)

Saint Margaret Clitherow was a holy wife and mother who lived in England during the reign of Queen Elizabeth I, when being a Catholic was considered a crime. A convert to Catholicism, she refused to abandon her faith, even secretly running a Catholic school in her home, right under the noses of the authorities. She also helped priests to celebrate secret Masses and hid them when they needed refuge despite the grave danger. Her husband, who was not Catholic, loved and supported her. This "Pearl of York" was martyred by being crushed to death, and her last words were, "Jesu! Jesu! Jesu! have mercy on me!" She is one of the forty Martyrs of England and Wales and is the patron saint of converts to the Catholic Faith.

PRAYER

Saint Margaret, your courage and zeal for the Faith inspire us to place all that we have and are in God's hands, to use as He will. Pray with us on your feast: Gracious Father, fill our hearts with courage and zeal for our faith, even in difficult and dangerous times. Grant us the virtue of fortitude. Protect and preserve our religious freedom and, in your mercy, correct all injustices. Defend those who are most vulnerable. Bless our priests and those suffering and being persecuted for the Faith. May all families rest on you as their firm foundation. We ask this in the name of Jesus. Amen.

MARCH 27

Blessed Giuseppe Ambrosoli (1923–1987)

Blessed Giuseppe grew up in a large family in Italy. Helping others was a commitment and priority in his life. During World War II, he served in the Italian underground, helping people of the Jewish faith get to safety in Switzerland. After the war he became a doctor, then a priest, and he joined the Comboni Missionaries of the Heart of Jesus, moving to Africa to serve as a missionary. He served in Uganda for thirty-two years, opening a hospital and midwifery school where he focused especially on care for people suffering with leprosy. He was deeply loved by the people he served, who called him "the saint doctor."

PRAYER

Blessed Giuseppe, pray for us, that we might love our neighbor and seek to serve others with the same charity that you showed throughout your life. Pray with us today: Righteous Father, fill us with the desire to know and love you better, and remove any obstacles in our lives that keep us from following you wholeheartedly. Guide us in living an ordered life, and help us to serve others with love, commitment, and dedication. May we use all the gifts and talents you give us for your glory. Enable us to use these gifts in an excellent way to serve others. Grant us the gift of hospitality, that we may welcome, encourage, and uplift others. Confirm us in love and make us saints. We ask this in the name of Jesus. Amen.

MARCH 28

Saint Tutilo (d. c. 915)

Saint Tutilo, an Irish Benedictine monk, was an intelligent and gifted artist who excelled as a musician, poet, painter, sculptor, and goldsmith. He was also a gifted orator, composer, and teacher. He spent most of his life in Switzerland in the Abbey of Saint Gall, named after the companion of Saint Columbanus, who died there, and he helped to make the monastery an influential center of learning and culture.

PRAYER

Saint Tutilo, you used your many gifts to give God glory. Pray for us to do the same, and pray with us: Dear Father, you are the source of all beauty and all goodness. Help us to see the beauty in the world you have made, and to cultivate that beauty wherever we find it. Make us obedient to your authority and help us follow your will in our lives. Instill in us a yearning to express our creative gifts, and grant us simplicity of life. Bless the Benedictine order, keeping it faithful to you and its founder. We ask this in the name of Jesus. Amen.

MARCH 29

Saint Cyril of Heliopolis (d. c. 362)

Saint Cyril, a deacon in Phoenicia (modern-day Lebanon), was so zealous to defend God's honor that he demolished pagan idols and destroyed pagan temples. When Julian the Apostate came to power, Cyril was arrested and martyred, along with his bishop, Mark, and many others.

PRAYER
Saint Cyril, pray for us to labor in God's service with zeal and courage, as you did, and pray with us: Loving Father, fill us with your Holy Spirit and give us the zeal to love and serve you courageously, no matter what it might cost us. You are the one true God; strengthen our faith and grant us strength and clarity to recognize and tear down idols — beginning with those in our own hearts. Bless all deacons and make them holy and zealous in their service to you and the Church. We ask this in the name of Jesus. Amen.

MARCH 30

Saint Leonard Murialdo (d. 1890)

Saint Leonard Murialdo had a strong love for the poor, orphaned boys of Turin, which led him to help his friends Saint John Bosco and Father Joseph Cafasso. He worked with them in the Saint Aloysius Oratory and also participated in the Union of Catholic Workers. Later he directed the Artigianelli College of Turin. Traveling extensively, he researched the latest methods of education and vocational training for boys, seeking opportunities to educate and support at-risk boys. He founded the Congregation of Saint Joseph (Giuseppini del Murialdo) and helped put these preventive methods into practice for the boys he served.

PRAYER

Saint Leonard, you wanted the young men in your care to experience the dignity of wholesome work. Pray for us to do our work faithfully, and pray with us: Gentle Father, we praise and thank you for the gift of meaningful work. Help us always to use our gifts to serve you and lead others to you. Grant us the virtues of diligence and generosity. Bless and protect all children, especially those who are orphaned or abandoned. Bless the Congregation of Saint Joseph, keeping it faithful to you and its founder. We ask this in the name of Jesus. Amen.

MARCH 31

Saint Balbina (d. c. 130)

Saint Balbina was the daughter of Quirinus, a Roman tribune who had been ordered to guard the imprisoned Pope Alexander I. Balbina was miraculously healed of an ailment when Alexander instructed her to kiss the chains of Saint Peter. After this healing, Quirinus had the pope released from prison, and he and Balbina converted to Christianity. Pope Alexander then built the church of Saint Peter in Chains in the place where the miraculous chains are still housed. Balbina, her father, and the pope were martyred during the persecution under Roman Emperor Trajan for holding fast to their Catholic Faith. Saint Balbina is the patron saint of throat diseases, goiter, and scrofula (tuberculosis of lymphatic glands).

PRAYER

Saint Balbina, you served God faithfully after your miraculous healing, and ultimately you gave your life for your faith. Pray with us today: Gracious Father, grant that we may always be living witnesses of our faith. Teach us to be faithful, and give us the courage to live and die for love of you. Bless all those who wish to become Catholic and help us to make them welcome in the Church. We ask this in the name of Jesus. Amen.

APRIL

THE MONTH OF
THE RESURRECTION OF JESUS

APRIL 1

Saint Melito (d. c. 180)

Saint Melito, a bishop in influential Sardis (present-day Turkey), was one of the authorities of the Church of Asia, revered as a prophet, and seen as "walking always in the Holy Spirit." He was a great writer, and among other things he wrote "An Apology for the Christian Faith" to the Roman Emperor Marcus Aurelius, appealing to him to stop the persecution of Christians. Sadly, most of Saint Melito's writings have vanished, but we have the names of the works he wrote when he was bishop, and historian Eusebius recorded them. Saint Jerome and Tertullian both wrote of him as well.

PRAYER

Saint Melito, you led the Church in the midst of persecution and wrote with great wisdom. Pray for us and with us today: Gracious Father, grant us the grace to know you and to make you known. Guide us to use all our gifts to help others and lead them to you. Strengthen in us the virtues of courage and obedience. Teach us to listen to and obey the Holy Spirit, and send us His fruits and gifts in abundance. Bless your Church and protect all Christians who are persecuted for their belief in you. We ask this in the name of Jesus. Amen.

APRIL 2

Saint Francis of Paola (1416–1507)

Saint Francis of Paola was a hermit with a deep devotion to Saint Francis of Assisi. His secluded and prayerful lifestyle was so attractive that people flocked to join him, and he had to begin a religious order to accommodate them. He wrote a Rule of Life for the friars, nuns, and laypeople of his order, the Hermits of Saint Francis, which came to be called the Minims, meaning "least." God worked many miracles through him and also gave him the gift of prophesy. When King Louis XI of France lay dying, Francis helped prepare him for death. His successor, Charles VIII, was so grateful that he constructed a monastery for him. Saint Francis of Paola is the patron saint of seafarers.

PRAYER

Saint Francis, you gave yourself completely to God, and He worked marvels through you. Pray for us to give ourselves to the Lord with complete trust, and pray with us: Dear Father, guide us to pray always, and grant us a love for silence and the gift of contemplation. Conform our thoughts, actions, and lives to Jesus. Grant us humility, the queen of all virtues. Instill in us a deep desire to assist others who are lonely, ill, and near death. Teach us how to be loyal friends and grant us stable, long-term friendships. Grant us many and holy priests. Bless the Order of Minims, keeping it faithful to you. We ask this in the name of Jesus. Amen.

APRIL 3

Saint Richard of Chichester (1197–1253)

Saint Richard knew poverty as a boy when his noble parents died and the guardian let the estate go to ruin. Through determination and hard work, he helped the family recover and then went to study law at the Universities of Oxford, Paris, and Bologna. After obtaining his degree, he served as chancellor and legal advisor for Saint Edmund Rich, Archbishop of Canterbury. Later he studied theology and became a priest. He was consecrated bishop of Chichester in 1245, despite the protests of King Henry III. Before he died, he preached the crusade for the recovery of the Holy Sepulcher.

PRAYER

Saint Richard, you were a faithful steward of all that God entrusted to you. Pray for us and with us today: Merciful Father, pour out your blessings on the pope and all bishops of the Church. Inspire them to be strong pastors and virtuous leaders. Bless your Church. Give us the virtues of prudence and diligence. Bless all families, and grant them the grace to forgive one another and to have strong relationships. Guide and direct our political leaders, and grant them success in advancing the culture of life. We ask this in the name of Jesus. Amen.

APRIL 4

Saint Isidore of Seville (560–636)

Saint Isidore, born into a family of saints, prepared himself through his studies to use his talents to carry out the mission God gave him to lead the Church in Spain. He fought the Arian heresy, worked for unity within the Church, and helped bring about a renewal of the Faith. He had a deep appreciation for music, of which he said: "Without music, there can be no perfect knowledge, for there is nothing without it. For even the universe itself is said to have been put together with a certain harmony of sounds, and the very heavens revolve under the guidance of harmony. For the enduring of laborers, too, music comforts the mind, and singing lightens weariness in solitary tasks." Isidore was totally committed to prayer, penance, and service, especially to the poor. He wrote an encyclopedia, a dictionary, a book of world history, and a Rule for monks. Saint Isidore is the patron saint of computers and the internet, and he is a Doctor of the Church.

PRAYER

Saint Isidore, God gave you many gifts, especially the gift of knowledge, and you placed all those gifts at His service. Pray with us today: Loving Father, inspire us to learn our faith, using our time, talent, and treasure for your glory, the salvation of souls, and the transformation of culture. Fill us with the virtues of studiousness and charity. Thank you for the many gifts you have given us, especially the gift of music. Instill in us confidence in speaking, gentleness in communicating your love, and courage in standing for the truth. We ask this in the name of Jesus. Amen.

APRIL 5

Saint Vincent Ferrer (1350–1419)

Saint Vincent Ferrer, a Dominican priest from Spain, was gifted with tears, tongues, prophecy, preaching, and miracles. In fact, he was such a great preacher and miracle worker that he helped God heal and convert thousands of people! When he preached, people repented of sin and changed their lives, and with hearts converted to God, they prepared for their final judgment. Through constant preaching on humility and Church unity, he helped end the Great Western Schism and build up the unity of the Church. Saint Vincent Ferrer is the patron saint of builders.

PRAYER

Saint Vincent, you helped many souls turn away from sin through your preaching. Pray for us to respond to the grace of conversion, and pray with us: Gracious Father, grant unity to your Church, and use us as you will to draw all people to yourself. Inspire us to believe in your miracles and hope in your mercy. Grant us the virtue of humility, and help us always to remember that we do not live for this life, but for the next. Bless the Dominican order, keeping it faithful to you. We ask this in the name of Jesus. Amen.

APRIL 6

The Martyrs of Persia (d. 345)

Thousands of Christians died in Persia (modern-day Iran) for adhering to their faith at different times in the Church's history. There are in total five groups of Persian martyrs, one of which is celebrated today. King Shapur II fiercely persecuted Christians from 339 to 379. The 120 martyrs celebrated today were killed in 345 after many months in prison, undergoing terrible tortures to try to get them to give up their faith. The group consisted of priests, deacons, and several consecrated virgins. They were supported and encouraged during their imprisonment by a wealthy woman named Jazdundocta, and after their deaths, she had them buried.

PRAYER

Martyrs of Persia, you would not allow torture or fear of death to deter you from your Christian faith. Pray for us to be steadfast in our faith, and on your feast, pray with us: Dear Father, grant us the grace to hold tenaciously to our faith, always seeking your truth, following the witness of the holy martyrs. Instill in us the courage to undergo whatever sufferings you may allow, and keep us loyal to you and to the Holy Catholic Church. Help us to cling to our faith when trials and obstacles prevent a smooth path to accomplishing the will of God in our lives. Confirm us in love and make us saints. We ask this in the name of Jesus. Amen.

Saint John Baptist de la Salle (1651–1719)

Saint John was only eleven when he started preparing for the priesthood. Although wealthy, he renounced his possessions and became poor to serve the poor. He developed a whole teaching system and founded the order that became the Brothers of the Christian Schools, focused on educating poor boys and training future teachers. The brothers also served those from wealthy families who had become involved in delinquent activities. Daily Mass and religious education were an important part of the schools. Saint John persevered through trials and opposition from many in the established education system at the time. Saint John Baptist de la Salle is the patron saint of schoolteachers.

PRAYER

Saint John, you provided and promoted education and formation for the young, especially the underprivileged. Pray with us on your feast: Loving Father, give us hearts to love and serve everyone you place in our lives, especially the poor. Give us the wisdom to teach children and lead them to follow you all their lives. With your help, may we overcome trials and obstacles without becoming discouraged. Bless the Brothers of the Christian Schools and keep them faithful to you. We ask this in the name of Jesus. Amen.

APRIL 8

Saint Julie Billiart (1751–1816)

Saint Julie suffered paralysis in her legs, likely as a result of trauma in her childhood. Yet she was so determined to help children that she taught them about God from her bed, even as the French Revolution raged around her. Father Joseph Varin encouraged her to begin the Sisters of Notre Dame of Namur to provide spiritual care for children, education for girls, and training for teachers. One day, after Saint Julie had been confined to bed for twenty-two years and while making a novena to the Sacred Heart, Father Varin challenged her to walk in honor of the Sacred Heart of Jesus. She obeyed, and miraculously she was able to walk again. After this miracle, she expanded the Sisters of Notre Dame, freely sharing her energy, enthusiasm, and joy with all the orphans and poor girls she and her community helped. No matter what obstacles or trials she faced, she firmly moved ahead, clinging to her persistent trust in Jesus, saying, "How good is the good God!"

PRAYER

Saint Julie, pray for us to trust in God's plan and to carry out His work even in the midst of our suffering, as you did. Pray with us today: Gracious Father, grant us cheerful hearts to give you praise in all circumstances. Make us clear and inspiring teachers of the Faith, able to understand and communicate the truth in simple terms. Bless all teachers and equip them to help children reach their highest potential, using all the gifts and talents you have given them. Fill us with joy at doing your will, and never let us be discouraged by obstacles. Bless the Sisters of Notre Dame de Namur and keep them faithful to you. We ask this in the name of Jesus. Amen.

APRIL 9

Saint Waldetrudis (d. c. 688)

Saint Waldetrudis (also known as Waudru) came from a noble family in Belgium. The family was filled with saints. She was daughter to Saints Walbert and Bertila, sister to Saint Aldegundis, wife to Saint Vincent Madelgarus, and mother to Saints Aldegundis, Landericus, Dentlin, and Madalberta. Waldetrudis formed her four children in the Faith and taught them to serve the poor and homeless. After her children were grown, Waldetrudis and her husband both entered religious life. She founded a convent and became a Benedictine nun. Saint Waldetrudis is the patron saint of Mons, Belgium.

PRAYER

Saint Waldetrudis, you sought holiness in the ordinary duties of your state of life, and you formed your children to love God above all else. Pray with us now: Heavenly Father, make us saints according to our state in life, and bless us with faith-filled families. Strengthen us in all the virtues, especially diligence and fidelity. Pour out your grace on all married couples. Guide all parents to form their children in the Faith, to provide stability for their families, and to serve the vulnerable. Bless the Benedictine order, keeping it faithful to you and its founder. We ask this in the name of Jesus. Amen.

APRIL 10

Saint Fulbert of Chartres (960–1028)

Saint Fulbert, gifted with intellectual ability, was a prolific writer and avid preacher with a strong devotion to the Blessed Mother. His professor at school in Rheims, France, was the future Pope Sylvester II, who recognized his ability and requested his assistance. After finishing his service to the pope, Fulbert returned to France and established a school at Chartres, which was so superb that students came from many countries to study there, calling him "venerable Socrates." He became bishop of Chartres and zealously spread the Faith, restored the cathedral, and promoted reform of the clergy and monastic life.

PRAYER

Saint Fulbert, pray for us to use our gifts, both small and great, to serve God and the Church as you did. Pray with us today: Merciful Father, inspire us to use our gifts to serve you and your Church without holding anything back. Bless the pope and all bishops, and make them strong pastors and virtuous leaders, wrapped in the mantle of Mother Mary. Guide all who teach the Faith and help them to understand and express the truth with clarity. Bless and reward all who live in monastic life for their prayers and sacrifices for the Church. We ask this in the name of Jesus. Amen.

APRIL 11

Saint Gemma Galgani
of Lucca (1878–1903)

Saint Gemma lost her mother when she was only a child. Her father died when she was nineteen, and she became mother to her younger siblings, earning a living as a maid. Among other mystical experiences, Gemma received the stigmata, including stripes of the scourging. The wounds appeared on Thursday nights and disappeared on Friday or Saturday each week. Health problems thwarted her dream of becoming a nun, so she took private vows. This "Flower of Lucca" died of tuberculosis when she was twenty-five. Saint Gemma is the patron saint of students, pharmacists, paratroopers, parachutists, and those suffering from back injury or spinal illness, headaches, or migraines, and is invoked against temptations, tuberculosis, and the death of parents.

PRAYER

Saint Gemma, your profound love of Jesus showed through in all you did, and He allowed you to share in the sufferings of His passion. Pray for us and with us on your feast: Loving Father, give us prayerful hearts, and fill us with a longing to be united with you. Grant us the gift of contemplation. May we fulfill your will for our lives, especially when it goes against our own desires. Help us to trust in your love and goodness. Give us the virtues of Saint Gemma, especially charity and self-control, and grant us the grace to accept our sufferings with joy as she did. We ask this in the name of Jesus. Amen.

APRIL 12

Saint Teresa of the Andes (1900–1920)

Saint Teresa, whose baptismal name was Juanita, grew up in Chile in a loving, devout family. From her childhood, God called her to himself. In her diary she wrote, "It was shortly after the 1906 earthquake that Jesus began to claim my heart for himself." By the time she was fourteen, she had consecrated herself as a Discalced Carmelite, and when she was nineteen, she entered the Monastery of the Holy Spirit in Los Andes. She faithfully cooperated with God's grace to eradicate her natural pride, selfishness, and stubbornness and to conform herself to Jesus and His love. A few months after she became a novice, she developed typhus and was allowed to make her vows while on her deathbed. She is the first Chilean to be declared a saint and the first Discalced Carmelite nun to become a saint outside of Europe.

PRAYER

Saint Teresa, pray for us to cooperate with God's grace to overcome all our sinfulness and become holy, as He wants us to be holy. Pray with us on your feast: Dear Father, grant us the determination, total dedication, and tenacity to hear and follow your will in all things, particularly your call on our lives. Like Saint Teresa, help us to cooperate with your grace to cultivate all virtues and detach from all worldly passions. Inspire children to seek to become holy in their everyday lives. Bless the Discalced Carmelite order and keep it faithful to you. We ask this in the name of Jesus. Amen.

APRIL 13

Saint Margaret of Castello (1287–1320)

Saint Margaret, a pious, gentle, humble child, had visual and physical disabilities. Her noble parents, ashamed of these disabilities, cruelly kept her in a walled-in room. When she was a young woman, her parents took her to a shrine in Castello, seeking a miraculous cure. When that did not happen, they abandoned her in the city and returned to their home. The poor of the city took care of "little Margaret," who eventually became a lay Dominican. She cared for the poor and sick, and visited prisoners. Always cheerful and serene, she accepted her afflictions, believing it a privilege to suffer for Christ. Her body is still incorrupt and can be venerated at the Church of Saint Dominic in Castello, Italy. Saint Margaret is the patron of people who are unwanted and those who suffer from blindness and physical deformities.

PRAYER

Saint Margaret, you loved and served God wholeheartedly, and you forgave those who hurt and rejected you. Pray for us to do the same, and pray with us: Gentle Father, may we never allow our weaknesses to keep us from serving you with all our hearts. Bless those who suffer from mental and physical disabilities. Grant us the grace to practice intentional acts of kindness, and to see serving and suffering for you as a privilege. Make us cheerful and serene like Saint Margaret. Bless the Dominican order and keep it faithful to you. We ask this in the name of Jesus. Amen.

APRIL 14

Saint Lidwina (1380–1433)

Saint Lidwina, born in Schiedam, Holland, had a beautiful devotion to Our Lady of Schiedam. She grew up poor, and when she was fifteen years old, she suffered a terrible skating accident, which caused her to be bedridden for years with sores and constant pain. She also suffered suspicion from others, as some thought her illness was caused by the devil. Despite all this, her prayers were powerful, and God worked miracles through her intercession. Eventually, she became so revered that holy men and women visited her bedside, and after her death a chapel was built there for pilgrims to the Netherlands. Saint Lidwina is the patron saint of ice skaters and the chronically ill, and her intercession is invoked by people with multiple sclerosis.

PRAYER

Saint Lidwina, you willingly accepted the sufferings God sent you, and He showed His great power and love through you. Pray with us on your feast: Merciful Father, we ask you for the strength to endure our trials with trust and confidence in your goodness. Allow us to serve you always, in suffering and sickness as well as in happiness and health. Teach us to accept trials and obstacles without complaining and in a true spirit of service to you. Allow us to intercede for others, and bless all for whom we have promised to pray. We ask this in the name of Jesus. Amen.

APRIL 15

Saints Basilissa and Anastasia (d. c. 68)

Saints Basilissa and Anastasia were noble women who were disciples of Saints Peter and Paul. After the two apostles were martyred, these women found and buried their bodies. For their faithfulness in performing this spiritual work of mercy — burying the dead — they followed in the footsteps of their holy teachers. Both were martyred by Emperor Nero, who had them beheaded for their pious action.

PRAYER

Saints Basilissa and Anastasia, you fearlessly cared for the bodies of the apostles after their martyrdom, and you accepted the crown of martyrdom yourselves. Pray with us today: Gracious Father, may we never shrink from serving you, even when it is dangerous or unpopular. Give us the grace to perform the works of mercy. Fill us with all virtues, especially charity and courage. Make us contemplatives in action, always ready to follow the witness of your martyrs. We ask this in the name of Jesus. Amen.

APRIL 16

Saint Benedict Joseph Labre (1748–1783)

Saint Benedict Joseph Labre, the oldest child of a large French family, longed to be a monk, but despite years of attempting to join various monasteries, he was never permitted to fulfill this dream. Finally, when he was twenty-five years old, he decided to become a pilgrim. He traveled to many shrines in Rome and all throughout Europe. Struggling with mental illness, he found consolation and comfort in the holy places he visited and the relics he venerated. He chose to live in radical poverty, owning nothing, and in all he did, he strove to gain virtue and become holy. He once said, "God is so good and so merciful, that to obtain heaven it is sufficient to ask it of Him from our hearts." Saint Benedict Joseph Labre is the patron saint (with Saint Dymphna) of people with mental illness.

PRAYER

Saint Benedict, pray for us to trust God even with our weaknesses and struggles, and to seek Him in all that we do. Pray with us on your feast: Gentle Father, be close to all who are suffering in any way, particularly those afflicted with mental illness. Give us the grace to be a source of comfort to anyone who is afflicted by any illness. Bless and protect all who are homeless and give them the help and hope they need, and a place to lay their heads. Comfort and support all who long to give their lives to you but struggle to discover their vocation. We ask this in the name of Jesus. Amen.

Saint Stephen Harding (d. 1134)

Saint Stephen Harding founded the monastery at Citeaux and had such a reputation for holiness that eventually Saint Bernard of Clairvaux joined him, along with many companions. Over the course of his life, thirteen monasteries were formed. He organized general chapter meetings and made regular visits (called visitations) to all the Cistercian monasteries. He wrote the Charter of Love to regulate all the monasteries associated with Citeaux, as well as the oldest history of the Cistercians.

PRAYER

Saint Stephen, your life shows us that holiness begets holiness, for you drew many souls to God through your humble example. Pray with us now: Merciful Father, inspire us to seek reform within ourselves and to be conformed to the image of Christ. Grant us the grace of a consistent prayer life and the gift of contemplation. Teach us how to serve you and others faithfully and loyally. Grant us the virtues of piety and humility and make us contemplatives in action. Bless the Cistercian order, keeping it faithful to you. We ask this in the name of Jesus. Amen.

APRIL 18

Saint Apollonius the Apologist (d. c. 185)

Saint Apollonius, a Roman senator who converted to Christianity, was so effective at defending the Faith through his authoritative *Apologia* that it is still considered irreplaceable in understanding how the Church functioned under Roman persecution. Unfortunately, a slave told the Roman prefect, Perennis, of his master's conversion, and Apollonius was arrested. He valiantly defended his faith to the Roman senate before he was beheaded.

PRAYER

Saint Apollonius, pray for us to have the courage to profess our faith even to the point of giving our lives for it, as you did. Pray with us on your feast: Heavenly Father, give us the same zeal that inspired the martyrs. Inspire us to learn our faith as well as we can, and to defend it when called upon. Make us fearless in standing firm in the truth. Grant us integrity and character so strong that we are powerful witnesses even to those who are not ready for conversion. Allow the Holy Spirit to speak through us, making us planters of seeds, trusting in your power even if we never see the fruit. We ask this in the name of Jesus. Amen.

APRIL 19

Saint Expeditus (d. fourth century)

Saint Expeditus was a Roman centurion in Armenia who was martyred along with his companions Hermogenes, Aristonicus, Galata, Gaius, and Rufus under the Roman Emperor Diocletian. Although not much is known about his life, many churches around the world are named in his honor, and his feast is especially celebrated in São Paulo, Brazil. Saint Expeditus is the patron saint of time and urgent causes, and his intercession is often invoked against procrastination and for success in lawsuits.

PRAYER

Saint Expeditus, you gave your life for the Faith, and we ask you to pray for us to do the same, whether in a physical or spiritual martyrdom. Pray with us now: Loving Father, grant us the grace always to serve you and your Church faithfully and to build up your kingdom. Give us the virtues of courage, fidelity, and perseverance. Support and protect those who are persecuted or dying for their faith, and never allow us to forget them and their needs. We ask this in the name of Jesus. Amen.

APRIL 20

Saint Agnes of Montepulciano
(1268–1317)

Saint Agnes was only nine years old when she entered a monastery at Montepulciano, Italy, and only fifteen when she became superior of another at Procena. She placed the monastery under the Dominican rule and stressed that charity is obtained through humility. Wise and revered, she was gifted with prophecy, visions, miracles (including supplying food for the convent), and levitating while in ecstasy during prayer. Saint Raymond of Capua wrote her biography, and, years after her death, Saint Catherine of Siena had miraculous experiences at her shrine. Her body was incorrupt until the sixteenth century, and her brain, hands, and feet are still incorrupt in the Sanctuary of Saint Agnes in Montepulciano.

PRAYER

Saint Agnes, pray for us to grow in humility and thus make room for charity in our hearts. Pray with us on your feast: Righteous Father, grant us the greatest gift of love, and keep us always close to you. Make us contemplatives in action. Grant us the virtue of humility, the queen of all virtues. Instill in us a hunger for holiness and fidelity to prayer. Bless the Dominican order, keeping it faithful to you. We ask this in the name of Jesus. Amen.

APRIL 21

Saint Anselm (1033–1109)

Saint Anselm had a wonderful gift for teaching and a beautiful way of working with others. Patient, kind, and well-spoken, he helped many people through his teaching and writing, which included treatises and many letters of spiritual direction. The leading philosopher and theologian of his time, the Father of Scholasticism, as he is known, famously described theology as "faith seeking understanding." Anselm was a reluctant leader in the Church. He was first made an abbot against his will, and later forced to become archbishop of Canterbury. He spoke out bravely and firmly against slavery, thus helping the passage of a law against selling people. Pope Clement XI named him a Doctor of the Church in 1720.

PRAYER

Saint Anselm, pray for us to grow in wisdom and to give our lives in God's service, even when it goes against our own desires. Pray with us today: Loving Father, give us hearts that long only to do your will in all things. May we learn the spiritual lessons you have for us, grow in holiness, and have the guidance of good spiritual directors. Grant us good skills of communication and patience with everyone, including ourselves. Make us fearless and consistent in defending the vulnerable and enslaved. Free and heal us from all spiritual enslavement. Free all people who are enslaved and convert their captors. We ask this in the name of Jesus. Amen.

APRIL 22

Saint Theodore of Sykeon (d. 613)

Saint Theodore of Sykeon was such a pious child that he preferred praying to eating. After increasingly withdrawing from the world during his childhood, he became a hermit when he was only a teenager. Later he became a monk and founded monasteries before he was eventually consecrated bishop of Anastasiopolis in Galatia, Asia Minor (modern Turkey). He practiced mortifications and ate very little, living on vegetables. God gifted him with prophecy and miracles, including bringing about rain during a drought and curing the emperor's son.

PRAYER

Saint Theodore, pray for us to prefer God over all things and to develop strong, consistent habits of prayer. Pray with us on your feast: Dear Father, grant us the grace to desire friendship with you, and give us prayerful hearts. Teach us to be consistent in our prayer life and grant us the gift of contemplation. Strengthen in us the virtues of self-control and piety. May we seek you in all things and lead others to you through our words and example. We ask this in the name of Jesus. Amen.

APRIL 23

Saint George (d. c. 300)

Saint George was a Roman soldier of high rank who publicly spoke out against Emperor Diocletian for his unjust and cruel treatment of Christians. For that, he was imprisoned and eventually beheaded. Saint Peter Damian said of him: "Saint George was a man who abandoned one army for another: he gave up the rank of tribune to enlist as a soldier for Christ. ... Bearing the shield of faith, he plunged into the thick of the battle, an ardent soldier for Christ." While little is known about his life, he is usually depicted as slaying a dragon because he spoke out against evil. He is the patron of soldiers and all who work for the good of their country. He is also a patron of England and the Boy Scouts.

PRAYER

Saint George, you courageously gave up everything to follow Christ and willingly died for your faith. Pray for us to love God so generously, and pray with us: Merciful Father, give us unwavering faith that will not be swayed even in the face of violence. Grant that we may never give in to evil but fearlessly and with great courage state the truth no matter the consequences. May we always pray and work for the advancement of your kingdom and through this live in union with you. We ask this in the name of Jesus. Amen.

APRIL 24

Saint Fidelis of Sigmaringen
(1577–1622)

Saint Fidelis was a German lawyer who helped the poor and oppressed, but becoming disillusioned with the legal system, he became a Capuchin Franciscan priest. He preached and wrote against Calvinism and Zwinglianism, zealously seeking to bring people back to the Catholic Faith. He was tireless in his efforts, once saying, "Woe to me if I should prove myself but a halfhearted soldier in the service of my thorn-crowned captain." While preaching in Switzerland, he was attacked and killed by a mob of Calvinists. Saint Fidelis is the patron saint of lawyers.

PRAYER

Saint Fidelis, pray for us to imitate you in your wholehearted service to God and the Church, and pray with us now: Heavenly Father, grant us the grace to thirst and work for true justice, and to give our lives completely to your service. Give us courage to speak the truth and share the Faith, even when it is difficult and unpopular. Make us strong enough to die for you if necessary. Give us the virtues of fortitude and perseverance. Bless the Franciscan order, keeping it faithful to you. We ask this in the name of Jesus. Amen.

APRIL 25

Saint Mark (d. first century)

Saint Mark, a cousin of Saint Barnabas, assisted Saints Paul and Barnabas on their first missionary trip and later helped Saint Paul while he was in Roman captivity. He is credited with founding the church in Alexandria, Egypt, and was the first bishop there. It is believed that Mark was a disciple of Saint Peter and that he wrote his gospel according to Peter's testimony. His is the shortest gospel and likely the first one to have been written. He died a martyr in Alexandria, Egypt, and his relics are in the cathedral in Venice, Italy. His symbol is a winged lion. Saint Mark is the patron of notaries, barristers, Egypt, and Venice.

PRAYER

Saint Mark, you were a true and unwavering disciple of Jesus, and your Gospel helps us to know Him and love Him more fully. Pray for us and with us: Loving Father, inspire us to read the Gospels daily, seeking always to understand and imitate the life and mission of Jesus. Grant us the strength and courage to proclaim the Gospel to all people. May we always accept trials and sufferings with patience and love, uniting our crosses to the cross of your Son. Grant us the grace to forgive those who hurt us and make amends to those we have harmed. Heal, convert, deliver, and protect us. We ask this in the name of Jesus. Amen.

APRIL 26

Saint Stephen of Perm (1340–1396)

Saint Stephen was a monk who became a missionary to the Komi peoples (also called Zyriane and Permiaks), in northeast Russia where he had been born. He developed a written form of the Zyriane language and set up schools to teach it so the local people could better understand the liturgy and Scriptures. He loved to help the poor and oppressed. He was the first bishop of Perm, and in that office he strongly opposed the Strigolniks (the first Russian dissenters). He truly lived up to his name, Stephen, from the Greek word *stephanos*, which means crown. Dignified with the titles Enlightener of Perm and Apostle of the Permians, his biography was written by Epiphanius.

PRAYER

Saint Stephen, pray for us to have a true missionary spirit, and to labor to bring the love of Jesus to everyone we encounter. Pray with us on your feast: Gracious Father, make us tireless in service to our neighbors for love of you. Inspire us to be faithful and consistent in prayer and give us the gift of contemplation. Make us sensitive and helpful to the poor and oppressed, as Saint Stephen was. Bless our pope and bishops, making them strong pastors and virtuous leaders. Teach us how to communicate with others and heal our relationships. We ask this in the name of Jesus. Amen.

APRIL 27

Saint Zita (1218–1272)

Saint Zita was only twelve when she became a servant for the Fratinelli family, who had a business in wool and silk weaving in Lucca, Italy. She remained in their service for forty-eight years. At first she bore disapproval and hardship from the family for her pious practices, but eventually she gained everyone's respect because of her goodness. She loved the poor and often gave them food and clothing. She also visited prisoners to encourage them. God gifted her with miracles. Saint Zita is the patron saint of maids and domestic workers.

PRAYER

Saint Zita, your faithfulness in service to your employers and to the poor and your example of charity moved all who knew you. Pray with us on your feast: Gentle Father, make us your faithful and tireless servants in everything we do. Give us a life of prayer and deepen our friendship with you. May we always finish the tasks you have given us to do. Fill us with determination, diligence, and humility like Saint Zita. Form us to be people of integrity who are good witnesses to you. Make us saints. We ask this in the name of Jesus. Amen.

APRIL 28

Saint Gianna Beretta Molla (1922–1962)

Saint Gianna was a wife, mother, and physician who gave her life for her preborn child. She was a successful doctor who formed her own medical clinic to treat the poor and elderly, women, and babies. She balanced the responsibilities of her medical practice and her family. Her husband, Pietro, and her three children loved her very much. She was also involved in serving the poor through organizations like the Saint Vincent de Paul Society and Catholic Action. When she was pregnant with her fourth child, she learned that she had a tumor, the removal of which might kill the baby. She chose to delay that surgery so the baby could be born safely, saying, "If you must decide between me and the child, do not hesitate, choose the child. I insist on it." Seven days after her healthy baby girl was delivered, Gianna died. Her daughter, Gianna Emanuela, was present along with her father at her mother's canonization in 2004, only forty-two years later. Gianna is the patron saint of the pro-life cause.

PRAYER
Saint Gianna, you willingly gave your life to save the life of your baby. Pray for us to be courageous and generous as you were, and pray with us: Heavenly Father, grant us grace to uphold the dignity of every human life, at every stage. Teach us to know and love the Church's social justice teachings. Assist us in making them known. Instill in all parents a deep love for and desire to protect their children. We ask this in the name of Jesus. Amen.

APRIL 29

Saint Catherine of Siena (1347–1380)

Saint Catherine, the youngest of a large family in Siena, Italy, had a deep life of prayer from an early age. She held direct conversations with God the Father, which she wrote about in her book, the *Dialogue*. She also received many visions, and she worked for unity within the Church, convincing the pope, who was living in Avignon, France, to return to Rome. As a Lay Dominican, she helped the sick and taught and encouraged those who gathered around her for spiritual guidance. She once wrote: "As a tree you should be planted deep in the earth of true humility, so that the wind of pride will not do damage to the tree of your soul. The soul is a tree of love created by God out of love and for love and can only live from love." She experienced the stigmata and lived for a long time on nothing but the Eucharist. She is one of only four women to be declared a Doctor of the Church.

PRAYER

Saint Catherine, you loved God passionately, and you teach us to do the same through your words and example. Pray for us and with us: Dear Father, give us the grace to be contemplatives in action, serving the poor and sick. May we use all the talents and gifts you have given us to be who you created us to be and thus change the world. Give us the virtues we need to fulfill your call in our lives, especially humility. Grant all nurses the knowledge needed to be your hands and presence in caring for the sick. Bless and unify our Church and our families. We ask this in the name of Jesus. Amen.

APRIL 30

Saint Pius V (1504–1572)

Michele Ghislieri was educated by the Dominicans and entered the order as a young man. He became novice master, then prior, and eventually was made bishop of Sutri, Italy. The pope made him an Inquisitor, and he filled this office until he became pope himself, taking the name Pius V. He virtuously led the Church during the Protestant Reformation and was instrumental in leading the Catholic Counter-Reformation, zealously enacting the reforms of the Council of Trent, including promulgating the Roman catechism, breviary, and missal. When the Turks threatened Christendom, he urged all the faithful to pray the Rosary, leading to the Christian victory at Lepanto. In thanksgiving, he initiated the feast of Our Lady of Victory, now called Our Lady of the Rosary.

PRAYER

Saint Pius V, pray for the Church today, to enact reforms and faithfully teach the truth. Pray with us on your feast: Righteous Father, inspire us to personal conversion, and grant us the grace to love your Church and be true reformers who are not critical, but active in bringing needed change. Give us the virtues of fortitude and prudence, that we may carry out your will no matter what obstacles we face. Guard and assist our pope and all bishops and make them faithful leaders and true shepherds. Bless the Dominican order, keeping it faithful to you. We ask this in the name of Jesus. Amen.

MAY

THE MONTH OF
THE BLESSED VIRGIN MARY

MAY 1

Saint Joseph the Worker

Pope Pius XII instituted the feast of Saint Joseph the Worker in 1955. Saint Joseph had the extreme privilege and responsibility of providing for the Holy Family, and in his example we see that work is good, it is a gift from God, and through our work we can give God glory. Through his work and provision for the Holy Family, Saint Joseph imaged God, participating in the continuing work of creation. As Pius XII reminded us: "The Spirit flows to you and to all men from the heart of the God-man, Savior of the world, but certainly, no worker was ever more completely and profoundly penetrated by it than the foster father of Jesus, who lived with Him in closest intimacy and community of family life and work. Thus, if you wish to be close to Christ, we again today repeat, 'Go to Joseph.'" Joseph is a guiding light for all who work in and outside the home. He is the patron saint of fathers and workers and a wonderful patron for those seeking employment.

PRAYER

Saint Joseph, pray for us to perform our work with diligence and justice, and pray with us on your feast: Dear Father, thank you for the gift of work, through which we participate in your creativity and provision. Allow our family to imitate the Holy Family by being faithful to our duties and using our talents to further your kingdom. May we always provide safe, loving environments for ourselves and our families. Bless and provide for all who are seeking employment and help those who are struggling in their work. We ask this in the name of Jesus. Amen.

MAY 2

Saint Athanasius (d. 373)

Saint Athanasius was tenacious in defending the truth of the Faith against the Arian heresy. He lived in Alexandria, Egypt, and he played an important role in the Council of Nicaea, which clearly defined the Church's teaching that Jesus is divine, sharing the same nature as the Father. Shortly after the council, Athanasius was made bishop of Alexandria. During his long episcopacy, he continued to teach and preach against Arianism, and he was misunderstood, falsely accused, humiliated, and exiled several times. At one point, he became a hermit in the Egyptian desert for several years, praying and writing many theological works and a biography of Saint Anthony of the Desert. Because of his writings and tireless work to promote the true faith, even when it was unpopular and dangerous, he is called the Father of Orthodoxy and is a Doctor of the Church.

PRAYER

Saint Athanasius, pray for us to love and defend the true faith as you did, and pray with us: Gracious Father, make us steadfast in serving you and clinging to the truth of our faith, even in difficult and dangerous times. Give us wisdom to communicate and defend the doctrines of the Catholic Faith. May we always pray the Nicene Creed with reverence and intention. Grant us the grace to be consistent in prayer and to keep studying and learning about our faith. Make us saints. We ask this in the name of Jesus. Amen.

MAY 3

Saints Philip and James (d. first century)

Saints Philip and James responded immediately when Jesus called them to be apostles. Philip, originally a disciple of Saint John the Baptist, brought Nathaniel to Jesus (and later, he also brought a group of Greeks to Jesus). He once asked Jesus to show His followers the Father. We read in Scripture: "Jesus said to him, 'Have I been with you so long, and you still do not know me, Philip? Whoever has seen me has seen the Father'" (Jn 14:9). James was the son of Alphaeus and is described in Scripture as "the brother of the Lord," meaning he was likely a relative of Jesus. He became bishop of Jerusalem. He is called "the Less" to distinguish him from the other Apostle James, the son of Zebedee and brother of Saint John the Evangelist.

PRAYER

Saints Philip and James, pray for the Church on your feast day, that we may remain faithful to Christ no matter what. Pray with us now: Merciful Father, inspire us to leave everything to follow you. Grant us the grace of detachment from worldly things and attachment to you. Conform our thoughts, actions, and lives to Jesus in total surrender to your will. Fill us with zeal to spread the Gospel so that everyone can come to know you. Make us saints. Bless all bishops, the successors of the apostles, and make them faithful leaders of your Church. We ask this in the name of Jesus. Amen.

MAY 4

Saint Florian (d. 304)

Saint Florian was an officer in the Roman army in the area that is now Austria. He converted to Christianity and then courageously and openly declared himself to be a Christian during the persecutions under Roman Emperor Diocletian. As punishment, he was tortured and finally killed by being thrown into the Enns River where it joins the Danube. People who are afraid of danger from fire or water have invoked his intercession, and healing miracles have occurred. Saint Florian is the patron saint of firefighters, Poland, and Upper Austria.

PRAYER

Saint Florian, you wholeheartedly embraced the Faith and gave your life for it. Pray for us to do the same, and pray with us: Loving Father, we thank you for the example of your martyrs, and we beg you to grant us the courage to die rather than give up our faith. Teach us to see our faith as the unifying principle of our lives. Make our characters so strong that we would never deny you or hurt our fellow Christians. Strengthen and protect all Christians who suffer persecution for their faith in you. Bless all firefighters and police officers who serve and protect others. We ask this in the name of Jesus. Amen.

MAY 5

Saint Angelo (1185–1220)

Saint Angelo (sometimes called Saint Angelo of Jerusalem) was born to a Jewish family in Jerusalem, and after his mother, Maria, converted to Christianity, he became Catholic as well. He joined the Carmelite order at eighteen years old, along with his twin brother, John. He lived for a time as a hermit, but he felt called to go to Sicily as a missionary to help convert the Jewish people and the many people falling prey to heresy there. He had the gift of miracles and of prophesy, foretelling that Saint Francis of Assisi would receive the stigmata. He was finally martyred for speaking out against sinful behavior. The Santa Maria del Carmine Church in Sicily houses his relics. Saint Angelo is the patron saint of those considering converting to the Catholic Faith, converts, and Palermo, Italy.

PRAYER
Saint Angelo, pray for us to have missionary hearts like yours, eager to spread the Gospel throughout the world. Pray with us today: Dear Father, open our hearts to you and grant us the grace of conversion. Give us courage and wisdom us to share the Faith with others and to strengthen one another to stand firm in our faith. Instill in us the deep desire to pray always and receive the gift of contemplation. Teach us how to serve from that deep place of contemplation as contemplatives in action. Bless the Carmelite order, keeping it faithful to you. We ask this in the name of Jesus. Amen.

MAY 6

Blessed Jacinto Veray Durán (1813–1881)

Blessed Jacinto was born on board a ship as his parents emigrated to Uruguay from the Canary Islands. He grew up on a farm and later felt inspired to become a priest. While attending the Jesuit college in Buenos Aires, he was known for his intelligence and cheerfulness. His pleasing personality endeared him to the people of Uruguay when he became the first bishop of Montevideo (the only diocese in the country at that time). As bishop, he helped his priests deepen their spiritual life by having them make the *Spiritual Exercises*. He traveled the country making sure the people received their sacraments, helping the poor and sick, and working for peace.

PRAYER

Blessed Jacinto, you led the Church in Uruguay and shepherded the souls in your care with tireless devotion. Pray for us and with us today: Gentle Father, grant us the virtues of Blessed Jacinto, especially cheerfulness and diligence. Help us to stop complaining and instead be encouraged by our ability to serve you and others. Give us a grateful attitude. Bless all bishops and make them virtuous leaders. We ask this in the name of Jesus. Amen.

MAY 7

Saint Domitian (d. 560)

Saint Domitian worked tirelessly to establish Christianity in the Netherlands, France, and Belgium. As bishop of Maastricht in the Netherlands, he became known as the "Apostle of the Valley of the Meuse," valiantly defending the Faith against heresy. He was extremely generous, building churches and hospices. An ardent lover of the poor, he assisted them in every way during a severe famine. His relics are in the Church of Notre-Dame in Huy, Belgium. Saint Domitian is the patron saint of those with fever and the city of Huy.

PRAYER

Saint Domitian, pray for us to love and serve the Church as you did, sharing the light of Christ and serving our neighbor with joy. Pray with us today: Loving Father, make us so committed to restoring all things in Christ that we help everyone we meet to find healing and conversion. Give us compassionate and generous hearts to serve those in need, especially the poor and vulnerable. Protect the people of the Netherlands, Belgium, and France, and draw them to yourself. Bless all bishops, making them true shepherds and virtuous leaders. We ask this in the name of Jesus. Amen.

Saint Maria Magdalene of Canossa (1774–1835)

Magdalene of Canossa was a marchioness, the daughter of the Marquis of Canossa. She was born in Verona and was just a child when her father died and her mother remarried, leaving her abandoned. Living with an uncle, she was treated harshly by her governess and fell ill. At seventeen she joined the Carmelites, but she soon discerned that the life was not for her. Instead, she felt God calling her to serve poor, sick children and women. She founded the Daughters of Charity (known as the Canossian Sisters) and told them that they should be "detached from everything … and ready for the Divine service and to go anywhere, even to the remotest country." Pope Pius XI said that, although others might serve the poor, she became poor with them.

PRAYER

Saint Magdalene, you became poor with the poor you served and generously gave of yourself. Pray for us and with us now: Gracious Father, give us compassionate and generous hearts to serve you in our neighbor, especially those who are most vulnerable. Comfort all those who grieve, and lead us to help one another in carrying our crosses. Teach us to be sensitive to the needs of all, especially those who are treated poorly and those who suffer from trauma. Bless the Canossian Sisters, keeping them faithful to you. We ask this in the name of Jesus. Amen.

MAY 9

Blessed Maria Carmen
Rendiles Martínez (1903–1977)

Blessed Carmen felt God calling her to religious life when she was fifteen years old. She entered the Congregation of the Servants of the Eucharist when the order came to Venezuela, then traveled to the motherhouse in France for formation. Upon returning to her native country, she served as novice mistress in Valencia, and then as mother superior in Caracas. She founded convents and schools throughout Venezuela and Colombia. Eventually she got approval for her order to become a separate congregation as the Servants of Jesus of Caracas (also called Servant Congregation of Jesus of Venezuela). She was a loving superior until her death and is the third Venezuelan to be beatified.

PRAYER

Blessed Carmen, pray for us to answer God's call in our lives and to do His will in all things, as you did. Pray with us: Merciful Father, inspire us to imitate Blessed Carmen, praying daily, listening carefully, and discerning your call for our lives. May we find and fulfill our vocation and mission. Give us determination, perseverance, and fortitude to overcome all obstacles in doing your will. Make us virtuous leaders who help others, especially children, in practicing virtue and learning their faith. Bless the people of Venezuela. We ask this in the name of Jesus. Amen.

MAY 10

Saint John of Ávila (1499–1569)

Saint John of Ávila, outstanding confessor, spiritual director, and Catholic reformer, served as a missionary in Andalusia, Spain. He helped with the formation of priests and supported the Discalced Carmelites, the Jesuits, and the Brothers Hospitallers. During his life, he influenced many great saints, including Teresa of Ávila, Francis Borgia, and John of God. He insisted on the importance of clerical reform and worked diligently to help all Catholics, especially children, receive the very best Catholic education. Though he was a preacher first, he was also a prolific writer, penning treatises, sermons, and letters. Encouraging all people to holiness, he once wrote: "The Father, the Son, and the Holy Spirit reside within us, and we already have a beginning here of that communion with God which will be perfect in the next life. Let us thank Him for all His mercies and prepare ourselves to receive the favors that still remain to be bestowed on us." He is the patron saint of diocesan priests and a Doctor of the Church.

PRAYER

Saint John, you encouraged people to reform their lives and to seek holiness, and your influence touched many hearts. Pray for us and with us: Heavenly Father, grant us a radical commitment to holiness, education of the faithful, and service to the poor. May we never cease to study our faith and grow in our understanding of your truth. Increase in us the virtues of humility and diligence, and provide us with wise spiritual directors. Bless all diocesan priests. We ask this in the name of Jesus. Amen.

Saint Antonio de Sant'Anna
Galvão (1739–1822)

Saint Antonio, born in Guaratinguetá in Brazil, was known as a "man of peace and charity." He grew up in a large, pious, and influential family in São Paulo, Brazil. His father, Antonio Galvão de França, was a Secular Franciscan, and his mother, Izabel Leite de Barros, was a generous helper of the poor. They had eleven children. When he was twenty-one, Antonio became a Franciscan friar and was eventually ordained a priest. He helped Sister Helena Maria of the Holy Spirit establish Our Lady of the Conception of Divine Providence convent, and later he founded the Saint Clare Convent. To this day, pilgrims flock to his tomb at the Saint Francis Friary in São Paolo.

PRAYER

Saint Antonio, pray for us to be, like you, people of peace and charity. Pray with us on your feast: Merciful Father, may we serve you each day with joy and generosity. Help us to follow your will for our lives, even when it is difficult or uncomfortable. Grant families the grace to raise and educate their children in the Faith, and bless all families with the support they need to thrive. Bless the Franciscan order, keeping it faithful to you. We ask this in the name of Jesus. Amen.

Venerable Edel Mary Quinn (1907–1944)

From childhood, Edel Quinn wanted to become a Poor Clare, but she was unable to do so because she suffered from tuberculosis. Denied this dream, she began to increase her involvement in the Legion of Mary, of which she was a member. The founder of the Legion of Mary, Servant of God Frank Duff, asked her to go to set up the Legion in East Africa. She moved to Kenya and established the Legion there, working faithfully, lovingly, and perseveringly for many years. She was beloved by the African people, and today many people in Africa are Catholic because of her love and caring evangelization. The generosity of her life is summed up in her own words: "What boundless trust we should have in God's love! We can never love too much; let us give utterly and not count the cost. God will respond to our faith in Him."

PRAYER

Venerable Edel, you gave of yourself without complaining or tiring, eager to win many souls for Christ. Pray with us now: Heavenly Father, fill us with joy and make us generous in your service like Venerable Edel. May we always use our talents and gifts to carry out your will for us, trusting in your infinite generosity and goodness. Grant us the grace to share our faith with others who do not know you yet. Bless the Legion of Mary, keeping it faithful to you. We ask this in the Name of Jesus. Amen.

MAY 13

Blessed Imelda Lambertini
(1322–1333)

Little Imelda was born in Bologna to a noble family. When she was only nine, she went to live in a Dominican convent. Always a pious child, she deeply desired to receive holy Communion, but she was considered too young. Still, she persistently asked Jesus to grant her desire, feeling sad that she could not join the nuns when they received Communion. Finally, one day when she was eleven, Jesus allowed it. As the nuns processed forward to receive, leaving her kneeling in her place, a host appeared above her head. Understanding that this was a sign from God, the priest gave her first Communion. Filled with joy, she made her thanksgiving. Sometime later, the nuns returned to the chapel to check on her and found her still kneeling in her place. She had died of love.

PRAYER

Blessed Imelda, pray for us to love the Blessed Sacrament as you did, and to receive communion as often as we can, with grateful joy. Pray with us today: Loving Father, grant us a fervent love for Jesus in the Holy Eucharist. May we always receive Him with profound reverence and thanksgiving. Give us wisdom to teach those preparing for their first Communion, especially children, about the True Presence of Jesus in the Blessed Sacrament. Bless all who are preparing to receive their first Communion. Guide and protect the Dominican order, keeping it faithful to you. We ask this in the name of Jesus. Amen.

MAY 14

Saint Matthias (d. first century)

Saint Matthias was the apostle chosen to replace Judas after Jesus' ascension. He had been a disciple of Jesus, and when Peter said they must choose a replacement for Judas, we read in the Acts of the Apostles: "And they put forward two, Joseph called Barsabbas, who was also called Justus, and Matthias. And they prayed and said, 'You, Lord, who know the hearts of all, show which one of these two you have chosen to take the place in this ministry and apostleship from which Judas turned aside to go to his own place.' And they cast lots for them, and the lot fell on Matthias, and he was numbered with the eleven apostles" (1:23–26). Not much is known about his life, but according to tradition, he labored in missionary work until he was martyred.

PRAYER
Saint Matthias, pray for the Church, and pray for each of us to love the Lord with all that we have and are. Pray with us today: Dear Father, set our hearts on fire with love for you and give us true apostolic zeal. Inspire us to live and die for our faith like the apostles. May we always use our gifts and talents to do your will and further your kingdom, sharing the Gospel with those who do not know you. Bless all bishops and make them virtuous leaders. Make us saints. We ask this in the name of Jesus. Amen.

MAY 15

Saint Isidore the Farmer (1070–1130)

Isidore was a laborer in Spain who worked on the farm of a land-owner named Juan de Vergas. His wife, Maria de la Cabeza, is also a saint, and they had one son, who tragically died when he was young. Working the land and living simply and piously, he was revered for his generosity to the poor and sick, and the miracles God worked through him. According to a story that is often told about him, God sent angels to help him with his work so he could attend daily Mass. His body is incorrupt. Saint Isidore the Farmer is the patron saint of farmers, laborers, the city of Madrid, Spain, and the U.S. National Rural Life Conference.

PRAYER

Saint Isidore, you were faithful to your daily work, and you always put God first in everything you did. Pray for us to do the same, and pray with us: Gracious Father, grant us the virtue of diligence to carry out our work with joy, for love of you. Inspire us to become holy and to support those around us, encouraging them to grow in holiness. Comfort all who mourn, especially those parents who have lost children. Assist married couples to work together to become holy and be holy witnesses of Jesus' love for His Church. Make us saints. We ask this in the name of Jesus. Amen.

MAY 16

Saints Alypius (d. 430) and Possidius (d. 437)

Saint Augustine referred to Alypius as the "brother of my heart." Possidius was another close companion who wrote a biography of Saint Augustine, the *Vita Augustini*. Both Alypius and Possidius belonged to the monastery Augustine founded in Hippo, Africa, and they worked hard to promote the truth in the face of the Donatist and Pelagian heresies. Both men attended the councils at Carthage in 403 and 407, and both had the great privilege of being with Saint Augustine when he died. Saint Possidius became a bishop and was forced into exile by the Arian King Huneric.

PRAYER

Saints Alypius and Possidius, pray for us to form holy friendships and to help one another to sainthood. Pray with us on your feast: Dear Father, bless us with holy friendships through which we can encourage and support one another on our journey through this life. Grant us wisdom to study and teach the Faith, and give us the grace to recognize the truth and avoid error. Bless all bishops, making them true shepherds and virtuous leaders. Bless the Augustinian order and keep it faithful to you. We ask this in the name of Jesus. Amen.

MAY 17

Saint Paschal Baylon (1540–1592)

Saint Paschal's extraordinary gifts included mystical experiences and working miracles. From the time he was seven until he was twenty-four years old, he helped his parents, Martin and Elizabeth, as a shepherd in Aragon, Spain. Then he joined the Alcantarine Franciscans and served as a lay brother and doorkeeper. His deep love of the Eucharist led him to spend countless hours of prayer with Jesus, and he once defended the doctrine of the Blessed Sacrament in a debate with a Calvinist preacher. So tenderly did he serve the sick and poor that God worked miracles of healing through him. Many people sought his counsel. After he died, fragrance and miracles accompanied the three-day veneration of his body, which was found to be incorrupt nineteen years after his death. Saint Paschal is the patron saint of shepherds and Eucharistic congresses and associations.

PRAYER

Saint Paschal, your love for the Eucharist was the source of all your good works. Pray for us to cultivate a deep love for the Blessed Sacrament, and pray with us: Heavenly Father, give us a deep love and reverence for Jesus in the Blessed Sacrament like Saint Paschal had. May we always seek to serve Jesus in the poor and the sick. Guide us to pray faithfully, and strengthen our friendship with you. Grant us the gift of contemplation. Assist us in telling others persuasively about the True Presence of Jesus in the Eucharist, especially those who do not believe. We ask this in the name of Jesus. Amen.

MAY 18

Saint Eric of Sweden (d. 1161)

Saint Eric, the faithful king of Sweden, with the help of Saint Henry, bishop of Uppsala, converted his country to Christianity. A strong and organized ruler, he ousted the pagans and wrote laws for the country. Unfortunately, he was sabotaged by his own nobles, who collaborated with the Danish to overthrow him. He was blessed to attend Mass before the attacking army killed him, reportedly saying, "Let us at least finish the sacrifice; the rest of the feast I shall keep elsewhere." He died a martyr for his faith and is buried in the Cathedral of Uppsala, Sweden.

PRAYER

Saint Eric, you were a faithful and just ruler, and you led your people to the Church. Pray for us and with us: Righteous Father, grant us the grace to long for your kingdom and to labor in your service. May we use our gifts and talents to complete the tasks you ask of us, and may we always rely on your help in carrying out your will. Help us to follow your just laws. Give us the virtues of justice, fortitude, and prudence, that we might serve you faithfully according to our state in life. Bless all those in positions of power and help them to work with humility, recognizing that all power is yours. We ask this in the name of Jesus. Amen.

MAY 19

Saint Dunstan (d. 988)

Saint Dunstan is considered one of England's greatest saints. Before he was born, his mother had a dream that he would be holy. When he grew up, he became a priest and eventually abbot of Glastonbury. With Saints Ethelwold and Oswald, he restored monastery buildings and discipline for the monks, built new monasteries, and reformed the clergy throughout England. He served as an advisor to Kings Edred and Edgar, helping bring about even more reform. After he became archbishop of Canterbury, he also took on the role of papal legate to England. He is buried at Canterbury Cathedral.

PRAYER

Saint Dunstan, pray for us to reform our own lives and to labor for healing and reform in our Church and world. Pray with us on your feast: Merciful Father, make us zealous to carry out the work you have given us. May we never shy away from doing your will, even when it is difficult or unpopular. Help us to reform ourselves and your Church and use our gifts and talents for your glory. Bless all bishops and help them to govern their flocks with virtue. Bless the Benedictine order, keeping it faithful to you. We ask this in the name of Jesus. Amen.

MAY 20

Saint Bernardine of Siena (1380–1444)

Saint Bernardine's parents died when he was six. When he was still a young man, he almost died from the plague after ministering to the sick. He survived, however, and joined the Franciscans of the Strict Observance, becoming a priest, then superior general. A gifted preacher, he was very successful in leading people to convert. He preached peace and promoted devotion to the Holy Name of Jesus, of which he said: "The Name of Jesus is the glory of preachers, because the shining splendor of that Name causes His word to be proclaimed and heard. … Was it not through the brilliance and sweet savor of this Name that God *called us into his marvelous light?*" He also urged churches to display the initials IHS to honor Jesus' name instead of arms of war. Saint Bernardine is the patron saint of public relations, advertising professionals, wool weavers, and Massa Marittima, and his intercession is sought for hoarseness, bleeding, and chest complaints.

PRAYER

Saint Bernardine, pray for us to love and honor the name of Jesus, and to serve Him in all that we do, as you did. Pray with us: Heavenly Father, grant us a great love for the Name of Jesus. May we invoke it with reverence throughout the day, especially in times of temptation. Teach us to make reparation for those who profane it by saying "Admirable is the holy name of God." Grant us the virtues we need to carry out your will, especially humility and charity. Bless the Franciscan order, keeping it faithful to you. We ask this in the name of Jesus. Amen.

MAY 21

Blessed Martyrs of
Mexico (d. 1915–1937)

The Blessed Martyrs of Mexico are twenty-five men (both priests and laity) who held fast to their faith in spite of the threats of the communist government, dying in union with Christ and His Church. They are some of the millions of Christians killed by the atheistic communists who overtook many governments in the early twentieth century. Blesseds Cristobal Magallanes Jara, Augustin Cortes, and Jose Maria Hurtado were priests, while Blesseds Manuel Morales, Salvador Puente, and David Roldán Lara were laymen. Blessed Cristobal was active in his community beyond his parish duties, founding schools, a newspaper, and cooperatives to help farmers. Refusing to obey the anti-Catholic restrictions of the unjust government, he continued to open seminaries. Like the other martyrs, he was arrested and executed without trial, saying on behalf of all of them, "I pray to God that my blood serves the unity of my Mexican brethren."

PRAYER

Blessed Martyrs of Mexico, thank you for your witness of fidelity to the Faith in spite of great suffering, which inspires us to hold fast to our faith. Pray with us today: Merciful Father, give us the virtues of faith, trust, strength, and courage. Inspire us to proclaim with steadfast loyalty, in union with these Mexican martyrs, "Long live Christ the King!" Free the world from the oppression of atheistic communism, with all its deception, destruction, and false ideologies. Free all peoples in countries still under communist oppression and deliver them from evil. Protect all who are being persecuted for their faith. We ask this in the name of Jesus. Amen.

MAY 22

Saint Rita of Cascia (1381–1457)

From the time she was a child, Rita had a deep love of prayer. When she reached adulthood, she wanted to enter religious life, but her parents wished for her to marry, as she was their only child. For eighteen years, she prayed for her husband's conversion from violence, and he repented just before he was murdered. When her sons wanted to avenge his murder, she begged God to take them so they would not sin, and they died of an illness. She then entered an Augustinian convent, where she received one of the wounds of Jesus in her forehead. The wound emitted such a foul odor that she had to live separately from the other sisters, but she bore all her sufferings with patience and sweetness. Her body, kept in the basilica that bears her name in Cascia, is still incorrupt. Saint Rita is the patron saint of those who struggle with infertility and of hopeless causes.

PRAYER

Saint Rita, you loved God passionately, and you accepted the sufferings He sent you without complaining. Pray for us and with us on your feast: Loving Father, give us the virtue of obedience and make us willing to do as you ask, no matter what. Fill us with your peace, and grant reconciliation in our marriages, families, communities, and nations. Assist and comfort those struggling with infertility and all who mourn the death of a child or a spouse. Bless the Augustinian order, keeping it faithful to you. We ask this in the name of Jesus. Amen.

MAY 23

Saint John Baptist de Rossi (1698–1764)

John Baptist de Rossi spent forty years committed to missionary work among the sick, prisoners, and homeless women in Rome. He taught them the doctrines of the Faith and even performed miracles. Talented, virtuous, a great student, and a member of sodalities including the Sodality of the Blessed Virgin Mary, he became a priest at the young age of twenty-three. As a confessor, he was greatly admired and sought after because he was tenderhearted and merciful. He understood the need for priests to preach well, saying: "The poor come to church tired and distracted by their daily troubles. If you preach a long sermon they can't follow you. Give them one idea that they can take home, not half a dozen, or one will drive out the other, and they will remember none." He brought spiritual and material assistance to so many people that he was called the "Apostle of the Abandoned" and the "second Philip Neri."

PRAYER
Saint John Baptist, you lived your life in service to those who were most abandoned. Pray for us to love as you did, and pray with us: Gentle Father, make us tender and gentle in our dealings with others, and give us merciful hearts toward all we meet. Guide us to help those in need, especially the sick, vulnerable, and those who seek our prayers. Protect priests and make them merciful confessors and powerful preachers. We ask this in the name of Jesus. Amen.

MAY 24

Blesseds Isidore Ngei Ko Lat (1918–1950) and Mario Vergara (1910–1950)

Blessed Ko Lat was a young boy in Burma when his parents died, and he was raised (along with his younger brother) by his aunt and uncle. After six years in the seminary, his path to priesthood was interrupted by World War II, and he returned to his village to teach children. He met Father Mario Vergara, a missionary priest to Burma, who had been originally assigned to another village and had set up an orphanage and services for the poor. Together, they taught the Burmese people the Catholic Faith. Unfortunately, when Burma won independence, lawless rebels persecuted Catholics. Because these two men spoke out, they were martyred. Blessed Isidore Ngei Ko Lat is the first native-born person from Burma to be beatified.

PRAYER

Blesseds Isidore and Mario, you taught and defended the Faith even when it was dangerous to do so. Pray for us and with us today: Righteous Father, give us a love of your children and determination to teach them the truth. Guide us to work together in the catechesis and evangelization of others. Give success to teachers and catechists. Make us courageous in defending the poor and vulnerable, even if it means that we will suffer. Bless and protect all who are persecuted for their faith. We ask this in the name of Jesus. Amen.

MAY 25

Saint Bede the Venerable (673–735)

Bede was so esteemed during his lifetime that he was known as Venerable Bede, and his writings were read in many churches. Kings and popes sought his advice. His excellent commentaries on Scripture are full of wisdom, and his *Ecclesiastical History of the English People* is a masterpiece of medieval history. From his monastery, Bede wrote and taught from the perspective of the classical scholastic foundation he received from Saint Benedict Biscop. One of his followers, Saint Cuthbert, testified that he returned thanks to God unceasingly. He encouraged others to be faithful and grateful in the ordinary circumstances of life, putting God at the center of their lives. As he attested of his own life, "I was no longer the center of my life, and therefore I could see God in everything." Saint Bede is the patron saint of historians and is a Doctor of the Church.

PRAYER

Saint Bede, you faithfully used the intellectual gifts God gave you to serve the Church and draw souls to Christ. Pray with us on your feast: Dear Father, be the center of our lives. Remove all selfishness and ambition from our hearts and draw us to yourself. Grant us grace to perceive and be grateful for your love and provision in our daily life. Fill us with the virtues of diligence, prudence, and humility. Inspire us to study the Faith and seek always to know you better. We ask this in the name of Jesus. Amen.

MAY 26

Saint Philip Neri (1515–1595)

Born in Florence, as a young man Philip Neri went to Rome to join the Jesuits and become a missionary. But God had other plans and made him an apostle to Rome to re-evangelize the city, which had become corrupted by worldliness. Radiating joy to all he met, he labored for many years as a layman, leading people to conversion. He taught that "the Name of Jesus pronounced with reverence and affection has a kind of power to soften the heart." Eventually, at his spiritual director's urging, he became a priest and, over time, formed the Congregation of the Priests of the Oratory. He taught his followers that humility is the safeguard of chastity. He also provided spiritual direction to many priests, including Saint Francis de Sales and Saint Charles Borromeo. He was known for his sense of humor and is called the Apostle of Joy.

PRAYER

Saint Philip, you joyfully served God by re-evangelizing Rome, leading many souls to conversion. Pray for us to have joyful hearts like yours, and pray with us: Loving Father, make us joyful witnesses of your love and goodness to all we meet. Like Saint Philip, may we follow your will for our lives, even when it does not seem to match our own desires, trusting that your plan is best. Protect youth and young adults and draw them to yourself. Grant us growth in all virtues, but especially humility. Bless the Congregation of the Oratory and keep it faithful to you. We ask this in the name of Jesus. Amen.

MAY 27

Saint Augustine of Canterbury (d. 604)

Saint Augustine, a Benedictine monk and prior of the Monastery of Saint Andrew in Rome, obeyed when Pope Saint Gregory the Great asked him to evangelize England. Along with forty companions, he traveled to England and was so successful that his ministry resulted in the conversion of King Ethelbert and all of England to the Catholic Faith. Augustine became the first archbishop of Canterbury and founded the Dioceses of London and Rochester. His witness and impact were so great that he is called the Apostle of England. Saint Augustine is the patron saint of England.

PRAYER

Saint Augustine, you served the Church faithfully, evangelizing England and bringing the Gospel to many. Pray for us and with us today: Merciful Father, allow us to be your witnesses in the world. Grant us missionary zeal, eloquence in speech, and unwavering charity, so that we can be strong witnesses of your love and faithfulness, drawing souls to you. Grant perseverance and success to all evangelists and missionaries. Bless all bishops, making them true shepherds and virtuous leaders. We ask this in the name of Jesus. Amen.

MAY 28

Saint Justus of Urgel (d. c. 527)

Saint Justus was a bishop of Urgel, Spain. He was so eloquent that Saint Isidore of Seville, who lived not long after he died, praised his writings, calling him "among the illustrious." He was committed to teaching God's truth in his preaching and writings, which include the *Commentary on the Canticle of Canticles*. He attended the two important Councils of Toledo and Lerida and guided his flock with wisdom and charity.

PRAYER

Saint Justus, you were a wise and prudent leader who tenderly cared for the flock entrusted to you. Pray with us on your feast: Heavenly Father, inspire us to be committed to learning and sharing the truths of our faith. Enable Catholic writers to reach many people and help them love you more deeply. Strengthen in us the virtue of prudence, and help us to exercise the Holy Spirit's gifts of wisdom and counsel. Bless all bishops, making them true shepherds and virtuous leaders. Make us saints. We ask this in the name of Jesus. Amen.

MAY 29

Saint Paul VI (1897–1978)

Due to ill health, Giovanni Battista Montini, the future Pope Paul VI, was schooled at home in Concesio, Italy. He was only twenty-three when he became a priest. Eventually, he became a Vatican diplomat. Pope Pius XII appointed him archbishop of Milan in 1954, and in 1958 Pope John XXIII made him a cardinal. When John XXIII died after the first session of Vatican II, Montini was elected pope and took the name Paul VI. He worked to implement the decisions of the council; wrote encyclicals on social issues, including *Humanae Vitae*; and instituted the World Day of Peace. He had a special concern for young people. He was canonized by Pope Francis in 2018.

PRAYER

Saint Paul VI, you led the Church with wisdom, humility, and, above all, charity. Pray for the Church, and pray with us on your feast: Gracious Father, help us to understand and live the commandments so that all people will be treated fairly and with love. Inspire us to read the *Catechism* and the encyclicals of the popes so we can fully put into practice the Church's teachings, especially those on social justice. Heal us of the effects of the culture that are against those teachings. Make our domestic churches safe, holy, and filled with love. Bless our pope and the bishops in union with him. We ask this in the name of Jesus. Amen.

MAY 30

Saint Joan of Arc (1412–1431)

Young Joan was a peasant girl who was given a unique mission from God to help save France from English attacks and dominance. When she was only fourteen years old, she heard the voices of Saint Michael, Saint Margaret, Saint Catherine of Alexandria, and others directing her. Though untrained in politics or warfare, she possessed the gifts of prophecy and leadership. Obedient to God's call, the Maid of Orleans led the French army against the British who had besieged Orleans, gaining victory so that King Charles VII was at last able to be crowned. She was captured and unjustly put on trial for unfounded accusations of heresy and witchcraft. She was burned to death when she was only nineteen years old. Years later, Pope Callixtus III and her mother were able to clear her name and let the truth be known. American author Mark Twain, though not himself a Catholic, was so impressed with her that he wrote a biography about her. Saint Joan is the patron saint of France, soldiers, and the military.

PRAYER

Saint Joan, pray for us to serve God faithfully no matter what He might ask of us, and pray with us: Merciful Father, grant us the courage to listen to your voice and follow your promptings. Make us strong and virtuous leaders like Saint Joan. Heal and convert all who have left the Church and bring them back to you. Bless and protect all who serve in the military and assist them in defending the most vulnerable. We ask this in the name of Jesus. Amen.

MAY 31

The Visitation of Our Lady to Elizabeth

When the angel Gabriel told Mary that she would be the mother of Jesus, he also revealed, "And behold, your relative Elizabeth in her old age has also conceived a son, and this is the sixth month with her who was called barren. For nothing will be impossible with God" (Lk 1:36–37). Mary believed what the angel said, and her compassion and concern moved her to go right away to help. When she arrived, the baby in Elizabeth's womb leaped for joy in the presence of Jesus, and Elizabeth, inspired by the Holy Spirit, recognized that Mary was "the Mother of my Lord." This joyful scene is called the Visitation, and we meditate on it in the second joyful mystery of the Rosary.

PRAYER

Mother Mary and Saint Elizabeth, pray for us to recognize God's presence in all we meet, and to serve and encourage one another in love. Pray with us now: Loving Father, inspire us to trust in your will for our lives. Grant us peace as you work out your plan for us and in us. Instill in us a heart of hospitality and service, that we might see the needs of others and hasten to help them. Bless our extended family relationships. We ask this in the name of Jesus. Amen.

JUNE

THE MONTH OF
THE SACRED HEART OF JESUS

JUNE 1

Saint Justin Martyr and Companions (d. 165)

Saint Justin Martyr (sometimes called the Philosopher) converted from paganism at age thirty and hosted debates in his school in Rome. He was so passionate about the Catholic Faith that he wrote beautiful works of apologetics during an incredibly dangerous time for Christians. He even wrote an "Apology" explaining Christianity to the Roman Emperor Marcus Aurelius. Many of his writings, including his *Apologies for the Christian Religion* and his *Dialogue with the Jew Trypho*, are still studied today. When the Roman prefect Rusticus commanded that Justin and his companions — Charita, Chariton, Euelpistus, Hierox, Libenianus, and Paeon — worship the Roman gods, they defied this order. Saint Justin famously replied, "No one who is right thinking stoops from true worship to false worship." They suffered martyrdom together.

PRAYER

Saint Justin and Companions, you defended the Faith with courage and grace, and you boldly gave your lives for it. Pray for us to practice our faith with that same zeal, and pray with us today: Gracious Father, make us bold in proclaiming and living our faith and diligent in studying it so that we can teach it to others. Grant us the grace to love you with mind, heart, and soul, and strengthen in us the virtues of faith and hope. Give us the wisdom to uphold the truth in a world that does not accept it, and bless our children, giving them wisdom to reject false ideologies. Bless and protect all who are persecuted for their faith in you. We ask this in the name of Jesus. Amen.

JUNE 2

Saints Marcellinus and Peter (d. 304)

Saints Marcellinus, a priest, and Peter, an exorcist, were so passionate for the Faith that they converted their prison guard and his family before being martyred. This occurred during the persecution of Christians in Rome by Serenus, magistrate under Emperor Diocletian. Their executioner told Pope Saint Damasus I about their martyrdom, and he wrote an inscription that was placed over their tomb in the catacombs. According to his description, the two men were forced to clear out a space in the forest for their own graves before they were beheaded. Later, a Christian woman named Lucilla received a revelation about where they were buried, and she had their remains moved to the catacombs. Emperor Constantine I later erected a basilica there, in which his mother, Saint Helena, is buried.

PRAYER

Saints Marcellinus and Peter, you kept preaching the Gospel even in prison, and your fidelity led to salvation for your guard and his family. Pray for us to preach the Gospel always, and pray with us: Merciful Father, give us unwavering faith and contagious zeal to share it with everyone we meet. Grant us the courage we need to proclaim your truth. Help us to show your love through our good works, especially the corporal and spiritual works of mercy. Bless all those who suffer persecution for their faith in you. We ask this in the name of Jesus. Amen.

JUNE 3

Saint Charles Lwanga and Companions (d. 1886)

Saint Charles, a Christian convert in Uganda, had charge of the pages in King Mwanga's court, several of whom were Christians or catechumens. These zealous young men refused to violate their chastity or to give up their faith, despite the king's demands. Charles's predecessor as head of the pages, Joseph Mukasa, had courageously suffered martyrdom in November 1885, when he spoke out against the king's immoral behavior. Charles and several others were baptized that very night, realizing that their lives were probably in danger. In May 1886, fifteen pages were sentenced to death for their faith and forced to walk two days to the execution site. Some were killed on the way. On the day of execution, Charles was burned first, separately from the others, and as he was dying, he said: "You're burning me, but it's like water you're pouring to wash me. Please repent and become a Christian like me." He is the patron saint of youth and Catholic action in Uganda.

PRAYER

Saint Charles Lwanga and Companions, your love for God led you to sacrifice your lives, yet you never wavered in the face of brutality. On your feast, pray for us and with us: Righteous Father, grant us the zeal and steadfast courage of your martyrs. May we recognize the gift of our faith, as they did, and share it joyfully even when it is dangerous to do so. Grant us the grace to set appropriate boundaries fearlessly, opposing anyone who would compromise our chastity. Guard and protect the chastity of children. Bless all those who are persecuted for their faith in you. We ask this in the name of Jesus. Amen.

JUNE 4

Saint Optatus of Milevis (320–387)

Saint Optatus was the bishop of Milevis in Numidia. His writings on Church doctrine have been compared to Saint Augustine's! Highly regarded by Saints Augustine and Fulgentius, he wrote six treaties excellently refuting Bishop Parmenian, who is credited as the most famous writer of the Donatist heresy. Donatists believed that sacraments were only efficacious if the minister was sinless. Optatus wrote in one letter to Parmenian: "The workers can be changed but the sacraments cannot be changed. If then, you can see that all who are baptizing are workers, not lords, and that the sacraments are holy of themselves and not by reason of men, what is it that you claim so urgently for yourselves." A truly faithful and virtuous bishop, Optatus worked tirelessly and peacefully to correct, convert, and bring back into unity with the Church those who were misled and caught up in Donatism.

PRAYER

Saint Optatus, pray for us to recognize and hold fast to the truth of our faith, and to teach it effectively to others. Pray with us today: Dear Father, bless the Church with unity, and draw all people to the Faith. Grant us a correct understanding of the Church's teachings, and help us to live by her doctrines. In everything we do, make us true witnesses and good examples. Teach us how to lovingly correct others who are misled, and to accept correction ourselves when we need it. Bless all bishops and make them virtuous leaders. We ask this in the name of Jesus. Amen.

JUNE 5

Saint Boniface (c. 673–754)

Saint Boniface, a Benedictine monk from Britain, followed God's call to be a missionary in Germany, which was still mostly pagan. To show how powerless the pagan gods truly were, Boniface chopped down the Oak of Thor, which the pagans worshiped, and built a church in its place. Rightly called the Apostle to Germany, Boniface labored for many years to spread the Faith in Germany and the Netherlands, setting up many monasteries, convents, and schools, and eventually becoming archbishop of Germany. Boniface also oversaw reform of the Church in Gaul and in Britain. Near the end of his life, he returned to the Netherlands to work for conversion there. While there, he and his companions were set upon by a band of pagans and killed. Saint Boniface is the patron saint of tailors, the country of Germany, and the town of Fulda.

PRAYER

Saint Boniface, you spread the Gospel in pagan lands and ultimately gave your life for it. Pray for us to be effective witnesses of God's love, and pray with us: Loving Father, grant us the courage and zeal to share the Gospel wherever we go and in all that we do. May we follow your will for our lives, using all our gifts and talents for your glory. Strengthen in us the virtues of fortitude, prudence, and diligence. Make us saints. Bless all bishops and help them to be true shepherds and virtuous leaders. We ask this in the name of Jesus. Amen.

JUNE 6

Saint Norbert (1080–1134)

Saint Norbert was so shaken after a dangerous fall from his horse in a storm that he converted from his worldly life. He sold his belongings, became a priest, founded monasteries and hospices, and taught others through his powerful preaching to live for God, rather than the passing pleasures of this world. Pope Gelasius II allowed him to preach across Europe as a missionary. A miracle worker, he taught respect for the Holy Eucharist, encouraging people to be devoted to the Blessed Sacrament. He founded the Premonstratensian order, more commonly known as the Norbertines, urging his followers to be "of one mind and heart in God." He was made archbishop of Magdeburg in Germany in 1126.

PRAYER

Saint Norbert, after your conversion, you helped many souls through your preaching and leadership. Pray for us to have the grace of conversion, and pray with us on your feast: Merciful Father, grant us the grace of conversion, and set us free from any worldly attachments that keep us from loving you as we should. Give us a deep love for the Eucharist and help us to grow in all virtues, especially temperance, piety, and charity. Make us saints. Bless all bishops, making them true shepherds and virtuous leaders. Bless the Norbertine order, keeping it faithful to you. We ask this in the name of Jesus. Amen.

JUNE 7

Blessed Marie-Thérèse de Soubiran (1834–1889)

Blessed Marie-Thérèse founded an order of nuns, the congregation of Mary Help of Christians, with the aim of helping the poor in France. Sadly, because of the devious manipulation of one of her religious sisters, she was falsely accused of mismanaging the community's money and ousted from the order. She felt the loss of her reputation and her community keenly, but with strong faith, she believed that God would continue to guide her. Eventually, in 1874, she entered the monastery of Our Lady of Charity in Paris, where she remained until she died. Only after her death did the order of Mary Help of Christians discover that she had been falsely accused, and her reputation was restored.

PRAYER

Blessed Marie-Thérèse, you suffered greatly from slander, yet you faithfully continued to serve God, not seeking human respect. Pray with us today: Loving Father, help us to trust in your guidance of our lives, even when everything seems to be going wrong. Give us firm hope and constant humility. Help us to live in the present moment with you, lovingly doing all that you ask of us in our state in life. Bring healing to all people who have been falsely accused and whose reputations have been unjustly damaged. Give them the grace to forgive and pray for their oppressors. Convert all who treat others unjustly. Make us all saints. We ask this in the name of Jesus. Amen.

JUNE 8

Saint William of York (d. 1154)

William Fitzherbert had a winning personality and was involved in Church affairs from an early age. When he was appointed archbishop of York, many people thought it was because of his political connections. After only a few years, Pope Eugene III had him step down from the post. He did so gracefully, withdrawing into contemplative, penitential life in a monastery for six years. Eventually, after the death of Eugene III, he was reinstated as archbishop of York, to the joy of his flock, who welcomed him back. In fact, the people were so excited for his return that they crowded the wooden Ouse Bridge, and it collapsed. Yet thanks to his prayers, no one was injured. He died soon after his reinstatement, and so many marvels occurred at his tomb that, after an inquiry, Pope Honorius III canonized him.

PRAYER

Saint William, you humbly accepted misunderstanding and remained close to God in the midst of challenges. Pray for us to do the same, and pray with us: Gracious Father, save us from fear of the opinions of others, and teach us to pray for our enemies and forgive those who speak poorly of us. Grant us a spirit of penance and conversion. Confirm your Church in peace and unity. Bless all bishops, making them true shepherds and virtuous leaders. We ask this in the name of Jesus. Amen.

JUNE 9

Saint Ephrem (306–373)

Saint Ephrem, often called Ephrem the Syrian, was a deacon in the early Church. A gifted teacher, he opened and taught at a theological school. Besides writing many theological works, including commentaries on the Scriptures, he composed poems and music through which to praise God and convey truths of the Catholic Faith. He was so musically gifted that some called him the "Harp of the Holy Spirit." He made sails for ships, was generous to the poor, treated women with respect, and taught that pondering our death helps us prepare for it. He is the only Doctor of the Church who was a deacon.

PRAYER

Saint Ephrem, God gave you the gift of wisdom, and you used it to draw souls to Him. Pray for us and with us today: Heavenly Father, we give you thanks and praise, and we ask for the grace to give you glory in all that we do. Help us to use all our talents, gifts, and creativity to do your will. Strengthen us in virtue, especially generosity, studiousness, and kindness. Bless the Orthodox and bring all Christians back into the unity of your Church. Guide and protect all deacons and those discerning the diaconate. We ask this in the name of Jesus. Amen.

JUNE 10

Saint Getulius (d. c. 120)

Saint Getulius was married to Symphorosa, and both are saints. Originally a Roman soldier, he became a Christian, left the army, and returned to his estate, not far from where Emperor Hadrian lived. The imperial legate Caerealis was sent to arrest him, but when Getulius spoke of Jesus, Caerealis was converted. Then another officer, Primitivus, was sent to arrest him, but he also was converted. Eventually, Getulius, his brother Amantius, Caerealis, and Primitivus were all martyred. Later, Saint Symphorosa and their seven sons were also martyred.

PRAYER

Saint Getulius, you held fast to your faith in spite of danger and won other souls for Christ through your fidelity. Pray with us on your feast: Gentle Father, grant us the grace to remain grateful even in suffering and to be fearless. May our witness and our love for you draw others to you. Bless married couples, helping them to be true to their vocation. Give parents the wisdom and patience to form their children in the Faith. Guard and protect all who are persecuted for their faith in you. We ask this in the name of Jesus. Amen.

JUNE 11

Saint Barnabas (d. c. 61)

Saint Barnabas, originally named Joseph, from the Jewish tribe of Levi, sold his land, donated the money to the Church, and introduced Saint Paul to the apostles. According to Saint Luke (author of the Acts of the Apostles), "he was a good man, full of the Holy Spirit and of faith" (Acts 11:24). Later, Barnabas became Paul's partner on his first missionary journey. He lived up to the name *Barnabas*, which means son of encouragement. He and Paul began their missionary work in his hometown of Cyprus in Greece, and he is considered the founder of the Church there. Later, it is believed that he was martyred for the Faith. Saint Barnabas is the patron saint of weavers, missionaries, those grieving, the Barnabite order, and the cities of Milan and Florence in Italy. His intercession is invoked for protection from hailstorms and quarrels.

PRAYER

Saint Barnabas, pray for us to be able to preach the Gospel effectively to all we meet, and to encourage one another in living our faith. Pray with us now: Loving Father, give us true missionary hearts to share your Gospel with the world in all that we say and do. May we always praise your name and teach others to do so. Grant us the gift of encouragement, and teach us to be faithful friends, ready to apologize for our wrongs and to forgive, building up the unity of the Church. Give us all the virtues we need to be your faithful witnesses. We ask this in the name of Jesus. Amen.

JUNE 12

Saint Onuphrius (d. c. 400)

Saint Onuphrius lived as a hermit in the Egyptian desert for seventy years, where he prayed and fasted. He was renowned for his holiness, and people came to consult him on spiritual matters. There are many legends about him, including one about an angel coming to give him the Eucharist each week. The one thing that is certain is that he was a holy man who loved God and lived only for Him. Saint Onuphrius is the patron saint of weavers.

PRAYER

Saint Onuphrius, pray for us to be detached from all worldly things and to desire God above everything. Pray with us on your feast: Heavenly Father, grant us the grace to leave behind whatever prevents us from following you. May we grow closer to you each day, seeking out silence and prayer, and may we find true spiritual directors and friends to help us live our Christian vocation to the fullest. Grant us wisdom to see your will in all things. Bless all who live as hermits for love of you. We ask this in the name of Jesus. Amen.

JUNE 13

Saint Anthony of Padua (1195–1231)

Saint Anthony knew how to give up his own plans and start again in order to follow God's will. Born of a noble family in Lisbon, Portugal, he spent several years as a member of the Augustinian order before he transferred to the Franciscan order, inspired by the example of two Franciscan martyrs. He longed to be a missionary and die for Christ in Africa, and this desire was partially fulfilled, as God did make him a missionary — but in Italy and France. Anthony was so popular as a preacher and confessor that huge crowds would come to hear him. He helped so many people convert that he was called the "Hammer of the Heretics." A gifted scholar and miracle worker, he even raised people from the dead. Saint Anthony is the patron saint of Portugal, the poor, oppressed, travelers, and women suffering from infertility. Many people to pray to him when they need help finding lost things. He is a Doctor of the Church.

PRAYER

Saint Anthony, you followed God's will for your life and brought many souls back into the true Church. Pray for us to be effective witnesses of the Gospel, and pray with us: Merciful Father, help us to carry out your will with joy and fervor, no matter where it leads us. Make us eager to study your word and learn all we can about you. Grant us sensitivity to our neighbors and allow us to lighten their burdens. Enrich your Church with great preachers and confessors like Saint Anthony. Bless the Augustinian and Franciscan orders, keeping them faithful to you. We ask this in the name of Jesus. Amen.

JUNE 14

Venerable María Beatriz del Rosario Arroyo y Pidal (1884-1957)

Venerable María Beatriz grew up in the Philippines and from a young age loved to perform the corporal works of mercy, following in her family's tradition of almsgiving. Her family was and still is involved in serving in the political life of the Philippines. She discerned a call to religious life and entered the Convent of Saint Catalina in Manila, giving them her inheritance. After a period of formation, she became a Dominican nun. Later, she discerned the call to form a new community, serving in schools, colleges, and retreat houses. With two other sisters, she founded the Dominican Sisters of the Most Holy Rosary of the Philippines. Thirty-two years later, Mother Rosario was elected the First Superioress General, serving in that capacity until she died of heart failure three years later.

PRAYER

Venerable María Beatriz, you served God with generosity, giving of the abundance that He gave you. Pray for us to be generous, and pray with us on your feast: Heavenly Father, give us the virtues of Venerable María Beatriz and all the saints, especially generosity and humility. Guide us to correctly discern our vocation. Help us to fulfill the mission you have given us. Grant us the grace to perform the spiritual and corporal works of mercy, especially prayer, fasting, and almsgiving. Bless the Dominican order and keep it faithful to you. We ask this in the name of Jesus. Amen.

JUNE 15

Saint Vitus (d. c. 303)

Very little is known about Saint Vitus, except that he was martyred as a child during the Diocletian persecutions, along with Saints Crescentia and Modestus. It is believed that he was the son of a Sicilian senator, and he was arrested along with his nurse, Crescentia, and her husband, Modestus. Vitus is one of the Fourteen Holy Helpers — saints who have traditionally been invoked against various illnesses and disasters. Saint Vitus is the patron saint of dancers, actors, and people with epilepsy. He is invoked for protection in storms.

PRAYER
Saint Vitus, although you were only a child, you bravely faced the pagan authorities and gave your life for your faith. Pray with us on your feast: Righteous Father, make us steadfast in our faith, no matter what obstacles or dangers we may face as a result. Thank you for the gift of your saints, especially the Holy Helpers, and their generous intercession on our behalf. Please grant us the grace to receive all your gifts and to suffer willingly for love of you. Increase in us the virtues of fortitude and perseverance. Through the example of the child saints and martyrs, encourage children to be magnanimous. Make us saints. We ask this in the name of Jesus. Amen.

JUNE 16

Martyrs of Lang Coc, Vietnam (d. 1862)

Daminh (Dominic) Nguyen, a doctor, and four peasant farmers — Andrew Tuong, Daminh Nguyen Duc Mao, Daminh Nhi, and Vinh Son Tuong — completely accepted the power of the cross of Jesus. When ordered to contemptuously step on a crucifix, they refused. As punishment, they were imprisoned and tortured before suffering martyrdom for their courage, tenacity, and ardor in refusing to deny Jesus and His sacrifice on the cross. These men are among the thousands of martyrs who suffered for their faith in Vietnam in the eighteenth and nineteenth centuries.

PRAYER
Holy martyrs of Lang Coc, pray for us to have the courage to stand firm in our faith even when it is dangerous. Pray with us on your feast: Gentle Father, help us to grow in virtue and holiness in imitation of these holy Vietnamese martyrs. Give us the sure knowledge of the truths of our faith and help us never to deny or denigrate them in any way. Grant us your grace to live the commandments with constancy and become strong witnesses to your truth and your Church. May we never boast, except in the cross of Christ Jesus, our Lord. Bless all who are persecuted for their faith. Make us saints. We ask this in the name of Jesus. Amen.

JUNE 17

Saint Albert Chmielowski (1845–1916)

Brother Albert, whose baptismal name was Adam, grew up in an area of Poland that was controlled by the Russians. As a young man, he participated in a military uprising and lost one of his legs to an injury. Later, he worked for a time as a successful artist but found that he yearned for a life of simplicity and dedication to the poor. He became a Secular Franciscan and later established the Albertine Brothers to serve the poorest people in Kraków. Several years later, he established a congregation for women, the Albertine Sisters. These houses for the poor and homeless have helped many. Pope Saint John Paul II felt a special affinity to him, calling Saint Albert "the Brother of Our Lord" and writing a play, *Our God's Brother*, in his honor. John Paul II beatified Brother Albert in 1983 and canonized him in 1989.

PRAYER

Saint Albert, you loved the poor and placed your many gifts at their service. Pray for us to serve our neighbor with love, and pray with us: Loving Father, inspire us to seek your will through consistent prayer and meditation and to follow it promptly. Teach us how to live a simple life and serve the poor and vulnerable in works of mercy. Grant artists the grace to use their talents, as Saint Albert did, to promote the good, true, and beautiful for your glory and the benefit of others. Bless the Franciscan order and the Albertines and keep them faithful to you. We ask this in the name of Jesus. Amen.

JUNE 18

Saint Elizabeth of Schönau (1129–1164)

Saint Elizabeth was an extraordinary Benedictine nun who received great mystical gifts. She lived in the convent of Schönau on the Rhine River in Germany and dictated her mystical experiences to her brother Eckbert, a Benedictine abbot, who served as her secretary and editor. Her writings include *The Book of the Ways of God*. Elizabeth stressed how critical it is to live for God, to do His work, and to do penance. Saint Elizabeth is the patron saint of those facing temptations.

PRAYER

Saint Elizabeth, you received extraordinary graces from God, and you shared them with others through your writing. Pray with us now: Dear Father, unite us to yourself and give us prayerful hearts. Heal those suffering from mental distress and their families who suffer with them. May we always follow your will and use our gifts and talents to serve you and give you glory. Bless the Benedictine order, keeping it faithful to you. We ask this in the name of Jesus. Amen.

JUNE 19

Venerable Matt Talbot (1856–1925)

Venerable Matt, born in poverty in Dublin, started drinking when he was twelve years old and struggled with alcoholism until he was thirty. His addiction led him into debt and even theft. Clearly seeing the state into which his soul had sunk, he turned to God and the sacraments. He later said, "I just asked the Holy Spirit for help, and He gave it to me." He went to confession and took the pledge, renouncing alcohol for three months, then six months, then for the rest of his life. Living the simple lifestyle of Saint Francis as a Secular Franciscan, he was sustained by prayer, daily Mass, penance, Scripture, and reading the lives of the saints. He once said: "Never be too hard on the man who can't give up drink. It's as hard to give up the drink as it is to raise the dead to life again. But both are possible and even easy for our Lord. We have only to depend on him." Venerable Matt is the patron saint of alcoholics, sobriety, and recovery from substance abuse and addiction.

PRAYER
Venerable Matt, you turned to God for help, and He healed you of your addiction and allowed you to help others. Pray with us today: Merciful Father, free us from all attachments that keep us from following your will for us. Grant us temperance in all areas of our lives. Give healing and recovery to people struggling with addiction and bless their families who suffer so much with them. Bless the Franciscan order, keeping it faithful to you. We ask this in the name of Jesus. Amen.

JUNE 20

Blessed Balthasar de Torres (d. 1626), Saint Vincent Kaun (d. 1626), and Blessed Francis Pacheco (1566–1626)

Blessed Balthasar was a Jesuit missionary from Spain who was sent to spread the Gospel in Japan. For his witness of the Faith, he was martyred in Nagasaki in 1626, along with Saint Vincent Kaun, a Korean who had converted to Catholicism and become a Jesuit, and Blessed Francis Pacheco, a Jesuit missionary from Portugal. With six other Jesuit priests, these men were burned alive just outside of Nagasaki. Between 1597 and 1873, different Japanese rulers had thousands of Christians — both European missionaries and natives — killed because they clung to their faith.

PRAYER

Blessed Balthasar, Saint Vincent, and Blessed Francis, pray for us to have the courage to hold fast to our faith no matter the cost, and pray with us on your feast: Gracious Father, inspire us to imitate Jesus and all the martyrs in times of trial, humiliation, and suffering for our faith. Grant us the strength and willingness to suffer and die if necessary to remain faithful to you. Strengthen in us the virtues of fortitude, perseverance, and hope. Bless and protect all missionaries and all who are persecuted for their faith in you. We ask this in the name of Jesus. Amen.

JUNE 21

Saint Aloysius Gonzaga (1568–1591)

Saint Aloysius was born to a noble family in Italy, but as a young man he gave up his inheritance to enter the Jesuit order. As a novice, he obeyed his superiors and moderated the penances he had been accustomed to performing. He was very intelligent and excelled at his studies in philosophy and theology. God also gave him the gift of prophecy so that he knew when he would die. When the plague broke out in Italy in 1591, he devoted himself to tending to the sick. Eventually, he contracted the plague himself, and after several months of illness, he died at the age of twenty-three. Saint Robert Bellarmine, his spiritual director, gave him last rites. Saint Aloysius is the patron saint of young students, Catholic youth, AIDS sufferers, and many Catholic schools and universities.

PRAYER

Saint Aloysius, you gave up wealth and a life of privilege to serve God. Pray for us to love God above all things, and pray with us: Heavenly Father, inspire us to make a generous gift of ourselves to others. Grant us the grace to be obedient to your will, always faithfully performing the duties of our state in life. Teach us to faithfully honor our parents. Instill in us a love for penance and sacrifice. Bless the Jesuit order, keeping it faithful to you. We ask this in the name of Jesus. Amen.

JUNE 22

Saints John Fisher (1469–1535) and Thomas More (1478–1535)

Saints John Fisher and Thomas More died because they refused to support King Henry VIII when he asserted himself as head of the Church in England to legitimize his divorce and remarriage. Saint John Fisher was bishop of Rochester and a cardinal, and he had been Henry's boyhood tutor. Saint Thomas More was a lawyer, Lord Chancellor, and Henry's good friend. Both men died upholding God's principles, the Church's teachings, and their consciences. In a letter he wrote to his daughter while in prison awaiting his sentence, Thomas wrote: "Nothing can come but what God wills. And I am very sure that whatever that be, however bad it may seem, it shall indeed be the best." Saint Thomas is the patron saint of attorneys, civil and public servants, court clerks, lawyers, and politicians. Saint John Fisher is the patron saint for the Diocese of Rochester in New York.

PRAYER

Saints John Fisher and Thomas More, pray for us to uphold the teachings of the Church with charity as you did, even when those teachings are unpopular. Pray with us now: Gracious Father, make us steadfast in our faith and in our adherence to your law, even to the point of death. Grant us fortitude and prudence to live and witness to our faith in the public square. Assist and protect political leaders and lawyers, and give them honesty, integrity, and a strong sense of justice to protect all people, especially the vulnerable. Bless all bishops, making them true shepherds and virtuous leaders. We ask this in the name of Jesus. Amen.

JUNE 23

Saint Alban (d. c. 304)

Saint Alban, believed to be the first person in Roman Britain killed under Roman Emperor Diocletian, was not even Christian when he hid a priest in his home to protect him from persecution. He was so moved by the priest's witness that he converted and was baptized. When the Romans came to arrest the priest, Alban protected him by putting on his cloak and was arrested in his place. So complete was his conversion that, when he was asked to deny Christ and sacrifice to Roman gods, he refused and zealously corrected the judge, saying: "If you want to know my religion, I am Christian. Your sacrifices are offered to devils. They cannot help you or answer your requests. The reward for such sacrifices is the everlasting punishment of hell."

PRAYER

Saint Alban, you boldly faced death for the sake of your newfound faith in Christ. Pray for us to recognize the great gift of our faith, and pray with us today: Dear Father, thank you for the gift of our faith. Increase our gratitude and our love for you each day. Grant us such a strong and committed love of you and your truth that we would willingly die for it. Convert our hearts from selfishness to selfless love and generosity, and keep us committed to protecting others, especially the vulnerable. Bless all who are persecuted for their faith in you. We ask this in the name of Jesus. Amen.

JUNE 24

The Birth of Saint John the Baptist (first century)

Saint Elizabeth was older and barren when God finally granted her prayer for a son. When her baby was still a tiny preborn child in his mother's womb, he sensed the presence of Jesus in Mother Mary's womb and, the Gospel tells us, leapt for joy. John the Baptist's mission to prepare people for Christ's coming was so significant that, besides Jesus and Mother Mary, he is the only person whose birthday is a feast day in the Church. His preaching and ministry were so powerful that people thought he must be the messiah. He told them firmly: "I am not the Christ, but I have been sent before him. The one who has the bride is the bridegroom. The friend of the bridegroom, who stands and hears him, rejoices greatly at the bridegroom's voice. Therefore, this joy of mine is now complete. He must increase, but I must decrease" (Jn 3:28–30).

PRAYER

Saint John the Baptist, you wholeheartedly fulfilled your mission to prepare the way for Jesus. Pray for us to prepare the way for Him in our hearts, and pray with us: Gracious Father, let us prepare the way for you in our own lives so that we can faithfully proclaim your goodness to all we meet. Grant us the grace of repentance and conversion. Inspire us to be witnesses to the truth without fear, and to know and follow your will, no matter what. Guide us to find our vocation and fulfill our mission. May we always faithfully proclaim your Gospel, keep the commandments, and live the beatitudes. We ask this in the name of Jesus. Amen.

JUNE 25

Saint William of Vercelli (1085–1142)

Saint William lost his noble parents when he was an infant and was raised by relatives. When he was fourteen or fifteen years old, he undertook a pilgrimage to Santiago de Compostela in Spain, after which he became a hermit on Monte Vergine in Italy. Eventually, he founded the Hermits of Monte Vergine (Mount of the Virgin), named after the Blessed Mother. His close friend, Saint John of Matera, helped him establish several monasteries in other Italian cities. He was so wise and well respected that King Roger I of Naples sought his advice and guidance. The monasteries William founded followed the Benedictine Rule, praying and working, blending contemplative prayer with manual labor.

PRAYER

Saint William, pray for us to love and serve God in our work and prayer, as you did, and pray with us: Loving Father, give us prayerful hearts and help us to build our life on a foundation of prayer and the works of mercy, always intent on doing your will. May we long for nothing else in this life, except to grow closer to you and draw others to you as well. Help us to grow in all the virtues, especially humility, piety, and diligence. Bless and protect all orphans and children who are abandoned or neglected, and grant them kind, loving, and faith-filled families. Bless the Benedictine order, keeping it faithful to you. We ask this in the name of Jesus. Amen.

JUNE 26

Saint Josemaría Escrivá de Balaguer (1902–1975)

Saint Josemaría had a unique mission to help people pursue holiness in every area of life, especially in their work. Born in Spain, he experienced the pain of loss, grief, and war from boyhood. As a young man, he followed God's call to become a priest. Later, he recognized that God was calling him to help people find holiness through their ordinary lives and work, and he founded Opus Dei (Work of God) for laypeople, and later, within it, the Priestly Society of the Holy Cross. He taught the importance of sanctifying work because it is the way in which God wants to make us holy. He wrote that "work is born of love; it is a manifestation of love and is directed toward love. We see the hand of God, not only in the wonders of nature but also in our experience of work and effort." He wrote many books, which are full of wisdom and practical help.

PRAYER

Saint Josemaría, you taught people to seek growth in holiness through their daily work. Pray for us to sanctify our work, and pray with us: Righteous Father, inspire us to pray, as Saint Josemaría did, "Lord, let me see what you want," and then give us the grace to follow where you lead. Grant us the grace to see our work as a gift, and teach us to sanctify it. Make us saints in our ordinary lives, teaching us to see each moment as an opportunity to grow closer to you. Bless Opus Dei and the Priestly Society of the Holy Cross, keeping them faithful to you. We ask this in the name of Jesus. Amen.

JUNE 27

Saint Cyril of Alexandria (370–444)

Born in Alexandria, Egypt, Saint Cyril became a priest, monk, and eventually bishop of Alexandria. He was intelligent and well-educated, and he used his gifts to write Scripture commentaries, letters, sermons, and treatises on the Incarnation and the Trinity. He presided over the Council of Ephesus in 431, where the Nestorian heresy (which taught that Mary was not the mother of God) was condemned. He said: "That anyone would doubt the right of the holy Virgin to be called the Mother of God fills me with astonishment. Surely she must be the Mother of God if our Lord Jesus Christ is God, and she gave birth to him!" A Doctor of the Church, he is called the Doctor of the Incarnation.

PRAYER

Saint Cyril, you used your intellectual gifts to serve the Church as a bishop and teacher. Pray with us on your feast: Merciful Father, we praise and thank you for the gift of the Incarnation, and for giving us Mary to be our mother. Grant us wisdom and inspire us to learn and defend the doctrines of the Church. Bless all bishops, granting them tenacity to teach and uphold the truth at all times, even when it is difficult. We ask this in the name of Jesus. Amen.

JUNE 28

Saint Irenaeus (130-200)

Saint Irenaeus, a disciple of Saint Polycarp, loved to relate how the martyr lived and spoke. He became the bishop of Lyon in what is now France. His theological writings, such as the treatise *Against Heresies*, were helpful in correcting the Gnostic heresy and illuminating Church doctrine. He is called the first great Catholic theologian, and he used systematic theology to demonstrate the coherence of faith. He taught that our free will allows us to cooperate with God's grace. He died a martyr like his friend and teacher, Polycarp. In 2022, Pope Francis named him a Doctor of the Church — the first Doctor of the Church who was also a martyr — calling him the Doctor of Unity.

PRAYER

Saint Irenaeus, you fearlessly defended the Faith and helped to teach and explain it, in the end giving your life for it. Pray for us to love and defend the Faith, and pray with us: Dear Father, grant peace and unity within our own hearts, in our families, in the Church, and in society. May we always recognize your truth and uphold it, even when it is difficult or unpopular. May we receive strong formation in our faith and share that formation with all those entrusted to our care. Strengthen the fruits and gifts of the Holy Spirit in us. Guide apologists, theologians, and those who teach theology, keeping them faithful to the teachings of the Church. Bless bishops, granting them wisdom and integrity in teaching and upholding the truth. We ask this in the name of Jesus. Amen.

JUNE 29

Saints Peter and Paul (first century)

Simon was a Galilean fisherman who met Jesus through his brother, Andrew, and he became one of Jesus' closest friends. He was the first of the apostles to confess that Jesus was the Christ, and Jesus commissioned him to lead the Church as the first pope. Jesus changed his name to *Cephas* (Rock), which is translated Peter (from the Latin *petrus*). Saint Peter led the Church after Jesus' ascension into heaven. Saint Paul, originally named Saul, was a devout Jew from Tarsus and a persecutor of Christians until his conversion. After he became a follower of Jesus, he was a great missionary, preaching to the Gentiles. Both Peter and Paul gave their lives for Christ during the persecutions under Emperor Nero.

PRAYER

Saints Peter and Paul, you loved Jesus passionately and gave your lives in witness to your faith in Him. Pray with us on your feast: Heavenly Father, grant us the grace to know you so we can make you known. Fill us with courage and give us perseverance to be missionaries of your great love and mercy. May we always be persons of integrity and authentic Christian witnesses. Bless the pope and all bishops, making them true shepherds and virtuous leaders. We ask this in the name of Jesus. Amen.

JUNE 30

Venerable Pierre Toussaint (1766–1853)

Venerable Pierre began his life as a slave of the Bérard family in Haiti. During the slave uprising that began in Haiti in 1797, Pierre and his sister, Rosalie, were brought to New York City. He apprenticed with a well-known hairdresser and became a successful hairdresser himself, eventually helping to provide for Mrs. Bérard after her husband died and the family fortune was lost. Upon her death in 1807, he was emancipated at forty-one years old. He purchased the freedom of a woman named Juliette and married her. Later, when Rosalie died, he also adopted and raised her daughter, Euphémie. They opened their home to the poor, orphans, and anyone in need. Pierre attended daily Mass, prayed the Rosary, and lived a holy life of generosity and kindness, helping raise funds for Catholic charities, opening a Catholic orphanage and Black Catholic school, and serving yellow fever victims. He kept working long after he could have retired comfortably, and when asked why, he replied, "I have enough for myself, but if I stop work, I have not enough for others."

PRAYER

Venerable Pierre, pray for us to live generously as you did, working not only for ourselves, but for others. Pray with us on your feast: Merciful Father, inspire us to be kind and merciful to others, serving them lovingly. Give us generous hearts, and set us free from all selfishness. Remove any prejudice from our minds and hearts and give us the courage to protect and defend victims of injustice. Free all who are enslaved. Bless married couples so they can assist each other to grow in holiness. We ask this in the name of Jesus. Amen.

JULY

THE MONTH OF
THE PRECIOUS BLOOD OF JESUS

JULY 1

Saint Junípero Serra (1713–1784)

Saint Junípero Serra, a Franciscan missionary priest from Spain, was a professor of theology who longed to share the Gospel with the people in the New World. Eventually he went to Mexico, where he worked for eight years with the Pame Indians, until he was put in charge of the former Jesuit missions in lower California. Over the next thirteen years, he walked many miles to found nine more missions along the west coast of California. He named these missions after saints. He labored to help the Native Americans come to Christ while educating them, helping them earn a living, and fighting for justice for them. Over time, he baptized six thousand people. Called the Apostle of California and the Father of the California Missions, he is buried in Mission San Carlos Borromeo del Rio Carmelo in northern California. He is the patron saint of California.

PRAYER

Saint Junípero, you traveled great distances to share the Gospel and draw souls to Christ. Pray for us to have the courage to share our faith, and pray with us now: Gracious Father, give us missionary hearts and fill us with your love for all souls, so we will work tirelessly to share you with others. Inspire us to labor for justice and to serve those in need. Bless all Native Americans, especially those who live in the areas where Saint Junípero served. Bless the Franciscan order, keeping it faithful to you. We ask this in the name of Jesus. Amen.

JULY 2

Saints Processus and Martinian (first century)

According to their legend, Saints Processus and Martinian, wardens in the Roman Mamertine Prison, came to faith through the preaching of Saints Peter and Paul, who were imprisoned there. The two wardens were baptized in a miraculous spring, and they followed in the apostles' footsteps, being martyred for their newfound faith. Their remains are buried in an altar in Saint Peter's Basilica in Rome.

PRAYER

Saints Processus and Martinian, you believed in the preaching of the apostles, and you gave your lives for your faith. Pray with us now: Loving Father, grant us the grace to proclaim your love wherever we are, even in the most painful circumstances. May we persevere in planting seeds of faith, even when they seem to bear no fruit. Grant us integrity of character rooted in you and anchored in virtue, and make us courageous when we face trials, obstacles, and persecution. Bless and protect all who are persecuted for their faith in you. We ask this in the name of Jesus. Amen.

JULY 3

Saint Thomas (d. first century)

Saint Thomas was absent when the other apostles saw the resurrected Jesus, and he refused to believe that Jesus was truly alive unless he could see Jesus' wounds as proof. Jesus met Thomas right where he was and with merciful love allowed him to see and touch His wounds. The Gospel of John recounts: "Then [Jesus] said to Thomas, 'Put your finger here, and see my hands; and put out your hand, and place it in my side. Do not disbelieve, but believe.' Thomas answered him, 'My Lord and my God!' Jesus said to him, 'Have you believed because you have seen me? Blessed are those who have not seen and yet have believed'" (20:27–29). It is believed that he preached and was martyred in India by Hindu priests. Saint Thomas is the patron saint of India, architects, construction workers, and cooks.

PRAYER

Saint Thomas, you doubted the Resurrection, and Jesus gave you the proof you needed to strengthen your faith. Pray for us to give our doubts to Jesus as you did, and pray with us: Dear Father, increase our faith, and help us to cling to you and your Church even when all seems hopeless. Grant us such a strong faith that, even when we cannot see what you are doing in our lives, we still trust you and remain faithful. Forgive our doubt, help our unbelief, and give us the grace to support and strengthen one another's faith. We ask this in the name of Jesus. Amen.

Blessed Pier Giorgio Frassati (1901–1925)

Blessed Pier Giorgio did everything — whether hiking and rock climbing, spending time with friends, or serving the poor — with zeal. Son of a wealthy and influential family in Turin, he became a lay Dominican and was involved in the Saint Vincent de Paul Society. He was a holy influence on his peers, but also notorious for his practical jokes. More than anything, he had a deep love for the poor, and he helped them in every way possible, saying, "It is an injustice to have health and not put it at the service of others." He paid bills for those who had no money, built a cart for a man to sell things from, and literally gave away the shoes off his feet and the coat off his back. It is likely he contracted polio from his visits to the sick, which led to his death at the age of twenty-four. Pope John Paul II called him "the man of the beatitudes." Blessed Pier Giorgio is the patron saint of young adults and World Youth Day.

PRAYER

Blessed Pier Giorgio, you served those in need without calling any attention to yourself. Pray for us to have generous hearts like yours, and pray with us: Heavenly Father, with Pier Giorgio, may we always keep our eyes fixed on the heights, desiring only to be united with you. Inspire us to pray, fast, and give alms generously. Give us the virtues of generosity, humility, and cheerfulness. Grant us the gift of contemplation, making us contemplatives in action, and keep us detached from material goods. May we always truly live the beatitudes and become saints. Bless the Saint Vincent de Paul Society and the Dominican order, keeping them faithful to you. We ask this in the name of Jesus. Amen.

JULY 5

Saint Anthony Mary Zaccaria (1502–1539)

Saint Anthony Zaccaria, born of a noble family in Cremona, Italy, became a physician for the poor before he sensed God calling him to be a priest. Inspired by Saint Paul's writings, he founded the Clerics Regular of Saint Paul, which came to be known as the Barnabites because they served in the Church of Saint Barnabas in Milan. To renew women religious and the laity, he also founded the orders of Angelic Sisters of Saint Paul and the Laity of Saint Paul. A forceful preacher, this Catholic reformer promoted meditation on Jesus' passion and Eucharistic adoration, popularizing the forty-hour devotion. He once wrote, "In His mercy, God has chosen us, unworthy as we are, out of the world, to serve Him and thus to advance in goodness and to bear the greatest possible fruit of love in patience." He died when he was only thirty-six years old and is the patron saint of physicians.

PRAYER

Saint Anthony, pray for us to serve God in our neighbor without wearying, and pray with us on your feast: Merciful Father, make us tireless in your service, always ready and willing to serve our neighbors with love. Grant us great empathy, and help us to lift one another up to hope and trust in you. Help us to grow in the virtues of generosity, humility, and charity. May we bear our trials and obstacles patiently and forgive those who hurt us. Give us a profound love for the Eucharist and help us to participate reverently in adoration of the Blessed Sacrament. We ask this in the name of Jesus. Amen.

JULY 6

Saint Maria Goretti (1890–1902)

Saint Maria, born in Corinaldo, Italy, was a cheerful and encouraging child who helped her mother, Assunta, after her father died of malaria. She willingly took her mother's place to cook, clean, and care for her younger siblings. Her service to her family allowed her mother to work on the land as her father had done. Unfortunately, when she was eleven years old, she was killed by Alessandro Serenelli for resisting his attempt to assault her. He cruelly stabbed her fourteen times, and she died of her wounds the next day. Before she died, she forgave her killer, saying she wanted him to be with her in heaven. Years later, she appeared in a dream to him while he was in prison, telling him she forgave him. Thanks to her intercession, Alessandro repented and went on to live a holy life, asking for and receiving forgiveness from Maria's mother. Saint Maria is the patron saint of rape victims, Catholic youth, the Children of Mary, and girls.

PRAYER

Saint Maria, your life was tragically cut short, but you forgave your killer and opened the way for his conversion. Pray with us on your feast: Loving Father, give us merciful hearts, and help us to forgive one another and ourselves, even as you forgive us. Inspire us to pray always for others, even our enemies. Protect our purity and the innocence of children. Deliver us from all violence, and grant healing and peace to all victims of assault. We ask this in the name of Jesus. Amen.

JULY 7

The Ulma Family (d. 1944)

Blessed Jozef and Wiktoria Ulma and their seven children were murdered on March 24, 1944, by the Nazis because they sheltered eight Jewish people in their home in Markowa, Poland. Sadly, their Jewish guests were also killed. The names of the Ulma children were Stanislawa, Barbara, Wladyslaw, Franciszek, Antoni, and Maria, and there was also an unnamed baby. The Jewish people they hid in their home were Saul Goldman and his sons Baruch, Mechel, Joachim, and Moses; Golda Grunfeld; and Lea Didner with her daughter Reshla. In their kindness, the Ulmas prepared meals for them according to kosher laws and prayed together like family. Called the Samaritans of Markowa, the Ulmas are the first family to be beatified together. They are buried at their parish, Saint Dorothy Catholic Church in Markowa.

PRAYER

Dear Ulma Family, pray for us to courageously and compassionately protect the vulnerable, no matter what it may cost. Pray with us now: Gracious Father, give us courage to stand up for those who are treated unjustly, even if it costs us everything. Give us compassionate hearts and a deep desire for justice. Convert all people from prejudice and hatred to love. Protect those suffering for their faith in you. Bless all families and help them to build their homes into true domestic churches. We ask this in the name of Jesus. Amen.

JULY 8

Saint Withburga (655–743)

Saint Withburga, the daughter of King Anna of East Anglia, was born into a family of saints. She became a Benedictine nun in Dereham, England, and after her death, her body was preserved incorrupt until Henry VIII destroyed it. The body of her sister, Saint Etheldreda, who was abbess at Ely Cathedral, was also incorrupt. Her other sisters were Saints Ethelburga, Erkenwald, and Sexburga (whose daughter was Saint Ermenilda). Saint Withburga's Well, the miraculous spring at the spot where her body was first buried at Dereham, is still there today.

PRAYER

Saint Withburga, pray for us to love our families and help one another grow in holiness, and pray with us: Righteous Father, grant us contemplative, prayerful hearts, and help us to seek your will in everything we do. Help us to grow in the virtues of piety, humility, and charity. Bless married couples and allow them to sanctify one another with joy. Give parents the graces they need to raise their children to be saints. Bless the Benedictine order, keeping it faithful to you and its founder. We ask this in the name of Jesus. Amen.

JULY 9

Saint Paulina of Brazil (1865–1942)

Saint Paulina, whose Italian parents immigrated to Brazil, taught catechism classes and helped sick people as a teenager. Later, she founded the Congregation of the Little Sisters of the Immaculate Conception to help both orphans and children whose parents had been slaves. Her religious name is Pauline of the Agonizing Heart of Jesus. Although she suffered from diabetes, that did not stop her from answering God's call to serve. She was removed from her position as superior of the order due to misunderstanding and conflict, but she bore this trial patiently. Later she suffered the loss of an arm to diabetes. In her spiritual testimony, she wrote: "Be humble. Trust always and a great deal in divine Providence; never, never must you let yourselves be discouraged, despite contrary winds. I say it again: trust in God and Mary Immaculate; be faithful and forge ahead!" Saint Paulina is the patron saint of people with diabetes.

PRAYER

Saint Paulina, you served God's people in spite of sickness and suffering. Pray for us to give of ourselves even when it is difficult, and pray with us: Dear Father, grant us loving hearts and give us the grace and strength to serve the people you place in our lives. Heal, assist, and encourage people with diabetes. Bless and comfort all who are misunderstood or falsely accused. Confirm us in love. Make us saints. Bless the Congregation of the Little Sisters of the Immaculate Conception, keeping it faithful to you. We ask this in the name of Jesus. Amen.

JULY 10

Blessed Emmanuel Ruiz and the Martyrs of Damascus (d. 1860)

Father Emmanuel Ruiz was a Franciscan missionary priest from Spain who served as superior of a Franciscan community in Damascus. He was one of eleven martyrs who died while ministering to the Christian faithful in Lebanon during the anti-Christian riots that took place in 1860. He, seven other Franciscan friars, and three Maronite laymen were captured and commanded to convert to Islam. When they refused, they were tortured and killed. Pope Pius XI beatified the Martyrs of Damascus in 1926.

PRAYER

Blessed Emmanuel and your fellow martyrs, pray for us to hold fast to our faith with courage, and pray with us on your feast: Gentle Father, make us courageous in living and proclaiming our faith, even to the point of death. Teach us how to cling to you in times of trial and adversity. In your mercy, protect and comfort all who suffer persecution for their faith in you. Bless the Franciscan order, keeping it faithful to you. We ask this in the name of Jesus. Amen.

JULY 11

Saint Benedict (480–547)

Saint Benedict, known as the father of Western monasticism, renounced his family's wealth to draw closer to God. He lived for a time as a hermit, and then established monasteries, including Subiaco and Monte Cassino, as other men came to join him in his way of life. He wrote his Rule, which still governs the Benedictine order today. During his life, he worked many miracles, including curing the sick and raising the dead. His sister, Saint Scholastica, founded a community of nuns who also followed his Rule. Once a year, they would visit with each other, and on their last visit before she died, Scholastica asked him to visit for a while longer. When he said no, she prayed, and it rained so hard he had to stay. Soon after that visit, Benedict saw her soul ascending to heaven. Saint Benedict is the patron saint of Europe, schoolchildren, poisonings, and those with kidney disease.

PRAYER

Saint Benedict, pray for us to pray and work for the glory of God, seeking sanctity in our daily lives as you did and taught. Pray with us: Heavenly Father, grant us a steady rhythm of prayer, work, study, and recreation in our lives, and help us to center our lives around you. Fill us with virtues, especially humility, piety, and diligence. May we persevere in the good works you have given us to do. Incline our hearts to constant prayer. Bless the Benedictine order, keeping it faithful to you. We ask this in the name of Jesus. Amen.

JULY 12

Saints Louis (1823–1894) and Zélie (1831–1877) Martin

Saints Louis and Zélie Martin faithfully lived the Sacrament of Matrimony and raised a devout family — including Saint Thérèse of Lisieux. Both desired to enter religious life, and both were refused before they met each other and married in 1858. Louis was a watchmaker, and Zélie owned a very successful lace-making business. They had nine children, four of whom died young. After nineteen years of marriage, Zélie died of breast cancer, leaving Louis to raise their five daughters. The girls all became religious sisters. Four entered the same Carmelite monastery in Lisieux: Marie (Sister Marie of the Sacred Heart), Pauline (Mother Agnes), Celine (Sister Genevieve of the Holy Face), and Saint Thérèse of the Child Jesus and the Holy Face. Venerable Léonie (Sister Francois-Therese) became a Poor Clare nun. Louis suffered terribly from mental illness before his death in 1894. Saints Louis and Zélie are the patron saints of illness, mental illness, marriage, parenting, and widowers.

PRAYER

Saints Louis and Zélie, your example of a God-centered marriage and holy family life inspires us. Pray for us to be examples of faith in our families, and pray with us: Dear Father, strengthen our family life, and may all that we do be centered on you. Grant married couples grace to be strong in living their vows. Teach parents how to faithfully form their children in the Faith and help them to grow in holiness. Comfort and heal women suffering with breast cancer and all people with mental illness. We ask this in the name of Jesus. Amen.

JULY 13

Saint Clelia Barbieri (1847–1870)

Saint Clelia, at twenty-one years old, was the youngest person ever to establish a religious order. Born near Bologna in Italy, she was only eight when her father died, leaving the family in poverty. She helped her mother earn money for the family. Later, following her parish priest's advice, she began educating poor girls like herself. Over time her love and zeal led her to form the Little Sisters of the Mother of Sorrows. Clelia had a special love for Jesus in the Eucharist and was favored with the gift of contemplation and ecstasies. She died of tuberculosis at the age of twenty-three, telling her sisters, "I'm going to heaven, and all those who will die in our community will enjoy eternal life." She is the patron saint of the Little Sisters of the Mother of Sorrows.

PRAYER

Saint Clelia, pray for us to love God by serving our neighbor, as you did. Pray with us today: Loving Father, set our hearts on fire with love for you and give us the virtue of magnanimity. No matter how young we are, allow us to do great things for you, always seeking your will and accepting your grace. May we be consistent and persevering in prayer and performance of the corporal and spiritual works of mercy. Bless the Little Sisters order, keeping it faithful to you. We ask this in the name of Jesus. Amen.

JULY 14

Saint Kateri Tekakwitha (1656–1680)

Saint Kateri was a Mohawk princess, daughter of a chief, who grew up in Auriesville, New York, which is today the site of the holy Shrine of the North American Martyrs. When Kateri was a small child, an outbreak of smallpox in the Mohawk tribe killed her parents and brother. She survived with facial scarring and vision problems. After she converted to Christianity, she dedicated her life to Christ, doing penance and works of mercy. Unfortunately, her tribe did not accept her faith. She was teased and even denied food. Seeking the support of a Christian community, she moved to Canada. There her character and holiness were formed by daily Mass, helping the sick, teaching children, and assisting the elderly until her death. Her last words were "Jesus, I love you." The "Lily of the Mohawks" is buried at the Saint Francis Xavier mission church near Montreal. She is the patron saint of people with facial deformities and visual impairments.

PRAYER

Saint Kateri, you were a quiet, humble witness of the Faith even when it meant separation from your tribe. Pray for us to give God all we have and are, and pray with us: Heavenly Father, we give you thanks and praise for the gift of our faith, and we ask for your help in living it fully. Strengthen in us the virtues of humility and faith. Heal, protect, and guide all who struggle with visual impairment or facial deformities. Grant strength and justice to those who are teased and bullied. Draw all people to yourself. We ask this in the name of Jesus. Amen.

JULY 15

Saint Bonaventure (1221–1274)

Saint Bonaventure almost died when he was four years old. His mother sought the intercession of Saint Francis of Assisi, and he was healed. As a young man, he became a Franciscan and was sent to study at the University of Paris, where he received his degree in theology along with Saint Thomas Aquinas. He was made Father General of the Franciscan order, a position he filled for seventeen years. Known as the Second Founder, he helped reform the Franciscan order and return it to its radical life of poverty. The pope appointed him a cardinal in 1273. He loved to look at the crucifix and meditate on the passion of Jesus, and he was devoted to Mother Mary. He wrote Saint Francis's official biography and many theological works, including *The Soul's Journey to God*. He is a Doctor of the Church, known as the Seraphic Doctor.

PRAYER

Saint Bonaventure, you eagerly studied and taught the truths of our faith, and you served as a leader in the Church. Pray for us and with us on your feast: Gracious Father, grant us the desire to know you better and to love you with our whole heart. Help us to grow in virtue, especially studiousness and diligence. Guide all teachers and writers of theology, keeping them firmly grounded in your truth and faithful to your Church. Grant all bishops and priests your grace and special protection. Bless the Franciscan order, keeping it faithful to you. We ask this in the name of Jesus. Amen.

JULY 16

Saint Marie-Madeleine Postel (1756–1846)

Saint Marie-Madeleine opened a girls' school when she was only eighteen years old. Sadly, the revolutionaries in France closed it down. Then she followed God's will and bravely sheltered priests despite the risk of death during the dangerous time of the French Revolution. Later, she began a religious order for women, the Sisterhood of Christian Schools of Mercy, securing a place for it in an abbey. Accepting suffering, she said: "O blessed cross! Come to my embrace. Yet more, O Lord: give me yet more to bear." The aunt of Blessed Placide Viel, she was known to be very holy and a virtuous leader, and she was gifted with miracles. Saint Marie-Madeleine is the patron saint of chastity, teenage girls, poverty, forgiveness, and apothecaries.

PRAYER

Saint Marie-Madeleine, you accepted God's will even when it was difficult, promoting the Faith with courage in the midst of danger. Pray with us on your feast: Loving Father, show us your will for our lives and give us the courage to follow it with love and patience. Bless all parents and help them to fulfill their role as first educators of their children, forming them in the Faith. Help all teachers as they labor to educate young people. Bless the order of the Sisterhood of Christian Schools of Mercy, keeping it faithful to you. We ask this in the name of Jesus. Amen.

JULY 17

The Carmelite Nuns of Compiègne (d. 1794)

Sixteen Discalced Carmelite nuns offered their lives to God in reparation during the French Revolution. They wanted God to allow them to make reparation so that the killing would stop, and God accepted their generous self-gift. Not long after their deaths, the Reign of Terror ended. The revolutionary forces trying to take over France and destroy the Catholic Faith were stopped because of the incredible sacrifice of these sixteen women: Sister Euphrasia of the Immaculate Conception; Sister Saint Louis, the subprior; Sister Henrietta of Jesus; Sister Saint Martha; Sister Therese of the Heart of Mary; Mother Teresa of Saint Augustine, the prioress; Sister Constance; Sister Julie of Jesus; Sister Mary Henrietta of Providence; Sister Jesus Crucified; Sister Marie of the Holy Spirit; Sister Charlotte of the Resurrection; Sister Therese of Saint Ignatius; and Sister Saint Francis; as well as Catherine and Therese Soiron (blood sisters), who were extern sisters.

PRAYER

Carmelite Martyrs of Compiègne, pray for us to love the Church as you did, and to entrust our lives to God. Pray with us now: Righteous Father, teach us true sacrificial love, so that we can give you everything we have and are. May we be willing to die for our faith and to give our very lives in reparation. Give us all the virtues we need to grow in holiness and fulfill your will for our lives. Bless all those who suffer persecution for their faith in you. Bless the Discalced Carmelite order, keeping it faithful to you. We ask this in the name of Jesus. Amen.

JULY 18

Saint Camillus de Lellis (1550–1614)

Saint Camillus became addicted to gambling while in the military and lost all his money. Later, he converted and changed his life, and he was able to get a job at Saint Giacomo Hospital in Rome, where he eventually became director. After meeting with Saint Philip Neri, his confessor, he realized God was calling him to be ordained a priest. Furthermore, he was to found an order, the Ministers of the Sick, to help men suffering from the plague and those wounded in battle. His religious order, known as the Camillians, became the first order to carry out this work. He built eight hospitals and fifteen communities before he died. Saint Camillus is a patron saint of nurses, nursing groups, and the sick.

PRAYER

Saint Camillus, you experienced a deep conversion and devoted your life to caring for the sick. Pray for us to experience the grace of conversion. Pray with us: Merciful Father, free us from all unhealthy attachments. Teach us how to clearly see our faults, and give us the grace and the courage to work to overcome them. Grant freedom to all those who suffer from gambling or other addictions, and comfort their families and loved ones who suffer with them. Bless the Camillian order, keeping it faithful to you. We ask this in the name of Jesus. Amen.

JULY 19

Saint Macrina the Younger (d. 379)

Saint Macrina the Younger was named after her grandmother Saint Macrina the Elder, and her parents were Saints Basil the Elder and Emmelia. She was the older sister of Saints Basil, Gregory of Nyssa, and Peter of Sebaste. Her brother Gregory wrote that her humility was a witness to them, and that she passed on her love of Scripture to them. She was well-educated and helped educate her siblings. Devoting her life to God in prayer and contemplation, she lived with her mother and a group of other women who consecrated themselves to God.

PRAYER

Saint Macrina, pray for us to love our faith and to teach it to those around us with kindness and love. Pray with us: Gentle Father, grant us the grace of a deep love and understanding of holy Scripture. Guide us to find and fulfill our vocations, so we can become the saints you created us to be. Make our families true domestic churches filled with charity, forgiveness, inspiration, and hospitality. Bless all siblings and give them strong relationships with one another. Strengthen and protect all consecrated women, and let their lives be a sign of your love in the world. We ask this in the name of Jesus. Amen.

JULY 20

Saint Aurelius (d. 429)

Saint Aurelius, lover of the poor, was the bishop of Carthage (modern Tunisia), the most influential see in Africa. With his close friend and fellow bishop Saint Augustine, he vigorously defended the Faith against the heresies of the time, particularly Donatism and Pelagianism, through preaching, writing, and even holding synods. In response to his concerns about the laziness of some monks, Saint Augustine wrote *On the Work of Monks*. These two bishops and friends died within a few weeks of each other.

PRAYER
Saint Aurelius, you were a true shepherd of the Church and a wise defender of orthodoxy. Pray with us on your feast: Gracious Father, make us committed in mind and heart to the truths of our faith. May we carefully study teachings of the Church and share and defend them whenever necessary. Grant us strength and courage to stand up to the false ideologies and heresies of our time. Bless and protect all bishops, helping them to be true shepherds and virtuous leaders. We ask this in the name of Jesus. Amen.

JULY 21

Saint Lawrence of Brindisi (1559–1619)

Saint Lawrence, an Italian Catholic reformer and missionary preacher, spoke eight different languages — Latin, Spanish, French, Italian, German, Bohemian, Greek, and Hebrew. His Hebrew was especially good, causing people to think he had been Jewish. This greatly helped him in showing people of Jewish faith the truth of the Christian religion, and many came to believe because of him. He relied on prayer, fasting, and mortification in union with his preaching to help God convert sinners. Besides languages, he was also gifted with prophecy and diplomacy. In 1602, he became Superior General of the Capuchin friars, but he resigned in 1605 and was sent on an evangelizing mission to Germany. Because of his leadership and communication skills, he was often enlisted to take part in political negotiations and even served for a time as military chaplain. He was also a gifted writer, and Pope Saint John XXIII declared him a Doctor of the Church in 1959.

PRAYER

Saint Lawrence, pray for us to use all our gifts to draw souls closer to God, just as you did, and pray with us today: Dear Father, grant us the grace to communicate your truth well. Fill us with the virtues of faith, hope, and charity. May we seek out opportunities to show our love in action by performing the spiritual and corporal works of mercy. Bless all bishops, making them true shepherds, virtuous leaders, and powerful preachers. Bless the Franciscan order, keeping it faithful to you. We ask this in the name of Jesus. Amen.

JULY 22

Saint Mary Magdalene (d. first century)

Saint Mary Magdalene was a close friend and disciple of Jesus. In His mercy, Jesus delivered her from seven demons, and she faithfully followed Him thereafter. She financially supported His ministry, followed Him to the cross, and remained there with Him as He died, faithful to the end. She also assisted in His burial on Good Friday and returned on Easter Sunday morning to anoint His body. Jesus granted her the extreme honor of being the first to see Him risen on Easter morning, as we read in the Gospel of Mark, "Now when he rose early on the first day of the week, he appeared first to Mary Magdalene, from whom he had cast out seven demons" (16:9). She told the apostles that Jesus was risen, earning the title "Apostle to the Apostles." Her role in the ministry of Jesus was so important that many saints write about her. Saint Mary Magdalene is the patron saint of penitent sinners.

PRAYER

Saint Mary Magdalene, pray for us to love Jesus and to proclaim His resurrection with joy, as you did. Pray with us on your feast: Merciful Father, inspire us to seek and follow Jesus, no matter the cost. Heal, convert, deliver, and protect us. Grant us true contrition for our sins, and help us to make amends whenever we do wrong. Protect the innocence of children and restore innocence to those who have been abused. Deliver and heal those who have been enslaved and used by others for financial gain. Convert all who oppress others. Make us saints. We ask this in the name of Jesus. Amen.

JULY 23

Saint John Cassian (d. 433)

Saint John Cassian, believed to be from the area that is now Romania, spent some time as a hermit in Bethlehem. From there he traveled to Egypt, where he spent many years in the desert learning from the hermits there. He is highly regarded for his theological works; in particular, his Institutes on the Monastic Life *(Institutes)* and Conferences on Egyptian Monks *(Conferences)* were widely praised, and Benedict used them in writing his Rule. Later in his life, John Cassian was a disciple of Saint John Chrysostom, who ordained him a deacon. When Chrysostom was unjustly exiled, Saint John Cassian defended him to Pope Saint Innocent I. Through the founding of French monasteries at Marseilles, he helped promote monasticism in Europe. His shrine is at the Monastery of Saint Victor in Marseilles, France.

PRAYER

Saint John Cassian, you loved God wholeheartedly and profoundly influenced the development of monasticism. Pray with us: Dear Father, inspire us to pray always and to cultivate silence in our lives so we can hear your voice. We thank you for the wisdom of your saints and ask for the grace to savor their writings. Root out all our vices and grant us integrity and growth in virtue, that we may be pleasing, faithful friends to you. Make us saints. We ask this in the name of Jesus. Amen.

JULY 24

Saint Sharbel Makhlouf (1828–1898)

Saint Sharbel Makhlouf's great miracles impressed even his Muslim neighbors. He was a contemplative monk who, it has been said, worked more miracles than any other saint. He belonged to the Maronite rite, living at Annaya Abbey monastery in Lebanon. A great mystic and prophet, he cautioned people not to cling to things of the earth, but to long for heaven, saying, "The ignorant man clings to the dust until he becomes dust; the wise and prudent man clings to Heaven until he reaches Heaven. You will belong to the place to which you cling." He spoke of success as "standing without shame before God." There is a shrine to Saint Sharbel behind the main altar at Saint Patrick's Cathedral in New York City. Saint Sharbel is the patron saint of Lebanon.

PRAYER

Saint Sharbel, you longed for heaven and lived detached from earthly things. Pray for us to be attached only to the things of God, and pray with us: Merciful Father, free us from all attachments that prevent us from loving you fully and grant us the grace to cling only to you. Heal us and help us to stand before you without shame. Strengthen us in all virtues, especially humility and holy detachment. Grant us the grace of a strong, consistent prayer life and the gift of contemplation. Strengthen our families in faith and make them holy. We ask this in the name of Jesus. Amen.

JULY 25

Saint James (d. first century)

Saint James was in Jesus' inner circle of close friends, along with his brother, Saint John, and Saint Peter. He and John were fishermen, the sons of Zebedee and Salome, before Jesus called them to follow Him. James has traditionally been called "The Greater" to distinguish him from Saint James the Lesser, the cousin of Jesus. He had the privilege of being present at key events, including Jesus' Transfiguration. He was martyred by King Herod Agrippa in Jerusalem, the first apostle to die for Jesus (see Acts 12:1–3). Santiago de Compostela in Spain remains one of the most famous pilgrimage sites in the world. Saint James is the patron saint of pilgrims, Spain, Guatemala, and Nicaragua.

PRAYER

Saint James, you were privileged to be one of Jesus' closest friends, and you willingly gave your life for Him. Pray with us on your feast: Loving Father, grant us apostolic zeal and enable us to imitate the apostles in sharing the Gospel wherever you send us, even if it means laying down our lives in martyrdom. May we always seek to be close friends with Jesus, inviting Him into every aspect of our lives. Bless and strengthen our family relationships and friendships. Make us saints. We ask this in the name of Jesus. Amen.

JULY 26

Saints Joachim and Anne (d. first century)

Saints Joachim and Anne are the parents of Mother Mary and grandparents of Jesus. Childless for many years, they prayed for God's mercy, and an angel appeared to Saint Anne telling her that she would conceive, and this child would be blessed by all the world. They consecrated their daughter Mary to God from her birth. Saint John Damascene spoke of them: "Joachim and Anne, how blessed a couple! All creation is indebted to you. For at your hands the Creator was offered a gift excelling all other gifts: a chaste mother, who alone was worthy of Him. … She alone for all time would maintain her virginity in mind and soul as well as in body." Saint Anne is the patron saint of pregnant women, childless women, nursemaids, grandmothers, widows, the cities of Florence, Naples, and Innsbruck, and the country of Canada.

PRAYER

Saints Joachim and Anne, God blessed you with a truly perfect child after many years of praying, fulfilling His promise of a Messiah through your family line. Pray with us today: Merciful Father, give us the virtues of trust, confidence, faithfulness, tenderness, and caring. Help all those who are praying to have a child and give consolation to those who are unable to have children. Inspire grandparents to help their grown children and grandchildren in the best way possible, offering a strong witness to the Faith and assisting in practical matters. We ask this in the name of Jesus. Amen.

JULY 27

Saint Titus Brandsma (1881–1942)

Saint Titus, a Discalced Carmelite priest, was known for his gentleness and intellectual gifts, and for his profound understanding of Carmelite spirituality and mysticism. An esteemed professor, author, and journalist from the Netherlands, he openly condemned Nazism and refused to participate in its propaganda. Like many other priests, he was targeted, arrested, and eventually killed. He died by lethal injection at the concentration camp in Dachau, Germany. Even during his imprisonment, he made himself available to others and spiritually supported his fellow prisoners. Saint Titus is the patron saint of Catholic journalists.

PRAYER

Saint Titus, you bravely defended the truth in spite of the dangerous political climate and gave your life for it. Pray for and with us now: Righteous Father, give us compassion and empathy for all who are vulnerable and suffering. May we provide them with a ministry of our presence and help them practically as well. Grant us prudence and fearlessness in proclaiming your truth even in the face of danger. Make us saints. Bless all journalists and help them to promote the truth even in dangerous times. Bless the Discalced Carmelite order, keeping it faithful to you. We ask this in the name of Jesus. Amen.

Saint Alphonsa of the Immaculate Conception (1910–1946)

Born to a noble family in India, little Annakutty lost her mother shortly after her birth and went to live with her grandparents, who taught her the Faith. By the time she was seven, she knew she was called to be a religious. At ten, she was taken to live with her aunt, who treated her harshly and continuously tried to force her to marry. She stood firm in her vocation and followed God's call to join the Congregation of the Franciscan Clarists, taking the religious name Alphonsa of the Immaculate Conception. She made her final vows in 1936. Plagued by sickness for the rest of her life, she survived a life-threatening illness through the intercession of Blessed Kuriakose Elia Chavara. She worked hard to be kind and "only speak sweet words to others," and to root out vice in her life, willingly doing penance for her sins. She once wrote, "I consider a day in which I have not suffered as a day lost to me."

PRAYER

Saint Alphonsa, you loved God passionately and willingly gave Him your whole life and all your sufferings. Pray for us and with us: Gentle Father, give us the virtues of patience, fortitude, and perseverance, and help us to see that you wish to use our sufferings to purify us. Guide us to form strong relationships by treating others with kindness, gentleness, and sweetness. Make us cheerful even when suffering from illness or discomfort. Bless the Congregation of the Franciscan Clarists, keeping it faithful to you. We ask this in the name of Jesus. Amen.

JULY 29

Saint Martha of Bethany (d. c. 80)

Saint Martha, along with her siblings, Mary and Lazarus, was a close friend of Jesus, who received Him into her home in Bethany. She is best remembered for getting angry when Mary sat at Jesus' feet and would not help her serve during one of their visits: "But the Lord answered her 'Martha, Martha, you are anxious and troubled about many things, but one thing is necessary. Mary has chosen the good portion, which will not be taken away from her'" (Lk 10:41–42). Jesus thus taught Martha that every act of service must flow from our relationship to Him. Later, Martha had faith that Jesus could intervene even after Lazarus died, making her beautiful statement of faith: "Yes, Lord; I believe that you are the Christ, the Son of God, who is coming into the world" (Jn 11:27). Jesus rewarded her faith by raising Lazarus from the dead. After the ascension of Jesus, it is thought that the family became missionaries in Gaul (modern-day France). Saint Martha of Bethany is the patron saint of waitpersons.

PRAYER

Saint Martha, pray for us that, with you, we might believe that Jesus is who He says He is and proclaim Him to the world. Pray with us: Loving Father, grant us the grace of hospitality, so that we may always welcome you in our prayer and our neighbor in joyful service. May we learn to pray always and receive the gift of contemplation so that every work we do flows from our relationship with you. Grant us the virtues of humility, diligence, and, most of all, love. Give us unwavering faith in you, even when all seems lost. We ask this in the name of Jesus. Amen.

JULY 30

Saint Peter Chrysologus (380–450)

Saint Peter Chrysologus's very name testifies to his effectiveness as a preacher and writer: *Chrysologus* means "golden worded." He is called the Doctor of Homilies, and we still have 176 of his sermons, which are brief and full of wisdom. Named bishop of Ravenna, Peter taught the importance of education in the Faith, and he taught that we should strive to learn our faith as much as we are capable of doing so. He was also a man of great virtue, witnessing powerfully to the importance of moderation in every part of our lives. Pope Benedict XIII named him a Doctor of the Church in 1729.

PRAYER

Saint Peter Chrysologus, your sermons led people to repentance, conversion, and deeper love of God. Pray for us and with us on your feast: Loving Father, fill us with the desire to learn our faith and never cease to study it. Teach us to order our lives, and grant us steady growth in virtue. Bless and inspire all bishops, priests, and deacons in their preaching and help us to hear your Holy Spirit speaking to us through them. Confirm our identity as your beloved children and make us saints. Bless all bishops, making them true shepherds and virtuous leaders. We ask this in the name of Jesus. Amen.

JULY 31

Saint Ignatius of Loyola (1491–1556)

Saint Ignatius, born to a Spanish noble family, dreamed of worldly glory. As a young soldier, he suffered a severe leg injury, and while recuperating, he had nothing to read but the lives of the saints. Inspired by their example, he became determined to change his life. His subsequent pilgrimage to Montserrat and retreat at Manresa confirmed his path and allowed him time to begin writing his *Spiritual Exercises*. He founded the Society of Jesus (called the Jesuits) at Montmartre, France, with Saint Francis Xavier, Saint Peter Faber, Alfonso Salmeron, Simon Rodriguez, Nicholas Bobadilla, and Diego Laynez. His famous "Suscipe" prayer beautifully encapsulates his spirituality: "Take, Lord, and receive all my liberty, my memory, my understanding, and my entire will. All I own and all I have, you gave to me; to you, Lord, I return it. Everything is yours, dispose of it according to your will. Give me your love and grace, this is enough for me." Saint Ignatius is the patron saint of spiritual exercises and retreats.

PRAYER

Saint Ignatius, pray for us to turn to the Lord with all our hearts and give up any worldly attachments or aspirations that prevent us from doing His will. Pray with us: Gracious Father, convert our hearts and give us a deep desire to be saints. Teach us to discern your voice and action in our lives, and make us eager to serve you. Strengthen us in virtue, especially the cardinal virtues — prudence, justice, temperance, and fortitude. Deliver us from all evil. Bless the Jesuit order, keeping it faithful to you. We ask this in the name of Jesus. Amen.

AUGUST

THE MONTH OF
THE ASSUMPTION OF MARY

AUGUST 1

Saint Alphonsus Liguori (1696–1787)

Saint Alphonsus emphasized God's mercy and having a concrete plan for prayer and devotion in serving Him. Originally a lawyer in Naples, he became a priest and later founder of the Congregation of the Most Holy Redeemer (called the Redemptorists), dedicated to mission work. With Sister Mary Celeste, he also founded the Redemptoristine nuns. In 1762, Pope Clement XIII made him bishop of the Diocese of Saint Agatha of the Goths. An expert in moral theology, a prolific writer, a poet, and a musician, he used his talents to give God glory and encourage people to pursue holiness. He once said in a sermon: "All holiness and perfection of the soul lie in our love for Jesus Christ our God, who is our redeemer and our supreme good. It is part of the love of God to acquire and to nurture all the virtues which make a man perfect." Later in life, he suffered from rheumatoid arthritis, a cross he carried until he died. Pope Pius IX declared Alphonsus a Doctor of the Church in 1871.

PRAYER

Saint Alphonsus, you encouraged everyone to pursue holiness, and you exemplified this pursuit throughout your life. Pray with us today: Merciful Father, grant us a firm commitment to prayer and pursuit of virtue, and help us order our whole life in pursuit of you. Guide us to make decisions in accord with your law. May we seek only you as our supreme good and trust you with every detail of our lives. Make us saints. Bless the Redemptorist order, keeping it faithful to you. We ask this in the name of Jesus. Amen.

AUGUST 2

Peter Julian Eymard (1811–1868)

When Saint Peter Julian was only five, he walked to the church one day and placed his head against the tabernacle, yearning to be near to Jesus and listen to Him. As he grew older, he wanted to be a priest, and he was ordained in 1834 in Grenoble. Encouraged by his friend Saint John Vianney, he went on to found the Congregation of Priests of the Blessed Sacrament with the mission to promote devotion to the Eucharist, especially through perpetual adoration, and to prepare people to receive the sacraments. He also founded the Servants of the Blessed Sacrament for women. Called the "Apostle of the Eucharist," this great preacher set up the Archconfraternity of the Blessed Sacrament and Priests Eucharistic League, and he wrote many books on the Eucharist. He lived his Eucharistic devotion fully, encouraging others to do so as well, saying, "Our whole life ought to be drawn to the Eucharist like a magnet."

PRAYER

Saint Peter Julian, pray for us to love the Blessed Sacrament as you did, and to make it the true source and summit of our lives. Pray with us on your feast: Gentle Father, fill us with a deep, abiding love for the Eucharist. May we receive communion often, visit the Blessed Sacrament, and through our witness help others believe in the Real Prescence of Jesus in the Eucharist. Transform us into yourself. Make us saints. Bless the Congregation of the Blessed Sacrament, keeping it faithful to you. We ask this in the name of Jesus. Amen.

AUGUST 3

Saint Lydia Purpuraria (d. first century)

Saint Lydia was a successful cloth merchant in Thyatira (in modern-day Turkey) and the first documented convert to Christianity in Europe. A friend of Saints Paul and Luke, she supported them on their missionary journey to Greece, lodging them in her home. Luke records their meeting in the Book of Acts: "One who heard us was a woman named Lydia, from the city of Thyatira, a seller of purple goods, who was a worshiper of God. The Lord opened her heart to pay attention to what was said by Paul. After she was baptized, and her household as well, she urged us, saying, "If you have judged me to be faithful to the Lord, come to my house and stay" (see Acts 16:14–15). Nothing else is known about Lydia, yet because of her faith the apostles were able to bring the Faith to Europe.

PRAYER
Saint Lydia, your faith paved the way for Christianity in all of Europe. Pray for us to have a strong faith, and pray with us: Loving Father, we give you thanks and praise for the gift of your Church. Increase our devotion and faith, and grant us true generosity and hospitality for others. Allow us to assist in sharing the Gospel even in seemingly small ways, especially within our own homes and in our families. Teach us how to support our priests and bishops in their ministry. We ask this in the name of Jesus. Amen.

AUGUST 4

Saint John Marie Vianney (1786–1859)

Saint John Vianney had to overcome many obstacles to become a priest, including learning difficulties and the French Revolution. Despite these challenges, he persevered, and at last he was ordained in 1815. He was assigned to the tiny parish of Ars, where he devoted himself to his flock through prayer, fasting, catechetical instruction, challenging homilies, and spending many hours in the confessional. His reputation as a holy confessor spread so much that people flocked to Ars from great distances to have him hear their confessions. Ars became a place of pilgrimage. Seeing the spiritual and physical needs of the people he served, he helped Catherine Lassagne and Benedicta Lardet set up La Providence, which was a school and eventually an orphanage for children. Saint John Vianney is the patron saint of priests.

PRAYER

Saint John Vianney, pray for us to be faithful in the work God gives us, even if it seems insignificant. Pray with us today: Merciful Father, we give you all that we are, and we ask for perseverance in following the plan you have for us, even when we face obstacles. Grant us a deep love for our faith, and help us to grow in perfection and to avoid sin. Strengthen us in virtue, especially the virtue of humility. May we love and serve our neighbors without counting the cost. Bless all priests and make them faithful servants to you and your Church. We ask this in the name of Jesus. Amen.

AUGUST 5

Saint Nonna (d. 374)

Saint Nonna was the mother and heart of a home full of saints. Because of her fasting, tears, and constant intercession, her husband eventually converted to Christianity and later became bishop of Nazianzus. Her older son, Saint Gregory of Nazianzus, became a bishop and Doctor of the Church. Her younger son, Saint Caesarius, became a physician, while her daughter, Saint Gorgonia, married and raised a family. Nonna practiced works of mercy and taught her children to do so. Gregory later wrote of his mother: "One woman may be distinguished for frugality, and another for piety, while she ... excelled all others in both of them. In each she attained the height of perfection, and both were combined in her. She was drawn to this each day before anything else, and she had complete faith that her prayers would be answered. Although greatly moved by the sorrows of strangers, she never yielded to grief. ... She subjected every human thing to God."

PRAYER

Saint Nonna, pray for us to imitate you in subjecting every human thing to God. Pray with us now: Gracious Father, help us to persevere in prayer for the conversion of our loved ones and of the world. May we never cease to trust in you and your mercy. Bless our families, and make our homes true domestic churches filled with love and tenderness. May we grow perfect in the virtues of piety, generosity, and tenacity. Help us to become saints. We ask this in the name of Jesus. Amen.

AUGUST 6

Saints Justus and Pastor (d. c. 304)

Saints Justus and Pastor, brothers, were only thirteen and nine when they were martyred during the persecutions under Roman Emperor Diocletian. The prefect Dacian set up court in what is now Alcala (not far from Madrid). He was trying adult Christians, but upon hearing of this, the brothers who were in school at the time ran to the tribunal and called attention to the fact that they were Christians. Dacian had them whipped, thinking that would take care of them, but they only became more confirmed in their faith. The fearful adult Christians who were wavering were inspired and renewed to stand firm for their faith. In fury that he could not force two children to do his will instead of God's, Dacian had the boys killed. They are the patron saints of Alcala, Spain.

PRAYER

Saints Justus and Pastor, you boldly proclaimed your faith in spite of the threat of death, and your courageous witness inspired others to give their lives. Pray with us on your feast: Gentle Father, give us the virtues of strength and courage that these child martyrs had and restore our innocence. Inspire us to know and profess our faith even when we face persecution. Guide us to remain faithful through all our trials and comfort us. Teach us how to overcome obstacles to doing your will and growing in our faith. Grant us integrity and character filled with virtue. Heal, convert, deliver, and protect us. Bring us to perfection in love and make us saints. We ask this in the name of Jesus. Amen.

AUGUST 7

Saint Miguel de la Mora (1874–1927)

Saint Miguel grew up in Mexico and learned how to raise cattle and ride horses. He became a priest at the time of the communist overthrow of the government. Known as a punctual and orderly priest, he served in the Cathedral of Colima. He refused to join the new government-approved church, but said Mass secretly at home and eventually left the city. He was apprehended along with his brother. General Flores, commander of the communist government, had him executed by firing squad. He died while saying the Rosary. He was fifty-three years old. His relics are in the Cathedral of Colima where he served. Saint Miguel is also celebrated May 21 as one of the Martyrs of the Mexican Revolution.

PRAYER

Saint Miguel, you willingly gave your life for the Faith, leaning on the intercession of Mother Mary for strength. Pray for us to hold fast to our faith, and pray with us: Righteous Father, help us to be punctual and to live in simplicity. Give us wisdom to know what you are asking of us and the courage to do it no matter what. Help us to prepare ourselves for the vocations you call us to, and give us the grace to fulfill the mission you have for us. Bless all priests and bishops, making them faithful to their duties and virtuous leaders. We ask this in the name of Jesus. Amen.

AUGUST 8

Saint Dominic (1170–1221)

Saint Dominic, born of a noble family in Caleruega, Spain, was beloved by people for his friendliness and kindness. He spent many years preaching the truth of Christ in southern France, where the Albigensian heresy (which taught, among other things, that the body is evil) was rampant. Eventually, he founded the Order of Preachers, now known as the Dominicans, to live in poverty and to preach the Gospel wherever they were needed. He and his friars sought personal holiness through prayer, community life, and the discipline of study to prepare them for preaching. It was said of him, "He seldom spoke unless it was with God — that is, in prayer — or about God; and in this matter he instructed his brothers." His order, like the Franciscans, which were founded just a few years earlier, was a mendicant (begging) order. Saint Dominic is the patron saint of astronomers and the Dominican Republic.

PRAYER

Saint Dominic, pray for us to speak always with or of God and to love Him with our whole hearts. Pray with us: Loving Father, grant us a burning love for the truth and a desire to share it with the world. May we always strive for holiness through prayer and study. Give us the wisdom to recognize the ways in which the Church needs repair and the courage to share in this work. Make us true friends who love to speak of you and who possess friendliness, kindness, and loyalty. Bless the Dominican order, keeping it faithful to you. We ask this in the name of Jesus. Amen.

AUGUST 9

Saint Teresa Benedicta of the Cross (1891–1942)

Saint Teresa Benedicta of the Cross was a highly educated Jewish philosopher and teacher whose birth name was Edith Stein. Her intellectual honesty moved her to constantly seek the truth, and after studying the *Autobiography of Saint Teresa of Ávila*, she realized the truth of Christ and His Church and converted to Catholicism. This was wonderful, yet painful, as she knew it would hurt her devout Jewish mother. A few years after her conversion to Catholicism, as the Nazis were gaining power, she became a Discalced Carmelite in Cologne. In 1939, her superior had her smuggled to a monastery in the Netherlands, and her sister Rosa came to join her there. In 1942, after the Nazis had invaded the Netherlands, she and Rosa were arrested and killed in the concentration camp at Auschwitz. She is a patron saint of Europe.

PRAYER

Saint Teresa Benedicta of the Cross, pray for us to seek the truth in all things and to willingly dedicate our lives to it. Pray with us on your feast: Righteous Father, give us prayerful hearts and a deep yearning for the truth, so that we will never be satisfied with anything less than you. Grant us the gift of contemplation. Guide us to be intellectually honest, and teach us to develop our gifts and talents so that you can work through us. Make us saints. We ask this in the name of Jesus. Amen.

AUGUST 10

Saint Lawrence (d. 258)

Saint Lawrence lovingly performed works of mercy, serving widows, orphans, the poor, and the sick, calling them the Church's treasures. He was one of the seven deacons of Rome under Pope Sixtus II who were martyred by the Roman Emperor Valerian. When commanded to bring the Church's treasures to the emperor, Lawrence brought the poor people in the Church before the prefect, saying, "These are the treasure of the Church." As punishment, he was burned alive slowly, but he kept his joy and integrity to the end, saying to the judge, "Let my body be turned; one side is broiled enough." So highly was he esteemed by the people of Rome that many converted to Christianity as they witnessed his death. Saint Lawrence is the patron saint of cooks, the poor, and the city of Rome.

PRAYER

Saint Lawrence, you kept your joy and sense of humor to the bitter end, witnessing to the joy of the Gospel even in death. Pray for us and with us: Gentle Father, make us generous and give us eyes to recognize where our true treasure lies. Guide us to see those in need and work diligently to meet their needs, especially those closest to us. Grant us pure hearts that expand to include the vulnerable, especially the preborn, your priests, and the enslaved. May we hold fast to our faith to the end, no matter the cost. We ask this in the name of Jesus. Amen.

AUGUST 11

Saint Clare (1194–1253)

Saint Clare, a noblewoman from Assisi, became a good friend of Saint Francis of Assisi, and with his support, she founded the Poor Clare Sisters. She remained abbess of the convent at San Damiano all her life. Long hours of prayer and silence before the Blessed Sacrament with Jesus gave her deep peace and joy, and often her face would shine after prayer. Besides her mystical gifts, she was so highly renowned for her wisdom and holiness that the pope, as well as other Church and secular leaders, consulted her. She once turned away an invading army by praying to the Blessed Sacrament and holding up the monstrance, which scattered the soldiers. Saint Clare is the patron saint of persons with blindness, laundry women, glass painters, glaziers, gilders, embroiderers, television and television writers, and the city of Assisi.

PRAYER

Saint Clare, you were renowned for your love of God and your wisdom, and you led many souls to God through your example. Pray with us now: Loving Father, grant us the grace to desire nothing but you and to give you our lives in complete trust. May we possess a deep reverence and love for Jesus in the Holy Eucharist. Teach us how to be true, loyal friends who listen deeply and love unconditionally. Grant us purity of heart, soul, and mind. Make us saints. Bless the Poor Clare sisters, keeping them faithful to you. We ask this in the name of Jesus. Amen.

AUGUST 12

Saint Euplius (d. 304)

Saint Euplius, an Italian deacon who was entrusted with the care of the Holy Scriptures, was arrested during the persecutions under Emperor Diocletian. His captors demanded that he turn over the Scriptures that he carried, and he steadfastly refused, saying: "Because I am a Christian, I will sooner die than deliver them. In them is eternal life, which is lost by him who would betray what God has entrusted to his keeping." In punishment, he was tortured and killed by Governor Calvisianus. He courageously died for his faith, holding firm to the responsibility he had been given.

PRAYER

Saint Euplius, pray for us to be faithful to the duties we are given and to remain steadfast in our faith. Pray with us: Dear Father, give us constancy, determination, and courage in serving you. Inspire us to learn Scripture and to keep it ever in our minds and hearts. May we never deny you or your Church's teachings. Guide us to find and fulfill our vocations and missions. Enable us to perform all the duties of our state in life faithfully and joyfully. Allow us to see and deeply understand that it is a privilege to suffer for love of you. Make us saints. Bless and protect all deacons, and keep them faithful to you and to the Church. Protect all who suffer persecution for their faith in you. We ask this in the name of Jesus. Amen.

AUGUST 13

Blessed Michael McGivney (1852–1890)

Blessed Michael McGivney, the "Apostle of Christian family life," was the oldest child of a large Irish Catholic family in Connecticut. When he became a priest, he was so cherished in his parish that people cried when he was transferred to a new assignment. He founded the Knights of Columbus to provide a Catholic alternative to the secret societies for men that were often openly hostile to Catholicism. He described the Knights thus: "It is an order composed of Catholics and instituted for the welfare of Catholic families. ... Not only in sickness, but when death takes the support of the family away, the Knights of Columbus comes to the relief of the widow and the orphan in a very substantial manner." Built on the principles of charity, unity, and fraternity, the Knights he founded have expanded to serve people in many countries all over the world through the spiritual and corporal works of mercy.

PRAYER

Blessed Michael McGivney, you were a loving priest who truly cared for his flock. Pray for us to live our vocations well, and pray with us: Merciful Father, help us to grow each day in generosity. May we always find ways to serve the poor, sick, and vulnerable, especially widows and orphans. Bless all families in need, and give us the opportunity to minister to them. Instill in us a love for living the liturgical traditions of the Church. Bless and protect all priests. Bless the Knights of Columbus, keeping them faithful to you. We ask this in the name of Jesus. Amen.

AUGUST 14

Saint Maximilian Mary Kolbe (1894–1941)

Saint Maximilian had a vision of Mother Mary when he was twelve. She offered him a choice between two crowns: a white one representing purity and a red one representing martyrdom. He chose both. When he grew up, he became a Conventual Franciscan and later founded the Militia of the Immaculata. He also established the City of the Immaculata to spread devotion to Jesus and Mary through the media, and a magazine, *Knight of the Immaculata*. Regarding devotion to Mary, he said: "Never be afraid of loving the Blessed Virgin too much. You can never love her more than Jesus did." He spoke out against the evils perpetrated by the Nazis. Kolbe was arrested in 1941 and sent to the concentration camp at Auschwitz. There, he offered himself to save a married man from execution. In the starvation bunker, he served and comforted his fellow prisoners through prayer and song before being killed by lethal injection.

PRAYER

Saint Maximilian Kolbe, you entrusted your life to the care of Mother Mary and taught others to do the same. Pray with us now: Loving Father, make us generous in serving you. Grant eloquence to those who write, teach, and speak about our faith, and give us the wisdom and courage to speak the truth. Give us a fervent devotion to the Blessed Mother. Make our hearts so generous that we would give our lives for another if necessary. Protect those being persecuted for their faith in you. Bless the Franciscan order, keeping it faithful to you. We ask this in the name of Jesus. Amen.

Assumption of the Blessed Virgin Mary

Jesus' mother, Mary, received the great privilege of being taken, body and soul, into heaven at the end of her life. While the faithful had held that Mary was assumed into heaven since the early Church, it was not officially declared dogma until 1950. Pope Pius XII wrote in *Munificentissimus Deus,* "We pronounce, declare, and define it to be a divinely revealed dogma that the Immaculate Mother of God, the ever-Virgin Mary, having completed the course of her earthly life, was assumed body and soul to heavenly glory." The Second Vatican Council beautifully stated in *Lumen Gentium,* "Just as the Mother of Jesus, glorified in body and soul in heaven, is the image and beginning of the Church as it is to be perfected in the world to come, so too does she shine forth on earth, until the day of the Lord shall come, as a sign of sure hope and solace to the people of God during its sojourn on earth" (68).

PRAYER

Mother Mary, you were assumed into heaven, body and soul, at the end of your life. Pray for us to live faithfully and to join you in heaven when our life on earth is over. Pray with us: Loving Father, thank you for the gift of the Blessed Mother. Through her intercession, help us to grow in all the virtues, and teach us to imitate her. Grant us a deep desire for prayer and contemplation. Help us to prepare for heaven each day, remembering that eternal life with you is our goal. May we do penance for our sins here on earth so we can go straight to heaven when we die. Make us saints. We ask this in the name of Jesus. Amen.

AUGUST 16

Saint Stephen of Hungary (977–1038)

Saint Stephen was the son of Geza, the Magyar chieftain. Both grew to love Jesus and became Catholic. After his father's death, Stephen came to power and was eventually crowned the first King of Hungary in the year 1000. He modeled Christian virtues and governed justly and prudently, spreading the Faith in his realm by establishing dioceses and building and supporting churches and monasteries. He was generous to the poor and the sick. In a letter he addressed to his son Emeric, he wrote: "Be humble in this life, that God may raise you up in the next. Be truly moderate. ... Be gentle so that you may never oppose justice. Be honorable so that you may never voluntarily bring disgrace upon anyone." Saint Stephen is the patron saint of bricklayers, stonecutters, masons, and Hungary.

PRAYER

Saint Stephen, you were a wise and righteous king and father. Pray for us to be prudent stewards of all God has given us, and pray with us: Heavenly Father, grant us magnanimity and wisdom, and give us the courage to exercise authority in those areas you have placed under our leadership. Guide us to find and fulfill our vocations. Teach us integrity and strengthen our character. Heal, convert, deliver, and protect us. Bless all our civil leaders, and help them to follow your law and govern with wisdom and justice. We ask this in the name of Jesus. Amen.

Blesseds Mary and Caspar Vaz and Blessed Bartholomew Laurel (d. 1627)

Blessed Mary and her husband, Blessed Caspar, were holy individuals who inspired and uplifted each other. This married couple was a beautiful witness to Christ and Christian marriage. These Secular Franciscans were martyred together in Nagasaki, Japan, united in death as they had been in life. Blessed Bartholomew Laurel, originally from Mexico, who had previously served as a missionary in Manila, was a Franciscan lay brother who went to Japan and was also martyred in Nagasaki. They are part of the huge number of Martyrs of Japan.

PRAYER

Blesseds Mary, Caspar, and Bartholomew, pray for us to have the courage to die for our faith if necessary, and pray with us: Dear Father, grant us the virtue of courage, that we may stand firm in our faith even to death. Bless all married couples and allow them to be beautiful witnesses to your covenant with your people. Bless your priests and make them holy. Grant us the grace to love and defend our faith. Uphold us and give us presence of mind in difficult situations, that we may remain true to our faith and draw others to you. Protect those who are suffering persecution for their faith in you. Bless the Franciscan order, keeping it faithful to you. We ask this in the name of Jesus. Amen.

AUGUST 18

Saint Jane Frances de Chantal (1572–1641)

Saint Jane Frances, a noblewoman from France, was well-educated, intelligent, gifted musically, and a gracious entertainer. She was married to a baron and had four children. After her husband died tragically in a shooting accident, she educated her children while caring for her father-in-law. When her children were older, she founded the Visitation Sisters with the help of Saint Francis de Sales, her spiritual director, who described her as "the perfect woman." Saint Vincent de Paul thought her one of the holiest souls he had ever met. She once told her sisters: "There is another martyrdom: the martyrdom of love. ... The martyrdom of love cannot be relegated to a second place, for love is as strong as death. For the martyrs of love suffer infinitely more in remaining in this life so as to serve God, than if they died a thousand times over in testimony to their faith, love, and fidelity."

PRAYER

Saint Jane Frances, pray for us to be martyrs of love, giving God all that we have and are, as you did. Pray with us: Dear Father, in everything we do, grant us diligence, fidelity, and patience. Inspire us to be generous with our time, talent, and treasure, and to serve you with our whole selves. Make us magnanimous in serving you so that we may be martyrs of love. Bless the Visitation Sisters, keeping them faithful to you. We ask this in the name of Jesus. Amen.

AUGUST 19

Blessed Joachim Firayama-Diz, Markus Shineiemon, and Bartholomew Monfiore (d. 1622)

Blessed Joachim Firayama-Diz was a ship captain who, along with Blessed Markus Shineiemon and Blessed Bartholomew Monfiore, both crew members, undertook a dangerous job. They transported missionary priests, Blessed Peter Zuniga and Blessed Louis Flores, aboard their ship to Japan, where intense persecution against Christians was occurring. They and all the crew belonged to the Confraternity of the Most Holy Rosary, and they strove to live their faith. They were all captured, and since they aided the priests, they were martyred with them in Nagasaki, Japan.

PRAYER

Blesseds Joachim, Markus, and Bartholomew, you bravely attempted to bring missionary priests into Japan despite the dangers. Pray for us to share our faith no matter the cost, and pray with us: Merciful Father, grant us the courage to live our faith and serve your Church, even when it is dangerous or unpopular. May we do your will in all things. Grant us the grace to be willing to die for you if necessary, and give us the virtues we need to live our lives in total dedication to you. Bless and encourage all missionaries and priests, keeping them faithful to you. We ask this in the name of Jesus. Amen.

Saint Bernard of Clairvaux (1090–1153)

Saint Bernard was such a virtuous leader, so encouraging, enthusiastic, and inspiring, that his four brothers and other relatives and friends followed him when he went to join the Benedictine monastery at Citeaux. Saint Stephen Harding, the monastery's founder, later chose Bernard to found and become abbot of the monastery of Clairvaux (the "monastery of light"). There Bernard and his monks lived a contemplative life of prayer according to the Benedictine Rule. Bernard also had a profound devotion to Mother Mary. Never too busy to receive visitors, he responded to letters from many people, including popes, who wrote to him seeking help and advice. He helped with disputes and difficult matters in the Church, including a schism that arose regarding who was the rightful pope. Saint Bernard is the patron saint of beekeepers and candlemakers.

PRAYER

Saint Bernard, your holiness attracted others to Christ. Pray for us to become holy, and pray with us now: Dear Father, make us humble, prayerful leaders, that we might grow close to you and lead others to you. May our lives be formed by prayer and penance, listening for your voice in the silence of our hearts. Grant us the grace to find and fulfill our vocations and missions. Guide us to go wherever you call us, to work for peace and unity, and to be the light of Christ in a dark world. Grant us a strong devotion to Mother Mary and make us saints. Bless the Cistercian order, keeping it faithful to you. We ask this in the name of Jesus. Amen.

AUGUST 21

Saint Pius X (1835 –1914)

Pope Saint Pius X, whose baptismal name was Giuseppe Melchiorre Sarto, grew up poor. He had such love and care for the poor that, as a young priest, he often gave away money, and sought to help and comfort everyone in need. Later, even after he became pope, he would say, "I was born poor, I lived poor, I will die poor." As bishop of Mantua in 1884, he reformed a liberal seminary. When he became pope, his motto was to "restore all things in Christ." He strenuously resisted the philosophy of Modernism, which was leading many people to try to "modernize" the Church and her teachings. Known as the "Pope of the Eucharist," Pius allowed children as young as seven years old to begin to receive holy Communion, and he promoted daily Communion and reading of Scripture and spiritual books.

PRAYER

Pope Saint Pius X, you served the Church with devotion and labored for needed reforms. Pray for the Church, and pray with us today: Dear Father, grant us a deep love of poverty and a desire to serve you in the poor. Help us to grow in the virtue of simplicity. Inspire us to work to restore all things in Christ, and grant us a deep love of the Holy Eucharist. Teach us to pray always and to perform the spiritual and corporal works of mercy, especially for the poor and vulnerable. May we live according to the Church's social teaching, promoting justice in our communities and families. Make us saints. We ask this in the name of Jesus. Amen.

AUGUST 22

Saint Sigfrid (d. 690)

Saint Sigfrid was a deacon in the monastery of Saint Peter at Wearmouth and a disciple of Saint Benedict Biscop. He was chosen to replace the abbot of Wearmouth, Saint Esterwine, after he died. Saint Benedict Biscop had established Wearmouth and the sister monastery of Saint Paul at Jarrow, where the Venerable Bede resided. The monasteries were a center for holiness and learning. Sigfrid was especially esteemed for his knowledge of Scripture, and he was deeply loved by the monks. Unfortunately, he suffered from poor health and died of a lung disease only a few years after becoming abbot. He is buried in the Abbey of Saint Peter with Saints Benedict Biscop and Esterwine.

PRAYER

Saint Sigfrid, you were a wise, gentle leader in the Church. Pray for us to use all our gifts in God's service, and pray with us: Gentle Father, give us the virtues that Saint Sigfrid had, especially goodness and kindness. Help us to love the Scriptures and to read them daily. Increase our knowledge and understanding of your word. Grant us close spiritual friendships with holy people who can help us to become better and more committed disciples. Bless the Benedictine order, keeping it faithful to you. We ask this in the name of Jesus. Amen.

AUGUST 23

Saint Rose of Lima (1586–1617)

Saint Rose, the first saint of the Americas, loved God so much that, when she was still very young, she made a prayer hut in her family's garden in Lima, Peru, and spent most of her time there. Consecrating herself to God, she became a lay Dominican, and she prayed, fasted, did penance, and performed works of mercy, especially caring for homeless children and the elderly. She prayed for the enslaved and native people of Peru while earning money for her poor family by selling flowers, needlepoint, lace, and embroidery handwork. Saint Rose is the patron saint of florists, vanity prevention, Peru, the Philippines, and Latin America.

PRAYER

Saint Rose, you devoted your whole life to God, spending time with Him in prayer and generously serving the poor. Pray with us on your feast: Loving Father, help us to grow in the virtues of piety, chastity, and generosity. May we always find your grace joyful and delightful, and may we live in a true spirit of penance. Give us the grace to pray, fast, give alms, and serve others with generosity. Make us saints. Bless the Dominican order, keeping it faithful to you. We ask this in the name of Jesus. Amen.

AUGUST 24

Saint Bartholomew (d. first century)

Saint Bartholomew, also called Nathanael in the Gospel of John, was one of the twelve apostles of Jesus. In John's Gospel, we read that Saint Philip brought him to Jesus. The Gospel of John recounts:

> Jesus saw Nathanael coming toward him and said of him, "Behold, an Israelite indeed, in whom there is no deceit!" Nathanael said to him, "How do you know me?" Jesus answered him, "Before Philip called you, when you were under the fig tree, I saw you." Nathanael answered him, "Rabbi, you are the Son of God! You are the King of Israel!" Jesus answered him, "Because I said to you, 'I saw you under the fig tree,' do you believe? You will see greater things than these." (1:47–50)

It is believed that Nathanael was martyred while on a mission to India and Armenia.

PRAYER

Saint Bartholomew, Jesus called you to be one of His apostles, and you followed Him willingly. Pray with us on your feast: Righteous Father, make us bold in preaching the Gospel and courageous in our service of you. Inspire us to joyfully bring your love to others. Grant us the grace to overcome our fear. May we always listen to Jesus and do whatever He tells us. Grant us all virtues and fill us with the Holy Spirit. Protect those who are persecuted for their faith in you. Confirm us in love and make us saints. We ask this in the name of Jesus. Amen.

AUGUST 25

Saint Louis IX (1226–1270)

Saint Louis was only twelve years old when he became king of France. His mother, Blanche, acted as regent until he was nineteen. He married Margaret of Provence, and they had eleven children. During his reign, he established peace and justice in France and reformed laws and court proceedings. He loved his people and showed it by founding hospitals, churches, libraries, and orphanages. He fed the poor at his own table, and he found time to perform works of mercy, including serving people with leprosy. He wrote in a letter to his son: "Be kindhearted to the poor, the unfortunate, and the afflicted. Give them as much help and consolation as you can. Thank God for all the benefits he has bestowed upon you, that you may be worthy to receive greater."

PRAYER

Saint Louis, pray for us to obey lawful authority and to act as wise stewards in our lives and families. Pray with us: Gracious Father, inspire us to love and work for peace and unity, and to make amends for wrongs we have committed. Grant us the virtue of self-control so that peace may reign in our families, our community, and the Church. Bless parents of large families, and parents of children who have special needs. May all parents be good guides to the souls you have entrusted to their care. Heal parents who are mentally ill or struggling with addiction and protect their children. Bless our civil leaders and help them to govern their people with wisdom, charity, and justice. We ask this in the name of Jesus. Amen.

AUGUST 26

Augustinian Martyrs of Capsa (d. 484)

The Augustinian Martyrs of Capsa (modern-day Gafsa in Tunisia) were seven men who lived in a monastery founded by Saint Augustine in northern Africa. They were arrested when King Homeric demanded that all monasteries be abolished. These faithful Augustinians — Abbot Liberatus, Father Rogatus, Father Septimas, Father Maximus, Deacon Boniface, Subdeacon Servus, and Subdeacon Rusticus — steadfastly refused to renounce their faith, and so they were martyred. Initially, they were to be burned, but the fire would not light, so they were beaten to death. Their martyrdom occurred only thirty-four years after Saint Augustine died.

PRAYER

Augustinian Martyrs of Capsa, pray for us to give our lives for love of God, as you did, and pray with us: Gentle Father, grant us the virtue of courage. Inspire us through the example of the martyrs to be fearless in proclaiming your truth. Give us the grace to hold fast to our faith no matter what happens. May we learn and be able to effectively communicate the teachings of the Church. Fill our hearts with heroic charity for our neighbor, and strengthen us to help those in need. Protect those who are being persecuted for their faith in you. Make us saints. Bless the Augustinian order, keeping it faithful to you. We ask this in the name of Jesus. Amen.

AUGUST 27

Saint Monica (322–387)

Saint Monica prayed for the conversion of the people she loved, especially her violent, pagan husband, her mother-in-law, and, most famously, her wayward son, Augustine. She prayed and fasted perseveringly for years, never giving up, even when it seemed like God was not answering her prayers. She trusted that God was working on His time, respecting her loved ones' free will, even when it was slower than she wanted. Yet God did hear her prayers, and over time her husband and mother-in-law converted and became Christians, and Saint Augustine became a great saint and brilliant Doctor of the Church. She died in Ostia, Italy, while en route home to Africa. Her relics are in the Basilica of Sant' Agostino in Rome. Saint Monica is the patron saint of married women and mothers.

PRAYER

Saint Monica, your example of persistent intercessory prayer continues to inspire us and give us hope. Pray with us today: Merciful Father, grant us the virtues of perseverance, patience, and forgiveness. May we pray without ceasing, even when it seems you do not hear us. Bless all mothers and guide them to be virtuous, kind, and loving. Bring those who have left the Church back into your fold, and grant that those who are not Christian may become part of your Church. Assist and give comfort to those who endure gossip and false accusations from others. Make us saints. We ask this in the name of Jesus. Amen.

AUGUST 28

Saint Augustine (354–430)

Saint Augustine was so gifted that he was made bishop of Hippo (modern-day Annaba, Algeria) only nine years after his baptism. Before his conversion, he led an immoral life, but he finally gave in to grace through the prayers of his mother, Saint Monica, and the teaching of Saint Ambrose. After baptism he was intensely zealous to promote the truth and help others overcome temptation. A prolific writer, he described his path to God through God's grace in his life in his *Confessions*, perhaps his most famous work. His preaching and eloquent writings helped counteract heresies in the Church of his day. Along with Saint Thomas Aquinas, he is recognized as one of the most brilliant minds the Church has produced. He founded the Augustinian order. Saint Augustine is a Doctor of the Church and the patron of the Augustinians, theologians, and Carthage.

PRAYER

Saint Augustine, your story of conversion continues to move hearts, and your wisdom is a guiding a light for the Church. Pray with us on your feast: Righteous Father, grant us the grace to accept our dignity as children of light, and free us from all immorality and disordered attachments. Grant us the virtues of chastity and self-control, and strengthen our desire to be holy saints, living for and in you alone. Bless the Augustinian order and all theologians, keeping them faithful to you. We ask this in the name of Jesus. Amen.

AUGUST 29

The Passion of Saint John the Baptist

Saint John the Baptist challenged people to follow God's law and to repent. His witness of simplicity and detachment was inspiring. His mission was to prepare the way for people to accept Jesus' new covenant, and he was faithful to this call to the end. He was not afraid to challenge the sinful behavior of King Herod Antipas, who had married his brother's wife, Herodias. As a result of this public censure, John was arrested and thrown into prison. Later, at the instigation of Herodias, Herod had John beheaded. Saint John is the patron saint of the monastic life.

PRAYER

Saint John the Baptist, you prepared the way for Jesus in your life and gave the ultimate witness in your death. Pray with us today: Merciful Father, grant us the virtues of zeal and fortitude in living our faith and sharing it with the world. May we always be completely committed to following your commandments and doing your will in our lives. Heal our hearts and remove from us any selfishness or worldliness. Keep us honest and true to you. Make us saints. We ask this in the name of Jesus. Amen.

AUGUST 30

Saint Margaret Ward (d. 1588)

Saint Margaret Ward, with the assistance of John Roche, an Irish waterman, bravely helped Father Richard Watson escape from Bridewell Prison in London during the English persecution of Catholics. Margaret undertook this dangerous mission knowing that helping or hiding priests meant a certain death sentence if she got caught. Though Father Watson did escape, she and Roche were arrested, imprisoned, and tortured. Offered freedom if they would attend a Protestant service after apologizing to the queen, they refused to violate their conscience. They were martyred at Tyburn. Margaret is honored among the forty martyrs of England and Wales.

PRAYER

Saint Margaret, you bravely gave aid to a priest imprisoned for his faith, though you knew the dangers. Pray for us to love the Church as you did, and pray with us: Gracious Father, give us the courage to hold fast to our faith and to seek justice for those who are oppressed. Grant us a firm and consistent prayer life to undergird the courageous actions you ask us to take. Bless and help those who are unjustly imprisoned, and give us the opportunity to serve and support them. Protect all who are being persecuted for their faith in you. Confirm us in love and make us saints. Bless and protect all priests. We ask this in the name of Jesus. Amen.

AUGUST 31

Saint Raymond Nonnatus (d. 1240)

Saint Raymond was truly a miracle baby, for his mother died while she was still pregnant, and they saved him through a caesarean birth. When he grew up, he became a Mercedarian, a religious order founded by Saint Peter Nolasco to ransom Christian enslaved people. At one point, he ran out of money to secure the ransom and allowed himself to be imprisoned to secure the freedom of Christian slaves. While in prison, he never stopped preaching about Jesus to his Muslim captors, and he was tortured for his courage. After his release from prison, he was made the second master general of the Mercedarian order in Barcelona and a cardinal of the Church. Saint Raymond is the patron saint of expectant mothers, midwives, newborn babies, victims of gossip, and women in labor. He is invoked for a safe birth.

PRAYER

Saint Raymond, you literally gave yourself when you had no money left to give. Pray for us to be so generous, and pray with us: Loving Father, make us courageous, joyful witnesses of your love to all we meet. Give us hearts of compassion, especially for the vulnerable and enslaved. Set free all who are enslaved and convert their captors. Keep mothers and children safe in childbirth, and guide all midwives and doctors who help them. May we never cease to proclaim the name of Jesus. Bless all bishops, making them true shepherds and virtuous leaders. Bless the Mercedarian order, keeping it faithful to you. We ask this in the name of Jesus. Amen.

SEPTEMBER

THE MONTH OF
THE SEVEN SORROWS OF MARY

SEPTEMBER 1

Saint Fiacre (d. c. 670)

Saint Fiacre's life as a hermit in Kilfiachra, Ireland, centered on prayer and contemplation. Seeking solitude, as people kept coming to learn from him, he moved to Meaux in northern France where he was supported on land given to him by the bishop, Saint Faro. This eventually became the village of Saint-Fiacre as people (including Queen Anne of Austria) came on pilgrimage to visit the oratory he built and dedicated to Mother Mary, and the travelers' hospice he established. Here, too, many followers came to live with him, and he eventually founded a monastery. He was given the gift of miracles in the laying on of hands. After his death, there were many miracles at his shrine. Saint Fiacre is the patron saint of drivers and gardeners.

PRAYER

Saint Fiacre, you loved spending time alone with God, yet you also received all who came to you for prayer and guidance. Pray for us on your feast: Righteous Father, through the intercession of Saint Fiacre, grant us the virtues of piety and simplicity. With your grace, may we center our lives around daily prayer and be open to receiving your gift of contemplation. Bless all who need healing and give us the opportunity to serve them through our prayers. Keep working miracles of healing in our world, using us as your instruments if that is your will. Heal, convert, deliver, and protect us. Make us saints. We ask this in the name of Jesus. Amen.

Saint Solomon Leclerq and Blesseds Leon Mopinot, Roger Faverge, and Uldaric Guillaume (d. 1792)

These four Brothers of the Christian Schools, along with many other priests and religious in France during the French Revolution, refused to take the oath to support the Civil Constitution of the Clergy, which would have forced them to compromise their faith. For refusing to go along with revolutionary forces, they were first expelled from their residences and schools. Saint Solomon, secretary to the superior general of the Brothers, was arrested and imprisoned at a Carmelite monastery in Paris, which had been turned into a prison. He was killed in the monastery garden, along with the other priests and religious imprisoned with him. Blesseds Leon, Roger, and Uldaric were thrown into ships with rotting debris, along with hundreds of other priests and religious who refused to take the oath. They died of illness from the terrible treatment they received on the prison ships.

PRAYER

Saint Solomon and Blesseds Leon, Roger, and Uldaric, you held firmly to your faith even in the face of great suffering. On your feast day, we ask for your prayers, and united in prayer with you, we pray: Heavenly Father, grant us the grace to be faithful and uncompromising in our commitment to our Catholic Faith. Make us fearless in trials and unwavering in persecution. Protect all who are being persecuted for their faith in you. Make us saints. Bless the Brothers of the Christian Schools and keep them faithful to you. We ask this in the name of Jesus. Amen.

Pope Saint Gregory the Great (540–604)

Saint Gregory was a nobleman, governor, Benedictine monk, and eventually pope. When he decided to leave his political office in Rome to become a monk, he donated his estates in Rome and Sicily for monasteries. He once preached in a sermon, "We make use of temporal things, but our hearts are set on what is eternal. Temporal goods help us on our way, but our desire must be for those eternal realities which are our goal." Always generous to the poor, as pope he used the Church's resources to help them. His political experience enabled him to make peace with the Lombard invaders. Known for his liturgical reforms, including music, he also encouraged the faithful to pray the Stations of the Cross. Pope Saint Gregory is the patron saint of singers, musicians, teachers, and scholars and is a Doctor of the Church.

PRAYER

Saint Gregory, you placed your many gifts at the service of God and His Church, even when it was difficult for you. Pray for us today, that we might imitate you, and pray with us: Merciful Father, give us generous hearts to serve you and our neighbor. Inspire those discerning vocations to listen carefully to your will. Grant us courage and patience in trials, in weariness, and in illness. Thank you for the gift of beauty that draws our souls to you, and help us to share this beauty with others. Bless our pope and all bishops, making them faithful shepherds of your Church. We ask this in the name of Jesus. Amen.

SEPTEMBER 4

Saint Cuthbert (d. 687)

Saint Cuthbert, a famous English bishop, had many gifts, including prophecy, healing, miraculously attaining food, and casting out demons. It is even said that animals sensed his purity and gentleness and paid homage to him. Immersed in prayer, he eventually became prior at Melrose Abbey in England, then at a monastery in Lindisfarne, Ireland, during which time he was made bishop. He helped victims of the plague by working miracles. After he died, his body was found to be incorrupt, and some of his vestments were discovered intact in 1828. Sadly, his shrine was destroyed in the sixteenth century under King Henry VIII. Saint Cuthbert is the patron saint of sailors and shepherds, and is invoked against the plague.

PRAYER

Saint Cuthbert, pray for us to place our lives in the service of God, as you did. On your feast day, please pray with us: Gentle Father, give us the virtues of humility, generosity, and mercy. Inspire us to pray always and in all that we do. Grant us the gift of contemplation and silence to discern your will. Guide us to find and fulfill our vocations and missions. Enable us to see the needs of others and perform spiritual and corporal works of mercy. Form us into virtuous leaders. Make us saints. We ask this in the name of Jesus. Amen.

SEPTEMBER 5

Saint Teresa of Calcutta (1910–1997)

Saint Teresa of Calcutta (known as Mother Teresa) was famous during her life for hearing, accepting, and following God's call to serve the poorest of the poor. She founded the Missionaries of Charity and helped thousands of poor, dying people in Calcutta, India, to die with dignity instead of dying alone, on the street, passed by and ignored. From there she went on to found houses for pregnant women in crisis, AIDS victims, orphans, and many others. She had a particular love for children and wanted to care for all of them. Saint Teresa of Calcutta is the patron saint of the Missionaries of Charity and co-patron of the Archdiocese of Calcutta (with Saint Francis Xavier).

PRAYER

Saint Teresa of Calcutta, you showed the world what it means to see the face of Christ in the poor, and your radical generosity knew no bounds. On your feast, join with us in praying: Loving Father, through the intercession of Saint Teresa of Calcutta, give us generous hearts of service to the Church and the world. Inspire us to live out the Church's teaching on social justice and to be steadfast in working for the vulnerable, poor, and oppressed. Guide us to trust absolutely in your providence and to perform the works of mercy, especially caring for the sick and burying the dead. Make us saints. Bless the Missionaries of Charity, helping them to be faithful to you. We ask this in the name of Jesus. Amen.

SEPTEMBER 6

Saints Donatian, Laetus, and Companions (d. c. 484)

Saints Donatian and Laetus, along with their companions Fusculus, Germanus, Mansuetus, and Praesidius, were North African bishops in what is now Algeria, Tunisia, and Libya, who were martyred by the Arian Vandals. Governor Boniface had invited the Vandals to help him against the Romans, which they did, but afterward, they refused to leave. The Vandal Kings Genseric and his son, Hunneric, were Arians, and they promptly began persecuting orthodox Christians, closing their churches. They deposed the bishops Donatian, Laetus, and their companions and had most of them tortured and left to die in the desert. Saint Laetus was thrown into a dungeon and then burned to death.

PRAYER

Saints Donatian, Laetus, and companions, we are humbled by your example of courage and fidelity even when it was difficult and dangerous. Pray for us and, on your feast day, pray with us: Heavenly Father, increase our faith, hope, and charity, and give us the virtue of fortitude. Help us to courageously follow you through difficulty and danger. Help us to learn our faith, and give us courage to defend it. Bless our bishops and help them to be holy shepherds and zealous pastors. Strengthen and protect all who are persecuted for their faith in you. We ask this in the name of Jesus. Amen.

SEPTEMBER 7

Blessed Frédéric Ozanam (1813–1853)

Blessed Frédéric earned a degree in law at the University of the Sorbonne in Paris. After undergoing a crisis of faith, he returned to the Church, zealously promising God "to devote my life to the services of truth which had given me peace." He began to do charitable work and urged others to join him in putting their faith into action. This was the beginning of what would become the Society of Saint Vincent de Paul, whose mission is to help the poor, under the patronage of Saint Vincent de Paul. Frédéric said: "We must do what is agreeable to God. We must do what Our Lord Jesus Christ did when preaching the Gospel. Let us go to the poor. Let us learn of Him. Let us do without hesitation whatever good lies at our hands." A devoted husband, father, and professor of law, he used his gifts of writing and teaching to share the Faith and show the Church's significance and influence in the world.

PRAYER

Blessed Frédéric, you showed your love for God and the Church by hastening to the service of others, especially the poor. Pray for us to love as you did, and pray with us: Gracious Father, through the intercession of Blessed Frédéric, inspire us to always do what is pleasing to you by imitating Jesus. Give us the virtues we need to serve you by serving and loving our neighbor. Teach us to practice spiritual and corporal works of mercy, and make us saints. Bless the Society of Saint Vincent de Paul, keeping it faithful to you. We ask this in the name of Jesus. Amen.

SEPTEMBER 8

The Nativity of the Blessed Virgin Mary

Mary was conceived without original sin, and the Holy Spirit was active in her from the beginning of her life. According to tradition, her parents, Saints Anne, and Joachim, prayed for many years for a child, and finally they had Mary. They consecrated her to the Lord from her childhood. She was a pious, faith-filled girl and a joy to her parents. Her birth, the birth of Jesus, and the birth of Saint John the Baptist are the only three births in the Church's liturgical calendar in honor of their special roles as Mother, Savior, and precursor.

PRAYER

Mother Mary, as we celebrate your birthday today, we ask for your prayers that we might become the saints God made us to be. Pray with us today: Dear Father, through the intercession of Mother Mary and in honor of her birthday, help us to grow in all her virtues, especially purity, chastity, modesty, humility, gentleness, kindness, simplicity, sincerity, and obedience. Grant us the grace to imitate her in everything we do. Thank you for the gift of our birthday and our baptism, when we were born to new life in Christ. Help us to honor our baptismal day and celebrate it as part of our liturgical year. We give you thanks and praise for giving us Mary as the mother of your Son and our mother. Under her protection, guide us to find and fulfill our vocations and missions, seeking always to do your will. Make us saints. We ask this in the name of Jesus. Amen.

SEPTEMBER 9

Saint Peter Claver (1581–1654)

Saint Peter Claver, a Spanish Jesuit priest, answered God's call to become a missionary to serve the African slaves in what is now Colombia, South America. He labored tirelessly, ministering to thousands of enslaved people who were brought by boat from Africa to the port city of Cartagena. He served through a ministry of presence, truly being with those forced into slavery in their hardship and suffering. While he was zealous about bringing these souls to Christ, he cared for their bodily needs first, saying, "We must speak to them with our hands before we try to speak to them with our lips." He encouraged, taught, and baptized thousands of people. Calling himself their slave, he brought food and medicine, and defended them whenever he could. Saint Peter Claver is the patron saint of African Americans and of enslaved peoples.

PRAYER

Saint Peter, your deep compassion and loving action won many souls for Christ, even in the most brutal conditions. On your feast day, join with us as we pray: Merciful Father, grant us the compassion and courage to serve and lift up the vulnerable. May we understand and live out the Church's teachings on social justice and witness to the dignity of every person. Grant us a ministry of presence to listen deeply and offer comfort to everyone we meet. Rescue, free, and heal all who are enslaved, especially in human trafficking, addiction, and abusive relationships. Heal and convert all oppressors. Deliver us from all prejudice. We ask this in the name of Jesus. Amen.

SEPTEMBER 10

Blesseds Anthony, Mary, and Peter Sanga and Charles Spinola (1615–1622)

Little Peter Sanga was only three years old when he was martyred in Nagasaki, Japan, along with his father, Blessed Anthony, his mother, Blessed Mary, and more than fifty others in what is known as the Great Genna Martyrdom. Blessed Charles Spinola, a Jesuit priest, was the leader of this brave group of Christians, which included priests and laypeople. Blessed Charles, along with his fellow priests, was burned to death, while many others were beheaded. All of them chose to die rather than renounce their Catholic Faith.

PRAYER

Martyrs of Japan, you held fast to the Faith in spite of threats of brutal torture and death, and your witness kept the flame of faith alive even when all seemed lost. Pray with us now: Righteous Father, through the intercession of all the Martyrs of Japan, give us the virtues of steadfast faith and courage. Help us always to witness in word and deed to your deep love and mercy for the world. Grant us the grace to stand firm and hold fast to our faith during persecution without fear, even to the point of giving our lives. May our words and deeds witness to you. Deliver us from the world, the flesh, and the devil, and bless all those who suffer persecution for their faith in you. We ask this in the name of Jesus. Amen.

Saint John Gabriel Perboyre (1802–1840)

Saint John Perboyre was a pious child raised in a devout family. He and two of his brothers became priests, and two of his sisters entered religious life. While accompanying his younger brother to seminary, John felt the call to the missionary priesthood. After being ordained in 1825, he served for a while as formation director in the seminary. Later, he set out on mission to China. After eight months of travel and five additional months of learning the Chinese language, he served in Hubei and zealously proclaimed the Faith, bringing many to conversion. Unfortunately, his time of ministry was cut short when persecutions of Christians began. His whereabouts were revealed, and he was stripped, tried, and tortured in multiple tribunals. Even people he had brought to the faith falsely testified against him out of fear. But he steadfastly affirmed, "I would sooner die than deny my faith." He was strangled while tied to a cross.

PRAYER

Saint John, thank you for your example of constancy in the faith. Pray for us to be unwavering in our faith, and pray with us on your feast day: Righteous Father, give us the zeal, courage, and constancy of the martyrs. Make us so strong in studying and living our faith that we will never renounce it. May we lovingly help others to understand and live the Faith as well. Bless all families to be devout domestic churches that raise up saints. We ask this in the name of Jesus. Amen.

SEPTEMBER 12

Blessed Maria Victoria Fornari Strata (1562–1617)

Blessed Maria Victoria, born in Genoa, lost her husband after they had been married eight years and was left to raise her six children alone. In this incredibly difficult time, she depended on the intercession of Mother Mary, who appeared to her in a vision, promising that she would protect her children and her, and encouraging her to strive to love God above anything else. Inspired by this vision, Maria vowed not to marry again, but to raise and educate her children until they were old enough that she could become a religious. In time, she founded a religious order, the Order of the Most Holy Annunciation. Both as a wife and mother, and as a religious sister, she performed many works of mercy.

PRAYER

Blessed Maria Victoria, you trusted in God's perfect plan and relied on Our Lady to help and guide you through the difficulties and sufferings of life. Pray for us to have that same trust, and pray with us: Merciful Father, help us to trust in your goodness and to follow your will for our lives. May we live our vocations with generosity. Make our homes true domestic churches, and help us to perform the spiritual and corporal works of mercy for love of you. Comfort all who grieve the loss of loved ones. Protect all children. Bless the Order of the Most Holy Annunciation, keeping it faithful to you. Make us virtuous leaders. We ask this in the name of Jesus. Amen.

SEPTEMBER 13

Saint John Chrysostom (347–407)

Saint John Chrysostom, bishop of Constantinople, was so gifted at preaching that he was called "Golden-Mouthed." He wrote: "Preaching makes me healthy. As soon as I open my mouth all tiredness is gone." His eloquent preaching helped people come to a deeper understanding and love of the truth and care for the poor. He urged everyone to always pray, fast, and give alms, calling almsgiving the "wing of prayer." As bishop, he called for reform of the people, the city, and the clergy, and he preached especially against the sins of greed and lust. The Empress Eudoxia, who felt personally attacked by his preaching, had him exiled, which ultimately led to his death. In everything he said, "Glory be to God for all things." A great theologian, he was named a Doctor of the Church. Saint John Chrysostom is the patron saint of preachers.

PRAYER

Saint John Chrysostom, you preached with eloquence and helped people come to a deeper understanding and love of the truth. Pray for us to seek the truth in all things, and pray with us: Gentle Father, grant us the virtues of magnanimity, tenacity, and eloquence. Teach us to be consistent in study of Scripture, prayer, fasting, and almsgiving. Form us into virtuous and fearless leaders. Comfort and assist those who are unjustly accused and ostracized. Bless all bishops and make them compelling teachers, competent administrators, and powerful preachers. We ask this in the name of Jesus. Amen.

SEPTEMBER 14

The Exaltation of the Holy Cross

The night before He died, Jesus asked His Father three times, "If it be possible, let this cup pass from me" (Mt 26:39, 42, 44). As God, He could have chosen any way He wanted to redeem us, but this was His Father's will, and He obeyed. The Romans killed people by crucifixion when they wanted to torture and humiliate them, making an example of them. Jesus endured this extreme form of execution to set us free from sin and open the door for us to have a relationship with our Father. The cross is the sign of His radical love for us, and He would have died that horrible death for each of us, even if we were the only person on earth. This feast in honor of the cross was established after Saint Helena found the True Cross in 320 and had a church built on the spot — the Church of the Holy Sepulcher in Jerusalem, dedicated in 335.

PRAYER

Merciful Father, in your great love, you sent your only Son, Jesus, to suffer and die to bring us back into a relationship with you. We praise and thank you for your great love, and we ask for the grace to love you completely. Give us the virtue of obedience and help us to trust in your will. May we always look at the crucifix with love, especially when we are tempted, going through trials, or feeling lonely or unhappy. Help us through the merits Jesus won for us to cooperate with your grace. Make us saints. We ask this in the name of Jesus. Amen.

SEPTEMBER 15

Our Lady of Sorrows

Mother Mary was full of love, kindness, sensitivity, and tenderness. As a mother, she felt great pain in her heart when something hurt or threatened her Son, Jesus. The prophet Simeon had predicted that she would suffer, and she did, sharing in Jesus' suffering. Traditionally, the Church has recognized seven particular moments of sorrow in Mary's life: 1) the prophecy of Simeon; 2) the flight into Egypt; 3) the loss of Jesus in the Temple in Jerusalem; 4) the meeting with Jesus on the way to Calvary; 5) standing at the foot of the cross; 6) receiving the body of Jesus when it was taken down from the cross and placed in her arms; and 7) the burial of Jesus. This memorial helps us to remember the unity of the two hearts, and the Liturgy of the Hours quotes Saint Bernard: "For only by passing through your heart could the sword enter the flesh of your son."

PRAYER

Mary, Mother of Sorrows, thank you for your witness of suffering with your Son and for offering Him to the Father for love of us. Pray with us on your feast day: Loving Father, grant us the grace to grow in all virtues and to suffer trials and crosses with calm and patient endurance as Mary did. Thank you for giving her to us to be our mother. Help us to bear our own sorrows and sufferings with patience, peace, and trust in your mercy. May we live in gratitude for the sufferings Jesus and Mary endured for our sake. Make us saints. We ask this in the name of Jesus. Amen.

SEPTEMBER 16

Saints Cornelius (d. 253) and Cyprian (d. 258)

Saints Cornelius and Cyprian were friends who helped each other and led the Church during difficult and dangerous times of persecution under the Roman Emperor Valerian. Saint Cornelius, pope from 251 to 253, fought for unity in the midst of schism. He had the difficult task of deciding how to respond to Christians who had apostatized during the persecutions under Emperor Decius and now wanted to return to the Church. He mercifully allowed them to be restored to the Church through penance. Saint Cyprian, bishop of Carthage, biblical scholar, and theologian, called the Council of Carthage to defend the Church's teachings with great zeal. He assisted Pope Saint Cornelius in showing mercy to those who had lapsed, even writing a treatise on how they could be formally reunited with the Church. Cornelius died in exile and is considered a martyr. Cyprian was beheaded. They are celebrated together because of their support for each other during their lives.

PRAYER

Saints Cornelius and Cyprian, you loved and led the Church in difficult times, and you remained faithful to the end. We ask for your prayers, that we too may remain faithful no matter the cost. Pray with us on your feast day: Merciful Father, grant us boldness and tenacity in living our faith. Give us the courage to follow the example of the saints and martyrs. May we use all our intelligence and gifts to bring others to you and your Church, fearlessly proclaiming your truth. Make us saints. Bless the Holy Father and all bishops, making them dedicated and effective shepherds. We ask this in the name of Jesus.

SEPTEMBER 17

Saint Hildegard of Bingen (1098–1179)

Saint Hildegard of Bingen was a Benedictine abbess and mystic who had a deep, contemplative prayer life. As a child, she began to have visions, which Saint Bernard of Clairvaux later encouraged Blessed Pope Eugene III to approve. She was entrusted to the care of Blessed Jutta at age eight and became a nun at fifteen. She became abbess of her community in 1136. When the Church hierarchy encouraged her to speak and teach, she obediently traveled throughout Germany to do so. She once said that "the spiritual life must be tended with great dedication." She also composed beautiful music, including hymns, canticles, and anthems, as well as scientific treatises. She used medicinal treatments, always using her many gifts to give glory to God. Because of her letters and theological writings, Pope Benedict XVI proclaimed her a Doctor of the Church in 2012, making her the fourth woman to be proclaimed a Doctor.

PRAYER
Saint Hildegard, thank you for your witness of using your gifts to glorify God and serve the Church. Pray with us on your feast: Gentle Father, give us obedience and humility to understand, accept, and use the gifts and talents you have given us for your glory and the good of our neighbor. Inspire us to appreciate music and to exercise our creativity in a loving way that calms and comforts the world. Bless the Benedictine order, keeping it faithful to you. We ask this in the name of Jesus. Amen.

SEPTEMBER 18

Saint Joseph of Cupertino (1602–1663)

Saint Joseph had such great difficulty with learning as a child that the people in his village thought he was mentally disabled. While this made it hard to for him to enter religious life, with God's help, he finally became a Franciscan priest. A humble soul, he took on the lowliest tasks. God gave him mystical gifts, including ecstasies, miracles, and the ability to rise off the ground (levitate) when praying. His fame as "the flying friar" caused disruption to the community life, so he was sent away to different communities, yet he bore all rejection with patience and love. His final words were: "Praised be God! Blessed be God! May the holy will of God be done!" Saint Joseph is the patron saint of astronauts, pilots, air travelers, and people with developmental disabilities.

PRAYER

Saint Joseph, you bore humiliation and rejection without complaint, and even with joy. Pray for us to seek only God with simplicity of heart, and on your feast day, pray with us: Dear Father, through the intercession of Saint Joseph, give us the virtue of humility. Inspire us to be patient with those who do not understand us. Grant us the grace to persevere, especially when we have difficulties with our concentration or memory. May we know your will and overcome all obstacles in carrying it out. Guide us to love and be patient with others who have learning or memory challenges, especially children. Teach us to forgive those who reject us. Bless the Franciscan order, keeping it faithful to you. We ask this in the name of Jesus. Amen.

SEPTEMBER 19

Saint Januarius (d. 304)

Saint Januarius was a bishop near what is now Naples, and one of many Christians martyred by the Roman Emperor Diocletian. We know almost nothing about his life, but he is said to have been killed along with several deacons. The executioners tried to burn him and, when that did not work, threw him and the others to the wild beasts in the arena, but they were again miraculously preserved. Finally, they were beheaded. His body was eventually brought to Naples. A vial containing his dried blood, which is kept in the Naples Cathedral, miraculously liquefies at different times each year. Saint Januarius is the patron saint of blood banks and blood donors and the city of Naples, Italy, and his intercession is invoked when there is danger of volcanic eruption.

PRAYER

Saint Januarius, you were a steadfast leader in the Church during difficult times, and you bravely gave your life for the Faith. On your feast day, pray for and with us: Gracious Father, through the intercession of Saint Januarius, give us the virtues of faith and courage. Inspire us to see our suffering as a gift that trains us spiritually and brings patience and empathy. Guide us to embrace the crosses you want us to carry, trusting that your will is only for our good. Be our strength in the spiritual battles we face. Bless all who suffer persecution for their faith in you. Guide and protect all bishops, making them true shepherds and virtuous leaders. We ask this in the name of Jesus. Amen.

SEPTEMBER 20

Saints Andrew Kim Taegon, Paul Chong Hasang, and Companions (1821–1846)

Saints Andrew Kim Taegon, Paul Chong, and their 101 companions were martyred in Korea during a brutal persecution that lasted from 1839 to 1867. Saint Andrew, son of Blessed Ignatius Kim, also a martyr, was the first native-born Korean to be ordained a priest. When he tried to help other missionaries enter the country, he was arrested, tortured, and killed. He bravely stated: "We have received baptism, entrance into the Church, and the honor of being called Christians. Yet what good will this do us if we are Christians in name only and not in fact?" Saint Paul was a married lay catechist. Saints Andrew and Paul and the other Martyrs of Korea represent the roughly ten thousand Christians martyred for their determination to keep the Faith during the persecutions of Christians in Korea.

PRAYER

Saints Andrew, Paul, and companions, pray for us to value our faith more than our lives, as you did. We ask you and all your fellow martyrs to pray with us on your feast: Heavenly Father, give us the courage and integrity to live as Christians, no matter the cost. May we help others come to the Faith by our words and witness. Enable us to stand firm in the face of persecution and fill us with the Holy Spirit. Bring us peace from our enemies. Protect those being persecuted for their faith in you. We ask this in the name of Jesus. Amen.

SEPTEMBER 21

Saint Matthew (d. first century)

Saint Matthew, a Jewish tax collector for the Roman government, was seen as a public sinner. His whole life changed when Jesus called him to be one of the twelve apostles, and he left everything and followed Him immediately. As we read in his Gospel: "As Jesus passed on from there, He saw a man called Matthew sitting at the tax booth, and He said to him, 'Follow me.' And he rose and followed Him" (Mt 9:9). He allowed Jesus to heal and convert him. It is believed that he wrote his gospel in the Hebrew language while he was in Antioch, and that he was martyred either in Persia or Ethiopia. Saint Matthew is the patron saint of accountants and bankers.

PRAYER

Saint Matthew, you left everything to follow Jesus and ultimately gave your life for Him and His Church. Pray for us to prize nothing except our friendship with Christ, and pray with us today: Righteous Father, inspire us to pray constantly and promptly obey when you ask anything of us. Grant us the grace to be careful stewards of our time, talent, and treasure, using our gifts for your glory and to serve others. Show your mercy to public sinners and give them the grace to repent and be converted. Guide all accountants to be fair and honest and all laborers to work justly for their wages. Heal, convert, deliver, and protect us. Confirm us in love and make us saints. We ask this in the name of Jesus. Amen.

Saint Thomas of Villanova (1488–1555)

Saint Thomas was a Spanish Augustinian priest, prior, and provincial, and court chaplain to Holy Roman Emperor Charles V. As provincial of his order, he sent Augustinian missionaries to the New World to evangelize. Eventually, against his own will, he became the archbishop of Valencia. He was revered for his piety and faithfulness, as well as his special love for the poor and their children, whom he often sheltered and fed in his own home. His love for the poor was so great that he was called the Beggar Bishop. Recognizing the importance of the virtue of humility, he once said: "Humility is the mother of many virtues because from it obedience, fear, reverence, patience, modesty, meekness, and peace are born. He who is humble easily obeys everyone, fears to offend anyone, is at peace with everyone, is kind with all."

PRAYER

Saint Thomas, you had many special gifts and were given much power in your life, but you remained humble, putting these gifts to the service of others. Pray with us on your feast day: Dear Father, give us the virtues of humility and kindness. Bless all evangelists and missionaries and give them success in the work you have given them to do. Help us to remain faithful in carrying out the duties in our state of life. Fill us with the Holy Spirit. Guide us to perform the works of mercy. Heal, convert, deliver, and protect us. Confirm us in love and make us saints. Bless the Augustinian order, keeping it faithful to you. We ask this in the name of Jesus. Amen.

SEPTEMBER 23

Saint Pius of Pietrelcina (1887–1968)

Saint Pius, better known as Padre Pio, was still a little boy when he began to have mystical visions. Later, as a Capuchin friar, he was the first priest ever to receive the stigmata. God granted him many spiritual gifts, including miracles, the ability to bilocate, and the ability to read people's souls in the confessional. Suffering from much spiritual warfare, he prayed the Rosary constantly, calling it a weapon against the powers of hell. He also suffered from the suspicion of others and was even made to stop his priestly service for a time. He built a hospital for the sick and spent long hours in the confessional. Because he often went into ecstasy while praying, his Masses were notoriously long. He famously urged Christians to "pray, hope, and don't worry. Worry is useless. What is needed is trust." Padre Pio is the patron saint invoked against stress.

PRAYER

Padre Pio, you showed by your example that we can trust God in all things. Pray for us to trust as you did, and pray with us on your feast day: Merciful Father, grant us the virtues of obedience and simplicity. Open our hearts to trust in your goodness and providence and remove any obstacles that keep us from trusting in you. May we always seek to serve others with complete selflessness. Grant us the grace to always be willing to pray for and assist others. Bless the Franciscan order, keeping it faithful to you. We ask this in the name of Jesus. Amen.

SEPTEMBER 24

Our Lady of Mercy

Something had to be done to ransom the Christians enslaved by the Islamic invaders of Spain. To provide for this need, Saint Peter Nolasco and his confessor, Saint Raymond of Penyafort, set up the Order of Our Lady of Mercy (known as the Mercedarians) with the help of King James of Aragon. Our Lady had appeared to each of these men separately and told them that the establishment of a religious order of men to free the captives would be pleasing to her Son. Courageously, they would either pay a ransom for the captives or, if necessary, be enslaved in their place. The feast of Our Lady of Mercy (formerly known as Our Lady of Ransom) was established in honor of Mary's special care for those in captivity.

PRAYER

Dear Father, through the intercession of Mother Mary, Saint Peter Nolasco, and the Mercedarian saints, give us the virtues of generosity, trust, and courage. Inspire us to perseveringly pray in intercession, especially for those enslaved in any way. Free all in captivity and convert their oppressors. May we always be ready to give every kind of help to others as we see their need. Protect those being persecuted for their faith. Enable us to have loyal and holy friends who help us in all the endeavors you ask us to undertake. Bless the Mercedarian order, keeping it faithful to you. We ask this in the name of Jesus. Amen.

SEPTEMBER 25

Saint Albert of Jerusalem (d. c. 1215)

Saint Albert, born in Parma, Italy, became a bishop of Vercelli. In this office, he mediated between Pope Clement III and Emperor Frederick I Barbarossa. He was eventually made the patriarch of Jerusalem, and despite the dangers (since Jerusalem at that time was governed by Muslims), he accepted the position. His wisdom and holiness won the respect of the Muslims. At the request of Saint Brocard and the hermits on Mount Carmel, he wrote a Rule of Life, which became the foundation for the Carmelite order. The rule, which was very rigorous, emphasizes the importance of silence and fasting. He was stabbed to death during a procession on the Feast of the Exaltation of the Holy Cross.

PRAYER

Saint Albert, you used your gifts of leadership and diplomacy to serve the Church, and you did not shy away from danger. On your feast day, we ask you to join us as we pray: Gentle Father, through the intercession of Saint Albert, give us the virtues of faithfulness and fortitude. Teach us to love silence and prayer and to offer sacrifices for love of you. Conform our thoughts, actions, and lives to Jesus, and help us to use all our talents and gifts for your service without reserve. Inspire us to truly live our faith in righteousness. Grant us the grace to be faithful to all the duties of our state in life. Make us saints. Bless the Carmelite order, keeping it faithful to you. We ask this in the name of Jesus. Amen.

SEPTEMBER 26

Saints Cosmas and Damian (d. c. 303)

Saints Cosmas and Damian were twin brothers from Arabia who both became physicians. They were so generous that they did not charge their patients for their services, and they earned the nickname *argyroi* ("the moneyless ones"). This allowed them to share their faith, and they were famous for curing people of all kinds of ailments. They were martyred in Syria with their brothers Anthimus, Euprepius, and Leontius under Roman Emperor Diocletian. Saints Cosmas and Damian are the patron saints of physicians, surgeons, pharmacists, barbers, chemists, dentists, and grocers, as well as the city of Florence, Italy.

PRAYER

Saints Cosmas and Damian, thank you for your generosity in serving God and your fellow man. On your feast day, pray for us and with us: Heavenly Father, strengthen in us the virtues of faith, generosity, and courage. May we use the gifts you have given us in service to others without holding anything back. Assist all physicians, surgeons, and pharmacists, and enable them to practice with a firm commitment to life. Guide us to live our faith and convictions with integrity. May we always act in good conscience and be protected in our rights of conscience. Protect those being persecuted for their faith in you. Heal, convert, deliver, and protect us, and make us saints. We ask this in the name of Jesus. Amen.

SEPTEMBER 27

Saint Vincent de Paul (1580–1660)

Saint Vincent de Paul, an ordinary farmer's boy from France, heard and followed God's call to the priesthood to serve everyone, especially the poor, sick, elderly, prisoners, and slaves. After his ordination, he was captured at sea by Turkish pirates and sold as a slave. He escaped two years later and returned to France. He labored tirelessly to serve the poor, founding hospitals, orphanages, and homes for the elderly. He founded the Vincentian priests to minister to spiritual poverty, and with Saint Louise de Marillac, he founded the Daughters of Charity. He even ransomed enslaved people! Saint Vincent is the patron saint of charitable societies.

PRAYER

Saint Vincent, in your compassion for the poor, you showed what it means to show true Christian love. On your feast day, pray for us and with us: Merciful Father, grant us the virtues of kindness and generosity. Give us merciful hearts that are attuned to the needs of the poor, sick, elderly, vulnerable, and those enslaved. Guide us to take all thoughts captive in Christ and rid us of negative, hopeless thoughts, inspiring us with confidence that you are taking care of us. Calm our minds and quiet our hearts. Make us saints. Bless the Vincentians and Daughters of Charity, keeping them faithful to you. We ask this in the name of Jesus. Amen.

SEPTEMBER 28

Saint Lorenzo Ruiz and Companions (1600–1637)

Saint Lorenzo Ruiz was the first Filipino to become a saint in the Catholic Church. An ordinary family man from the Philippines, he was falsely accused of murder and fled the country with Dominican priests and others who were going to Japan. Unfortunately, they arrived during the intense persecution of Christians in Japan by the Tokugawa Shogunate and were tortured and killed when they refused to renounce their faith. Before he died, he declared: "I am a Catholic, and I wholeheartedly accept death for God. If I had a thousand lives, I would offer them all to Him." Also called Saint Lorenzo of Manila, he and the others are some of the thousands of Martyrs of Japan. Saint Lorenzo is the patron saint of Filipino youth, altar servers, people working overseas, and the Philippines.

PRAYER

Saint Lorenzo and companions, you remained firm in your faith when you suffered misunderstanding and injustice, and even more when you were being tortured and killed for your fidelity to God. Pray with us on your feast day: Righteous Father, grant us the virtue of courage in living our faith. Give us magnanimous hearts willing to offer a thousand lives to you if we had them. Bring peace, reconciliation, and unity to all families, that they may be true domestic churches. Grant strength, patience, and protection to all those falsely accused and imprisoned and bring them justice. Guide us to pray for and assist all who are persecuted, imprisoned, and enslaved. Fill us with joy and make us saints. We ask this in the name of Jesus. Amen.

SEPTEMBER 29

Saints Michael, Gabriel, and Raphael, Archangels

This feast, traditionally known as Michaelmas, celebrates three archangels: Saints Michael, Gabriel, and Raphael. Saint Michael (whose name means "Who is like God?") drove out the devil and his legions from heaven after their defiance of God, and he is mentioned in Revelation 12:7–9. Saint Gabriel ("The strength of God") told Mary that she would be the mother of Jesus and also announced the birth of Saint John the Baptist (recorded in the Gospel of Luke). Saint Raphael ("God's remedy") helped Tobias find a wife and healed his father, Tobit (recorded in the book of Tobit). Together these angels are the patron saints of death, Germany, grocers, police officers, and radiologists. Saint Michael is the patron saint of police officers, sailors, peril at sea, battle, and those in temptation. Saint Gabriel is the patron saint of messengers and postal workers, broadcasters, and those who work in the telecommunications industry. Saint Raphael is the patron saint of druggists, those with eye diseases or blindness, lovers, safe journeys, and sheep raisers.

PRAYER

Saints Michael, Gabriel, and Raphael, pray for us to follow God's will in all that we do. On your feast day, pray with us: Heavenly Father, grant us the virtues of obedience and strength. May we always remember to call upon the archangels to help us. Guide us to find and fulfill our vocations and missions. Teach us how to live lives worthy of our calling. Make us saints. We ask this in the name of Jesus. Amen.

SEPTEMBER 30

Saint Jerome (345–420)

Saint Jerome was a priest, a spiritual director, and a master translator of Scripture. This Doctor of the Church was trained in the classics and taught and inspired by another Doctor of the Church, Saint Gregory of Nazianzus. He is perhaps best known for his work of translating the Bible into Latin, and he also wrote commentaries on Scripture, biographies, many letters, and translations of the works of Origen. He believed that "ignorance of Scripture is ignorance of Christ." While he struggled with anger and impatience, he worked very hard to cooperate with God's grace and gained the virtues of meekness and patience. Saint Jerome is the patron saint of librarians and Scripture scholars.

PRAYER

Saint Jerome, pray for us to use all our gifts for God's glory while overcoming our weaknesses and sins. On your feast day, pray with us: Gracious Father, grant us the virtues of patience and perseverance. Help us to study Scripture that we may know you through your word and help others to know you. Give us the discipline to study the truths of the Faith throughout our lives, and give us wise teachers to help us know you better. Calm our minds. Quiet our hearts. Enable us to cooperate with your grace to grow in virtue and overcome sin. Make us saints. We ask this in the name of Jesus. Amen.

OCTOBER

THE MONTH OF
THE HOLY ROSARY

OCTOBER 1

Saint Thérèse of the Child Jesus and the Holy Face (1873–1897)

Saint Thérèse was the youngest child in a family of saints. Her mother, Saint Zélie Martin, died when she was only four years old, and her older sister Pauline raised her before entering the Carmelite monastery. When Thérèse was fifteen years old, she was finally able to follow her sister's footsteps and became a Carmelite nun. In her short life, she developed her now famous "little way of childlike trust and surrender" to God, doing little things with great love. She was a member of the Archconfraternity of the Holy Face, making reparation for sins against the first three commandments through her devotion to the Holy Face of Jesus. She died after a painful battle with tuberculosis when she was twenty-four. Saint Thérèse is the patron saint of florists, missionaries, and pilots.

PRAYER

Saint Thérèse, you taught us that the path to God is through littleness, doing small things with great love. Teach us to be little, and pray for us and with us today: Dear Father, give us the virtues of charity, trust, and humility. Inspire us to confidently surrender to your will, and teach us to be little like Saint Thérèse. Grant us the gift of contemplation and make us saints who are always conscious of living before your Holy Face. We ask this in the name of Jesus. Amen.

OCTOBER 2

Holy Guardian Angels

The Holy Guardian Angels are assigned to protect us through this life and help bring us to heaven. From the moment we are conceived in our mother's womb, we have a guardian angel whose mission is to help us love God, do good, and become the saints God made us to be. The *Catechism* quotes Saint Basil, who wrote, "Beside each believer stands an angel as protector and shepherd leading him to life" (336). Saint Bernard of Clairvaux encourages us to remember our guardian angels, writing: "Let us be devoted and grateful to such great protectors; let us return their love and honor them as much as we can and should. … They who keep us in all our ways cannot be overpowered or led astray, much less lead us astray. They are loyal, prudent, powerful."

PRAYER

Holy Guardian Angels, thank you for your watchful presence and love. On your feast day, pray with us: Merciful Father, through the intercession of our guardian angels, give us all virtues and help us to grow in holiness. Help us to remember our guardian angels, to pray to them for help, and to cooperate with them as they strive to help us follow your will. With their guidance and help, make us saints. We ask this in the name of Jesus. Amen.

OCTOBER 3

Blessed Theodore Anne-Thérèse Guerin (1798–1856)

When Anne-Thérèse Guerin was fifteen years old, her father was murdered. Thus, she understood the trauma of loss and grief. Later, she joined the Sisters of Providence, where she took the religious name Theodore. She struggled with physical illness during her novitiate, which impacted her for the rest of her life. In 1840, she was sent to America with a small group of sisters to open a motherhouse and a school in Indiana. She established the Sisters of Providence of Saint Mary-of-the-Woods, opened schools, and set up two orphanages and a free pharmacy. Persevering despite many setbacks, she once wrote: "Have confidence in the Providence that so far has never failed us. The way is not yet clear. Grope along slowly. Do not press matters; be patient, be trustful." Because of her fidelity, she profoundly influenced Catholic education in the United States.

PRAYER

Mother Theodore Guerin, pray for us to have the courage and obedience to go wherever God sends us, just as you did. Pray with us today: Loving Father, grant us greater trust in your divine providence. Give us strength to do all that you ask of us and courage to do your will. Strengthen in us the cardinal virtues of prudence, temperance, fortitude, and justice. Comfort those suffering from loss, grief, and trauma, and help us to be a comforting presence to those who are grieving. Strengthen Catholic education. Bless the Sisters of Providence, keeping them faithful to you. We ask this in the name of Jesus. Amen.

OCTOBER 4

Saint Francis of Assisi (1181-1226)

Saint Francis, son of a wealthy merchant in Assisi, Italy, took part in a campaign against Perugia, a neighboring city, and he was captured and imprisoned, becoming very ill. After his release, as he slowly recovered, he underwent a profound conversion. He longed for simplicity, innocence, and detachment from material goods, and he wanted to live his life radically for God. One day as he prayed in the church of San Damiano, he heard Jesus speak to him from the crucifix, asking him to repair the Church. He began right away to repair the physical church of San Damiano, but over time he understood that the whole Church needed spiritual repair. He formed the Franciscan order to do this work by living in extreme poverty and sharing the love of Christ through works of mercy. Shortly before his death, he received the gift of the stigmata.

PRAYER

Saint Francis you sought always to be conformed fully to Christ, and you labored with generosity to repair the Church as He asked. Pray with us on your feast day: Gentle Father, give us the virtues of humility, simplicity, and magnanimity. Detach us from all worldly things and teach us to care only for your good opinion. Give us the grace to perform spiritual and corporal works of mercy and to care for your creation as good stewards. Make us saints. Bless the Franciscan order, keeping it faithful to you. We ask this in the name of Jesus. Amen.

OCTOBER 5

Saint Maria Faustina
Kowalska (1905–1938)

Saint Faustina, a Sister of Our Lady of Mercy in Poland, received many spiritual gifts, including visions, prophecy, bilocation, levitation, the ability to read souls, and the stigmata. On February 22, 1931, Jesus appeared to her and gave her the mission to promote the message of His Divine Mercy to the world. Following His direction, she had an image painted of the Divine Mercy with the caption, "Jesus, I trust in You." She recorded what Jesus told her in her *Diary*. God allowed her many sufferings in her life, and she accepted them bravely, saying: "The purer our love becomes, the less there will be within us for the flames of suffering to feed upon, and the suffering will cease to be suffering for us; it will become a delight! By the grace of God, ... I am never so happy as when I suffer for Jesus, whom I love with every beat of my heart."

PRAYER

Saint Faustina, thanks to your obedience to God, the world received the message of Divine Mercy. Pray for us to trust in God's great mercy, and pray with us: Merciful Father, give us the virtues of humility, simplicity, and obedience. Open our hearts to accept the reality of your unfathomable mercy and help us to trust completely in it. Grant us the gift of contemplation, that we may always know you are present. We thank you for all the ways in which you continually show us mercy, and we ask for the grace to show that mercy to others. We ask this in the name of Jesus. Amen.

OCTOBER 6

Blessed Marie Rose Durocher (1811–1849)

Blessed Marie Rose, whose baptismal name was Eulalie, was a pious girl from a large family, and she went to school in Montreal, Canada. She experienced so much sickness at boarding school that she had to return home after only two years. After her mother died, she went to live with her brother Theophile, a priest in Beloeil, and she managed his house for him. There she observed a severe shortage of schools, especially for girls. Her spiritual director, Fr. Pierro Telmon, OMI, and Bishop Ignace Bourget urged her to establish a congregation of teaching sisters. She obeyed and began the Sisters of the Holy Names of Jesus and Mary, serving as the order's first superior general. She died when she was only thirty-eight years old. Blessed Marie Rose is the patron saint of the sick.

PRAYER

Blessed Marie Rose, you saw the need for education for young people, and you took action. Pray for us to have the grace to step in and serve where we are needed. Pray with us on your feast: Gentle Father, help us to hear and obey your will for our lives. Grant us the grace to be faithful to all the duties of our state in life, and to step in and serve where we are needed. Guide teachers and parents to love the children entrusted to them, and to teach them with patience and kindness. Bring all children to knowledge and love of you. Bless the Sisters of the Holy Names of Jesus and Mary, keeping them faithful to you. We ask this in the name of Jesus. Amen.

OCTOBER 7

Our Lady of the Rosary

We celebrate the feast of Our Lady of the Rosary as a reminder of Mary's love for us and the power of her intercessory prayers. In 1571, Pope Saint Pius V called upon Christians to recite the Rosary, begging for Mother Mary's intercession and protection as the naval Battle of Lepanto raged. The Ottoman Turks posed a severe threat to Christian Europe, and this battle was a critical one. Thanks to Mary's protection, the Christians were victorious, keeping the Turks from overrunning the Christian nations. In thanksgiving, Pope Saint Pius V declared this a feast day, Our Lady of Victory, which later came to be known as Our Lady of the Rosary.

PRAYER

Our Lady of the Rosary, pray for us to have greater trust in your love and the power of your intercession. On your feast day, pray with us: Gracious Father, grant us all virtues and help us to imitate Mother Mary in all that we do. May we come to know her intimately and have confidence in her intercession and in the power of the Rosary. Grant us the grace to accept your will for our lives in trust and obedience, in imitation of Mary. Bring peace to the world through the Rosary, beginning in our marriages and families. Confirm us in love. Make us saints. Bless the pope and keep him faithful to you. We ask this in the name of Jesus. Amen.

OCTOBER 8

Saint Reparata (d. third century)

Saint Reparata was only twenty-one when she died in Palestine during the persecution of Christians under the Roman Emperor Decius. She was pressured to sacrifice to the Roman gods and give up her faith. When she would not deny Jesus and His Church, she was tortured and thrown into a furnace. God intervened, and she miraculously survived to give an even greater witness. When the authorities saw this, they tried again to force her to sacrifice to pagan gods and renounce her faith, which she steadfastly refused. Finally, she was killed by beheading. The Cathedral of Florence was named after her. Saint Reparata is the co-patron (with Saint John the Baptist) of Florence, Italy.

PRAYER

Saint Reparata, your steadfast faith in the face of death inspires us to live our faith boldly. Pray for us to love God with our whole hearts, and on your feast day pray with us: Righteous Father, help us to love you with all our hearts and grow in the virtues of faith and courage. May the witness of the martyrs inspire us to live our faith boldly and give us courage to hold fast to the truth we have received, and to share it with others. Keep us loyal to you and confident in your mercy, remembering that, no matter how young or old we are, we have your grace and power to remain faithful. Protect those being persecuted for their faith in you. Confirm us in love and make us saints. We ask this in the name of Jesus. Amen.

OCTOBER 9

Saint John Henry Newman (1801–1890)

Saint John Henry was born in London to a devout Anglican family. Throughout his life, he searched for the truth, and from a young age, he wanted to dedicate his life to God. He became an Anglican priest and, over time, a very influential preacher at Oxford, where he and some friends launched the Oxford Movement. As he continued to study his faith, he delved deeply into the writings of the Church Fathers, and as a result of this study, he converted to Catholicism. His conversion caused him much suffering, including losing his fellowship at Oxford. Yet he continued to write insightful theological works, which had a huge impact on the Church in England. He helped begin the Catholic University of Ireland and wrote many important works of theology, including *The Idea of a University*. Pope Leo XIII made him a cardinal in 1879, and he continued to serve the Church faithfully until his death at the age of eighty-nine.

PRAYER

Saint John Henry, your desire for truth led you to seek God with all your heart. Pray for us to have that same longing for truth, and pray with us: Heavenly Father, grant us a deep desire for truth and the honesty and the courage to seek and live according to the truth. Guide all teachers in Catholic schools, homeschools, and universities to be living examples of holiness and obedience to your Church. Help all Catholic universities to be faithful to the Church's teachings. We ask this in the name of Jesus. Amen.

OCTOBER 10

Saint Francis Borgia (1510–1572)

Saint Francis Borgia was one of the great Catholic reformers during the Protestant Reformation and one of the few male saints to have a double vocation. As a young man, he married Eleanor de Castro, and together they had eight children. He was a Spanish duke and member of the court of Holy Roman Emperor Charles V. Saints Peter of Alcantara and Peter Favre guided him to grow in his spiritual life. After Eleanor died, Francis became a Jesuit priest. He helped and advised Saint Ignatius of Loyola, and he founded many institutions and colleges, including the Gregorian University in Rome. Ever faithful, he served as general of the Jesuit order for seven years before he died, and he is sometimes called the second founder of the order. Saint Francis Borgia is the patron saint of earthquakes.

PRAYER

Saint Francis, pray for us to love God with all that we are and to follow His call wherever it leads us, just as you did. Pray with us on your feast day: Loving Father, through the intercession of Saint Francis Borgia, inspire us to reform our lives. Make our homes into true domestic churches, and grant us the gift of hospitality to attract others to you with kindness. Guide us to undertake everything you direct us to do with obedience and confidence in your help. Inspire more people to respond to their vocations to the priesthood and religious life. Make us saints. Bless the Jesuit order, keeping it faithful to you. We ask this in the name of Jesus. Amen.

OCTOBER 11

Saint John XXIII (1881-1963)

Pope Saint John XXIII was born Angelo Giuseppe Roncalli, a farm boy in Sotto il Monte, Italy. He became a Secular Franciscan while in seminary, was ordained a priest, and later served as a seminary professor. During World War II, he served as a diplomat in Turkey and Greece, and in this role, he helped save thousands of Jews. He was elected pope on October 28, 1959, taking as his motto *Oboedientia et Pax* ("Obedience and Peace"). He called the Second Vatican Council and promoted dialogue with Protestant denominations and other religions. Known as Good Pope John, he visited prisoners, the sick, the aged, and children. Pope Saint John XXIII is the patron saint of leaders and papal delegations.

PRAYER

Saint John, everyone who knew you recognized your goodness and your gifts, which you always used in service to God and the Church. On your feast day, pray with us: Loving Father, give us the virtues of joy, humor, and simplicity. Make us obedient, and help us to be hopeful and to see the good in all people and situations. Thank you for the gift of the Second Vatican Council, and guide us to continue to learn and live its teachings. Teach us to work for peace and justice, and form us into virtuous leaders. Make us saints. Bless our Holy Father, helping him to be a shepherd after the Sacred Heart of Jesus. We ask this in the name of Jesus. Amen.

OCTOBER 12

Blessed Carlo Acutis (1991–2006)

Blessed Carlo was an Italian teenager who loved computers. Even more than that, he loved God, and he combined these two loves by creating a website to document Eucharistic miracles. He wanted to help people believe in the truth of Jesus' Real Presence in the Eucharist. Carlo said that his life plan was "to always be united with Jesus," and he lived this out by serving the homeless, praying the Rosary, and attending daily Mass and Adoration. He made the Eucharist the center of his life and his "highway to heaven." His deep faith eventually converted his mother. When he was still very young, Carlo was diagnosed with leukemia, and he died when he was only fifteen. He is buried in Assisi near his beloved Saint Francis. The first millennial saint, he is the patron saint of computer programmers.

PRAYER

Blessed Carlo, your deep devotion reminds us of the treasure we have in the Eucharist. Pray with us on your feast day: Gentle Father, grant us reverence and longing for Jesus in the Eucharist. Make us joyful, even in the midst of suffering. Give us generous hearts that always seek to serve and uplift those around us. Instill in us a love for praying the Rosary, going to Mass, and doing works of mercy. Make us saints. We ask this in the name of Jesus. Amen.

OCTOBER 13

Saint Edward the Confessor (d. 1066)

Saint Edward, the son of King Ethelred the Unready and Emma of Normandy, was king of England from 1042 to 1066. He was married to Queen Edith, and he was a prayerful, just, and holy ruler who was loved by all. He loved to hunt and pray. Devoted to Saints Peter and John as his patrons, he built Westminster Abbey in honor of Saint Peter, as he wanted to make a pilgrimage to Saint Peter's in Rome but was never able to do so. He is buried in Westminster Abbey. Miracles occurred at his tomb, and many biographies have been written about him.

PRAYER

Saint Edward, you were faithful to your office even when it was difficult, and you were a wise and virtuous ruler for your people. Pray with us on your feast day: Heavenly Father, grant us the virtues of wisdom, commitment, and prudence. Inspire us to always be faithful to the duties of our state in life, ever faithful in small and large matters. Help all married couples to assist one another to heaven. Bless all who hold political office and make them just and faithful leaders. Form each of us into virtuous leaders in our spheres of influence. Confirm us in love and make us saints. We ask this in the name of Jesus. Amen.

OCTOBER 14

Pope Saint Callistus I (d. 222)

Pope Saint Callistus I began life as a slave in Rome. After his master freed him, he took charge of a bank, but later lost all the money and fled for his life before he was captured and sent to the mines in Sardinia. After his release, he eventually became a deacon of the Roman Church and served as director of the Christian cemetery on the Appian Way. He also served as secretary and advisor to Pope Zephyrinus, eventually succeeding him as pope. He was a faithful, merciful, and wise pope, known (and condemned by some) for his lenience toward sinners. He was martyred in a riot.

PRAYER
Saint Callistus, thank you for your witness of perseverance in difficulty and your exercise of wise leadership in the early Church. Pray with us on your feast: Heavenly Father, through the intercession of Pope Saint Callistus, give us the virtues of honesty and long-suffering. Inspire us to be responsible and hardworking, using all the talents and gifts you have given us for your glory. Grant justice to those falsely accused and free those enslaved. Teach us how to be patient and merciful to all who are weak in their faith. Heal, convert, deliver, and protect us. Form us into virtuous leaders. Bless the pope and bishops, making them strong pastors, true shepherds, and virtuous leaders. We ask this in the name of Jesus. Amen.

OCTOBER 15

Saint Teresa of Ávila (1515–1582)

As a child of seven, Saint Teresa set out for Africa to become a martyr, but her uncle found her and returned her to her home. Though she struggled with illness during her teens, she was inspired by the letters of Saint Jerome and the Carmelite Convent of the Incarnation in Ávila. Living there for many years, she came to long for a return to a more austere Rule of Life. Saints Francis Borgia and Peter of Alcantara advised her to follow the conviction God placed in her heart to reform the order, returning to strict observance of the ancient Carmelite rule. As a result, the Discalced Carmelites were born. Propelled by fierce determination and zeal, she founded sixteen convents throughout Spain and wrote many works on prayer and spirituality, despite suffering from migraine headaches and illness. Pope Saint Paul VI named her a Doctor of the Church in 1970, and she is known as the Doctor of Prayer.

PRAYER

Saint Teresa, pray for us to love the Lord as you did, with energy and fervor, despite setbacks. On your feast, pray with us: Gentle Father, give us the virtues of hope and joy. Inspire us to follow your will for our lives, not worrying about the trials or obstacles that come but persevering with determination and courage. Detach us from the opinions of others. Make us saints. Bless the Discalced Carmelite order, keeping it faithful to you. We ask this in the name of Jesus. Amen.

OCTOBER 16

Saint Margaret Mary
Alacoque (1647–1690)

After the death of her father, Saint Margaret Mary's family suffered from poor treatment by a relative, which caused them to lose their fortune. Later, her family was restored, and despite her mother's hesitations, she became a sister in the Convent of the Visitation at Paray le Monial, France. Jesus appeared to her in visions and asked her to promote the Work of Reparation through devotion to His Sacred Heart. This work led to her holiness, and she was crucial to it becoming known throughout the Church. She suffered criticism and rejection, yet she obeyed Jesus' request, "If you love Me, pray and sacrifice for those who do not believe in My love or do not care about My love." Because of her fidelity, devotion to the Sacred Heart spread throughout the Church, and many people observe the Five First Fridays in reparation for the coldness and indifference of Catholics toward the Eucharist.

PRAYER

Saint Margaret Mary, pray for us to have a deep devotion to the Sacred Heart of Jesus, and pray with us on your feast: Merciful Father, thank you for your great love, which we see poured out in the Sacred Heart. Inspire us to make reparation for our sins and for the coldness and indifference that so many show toward you. Teach us to love the Eucharist and to offer sacrifices for those who do not believe. Grant us a deep devotion to the Sacred Heart. Confirm us in love and make us saints. We ask this in the name of Jesus. Amen.

OCTOBER 17

Saint Ignatius of Antioch (d. c. 107)

Saint Ignatius likely knew Saint John the Apostle. The third bishop of Antioch, he is still known and beloved because of the seven letters he wrote on his way to martyrdom in Rome under escort of Roman Emperor Trajan's soldiers. These letters call for unity and stability in the Church, urging the faithful to "persevere in your concord and in your community prayers." His beautiful letter to his friend and fellow bishop, Saint Polycarp, is a testament to friendship and fraternity. He saw martyrdom as a blessing and privileged testimony to his friendship with God. He urged his fellow Christians not to try to stop his death, writing in his letter to the Romans: "I would rather die and come to Jesus Christ than be king over the entire earth. Him I seek who died for us; Him I love who rose again because of us." He was killed by wild beasts in the arena.

PRAYER

Saint Ignatius, you showed us by your example what true Christian fidelity looks like. Pray with us on your feast: Righteous Father, grant us the virtues of strength and courage, and inspire us to work for peace and unity within the Church and society. Give us the grace to be steadfast in suffering, offering up all our sufferings in union with Jesus. Teach us how to overcome obstacles, trials, and temptations gracefully and peacefully. Bless all bishops and help them to be true shepherds and virtuous leaders. We ask this in the name of Jesus. Amen.

OCTOBER 18

Saint Luke (d. first century)

Saint Luke had the privilege of being Saint Paul's assistant on many of his missionary trips. He faithfully accompanied Saint Paul to Rome for martyrdom, offering him comfort and support. A Gentile physician who converted to Christianity, he was also privileged to write one of the four Gospels, emphasizing Jesus' mercy, His consistent prayer, and His death for all people — Jews and Gentiles alike. Luke also wrote the Acts of the Apostles, in which he recorded the beginnings of the Church. He is said to have spent time with Jesus' mother, Mary, and after the death of Saint Paul in Rome, he returned to Greece, where he died. Saint Luke is the patron saint of physicians and painters.

PRAYER

Saint Luke, your writings have taught generations about Jesus and the early Church. On your feast day, pray for us and with us: Loving Father, help us to seek to know Jesus and give us a deep love for the Church. Make us true friends in joy and in sorrow. Grant us the grace to use all our gifts and talents for your glory. May we read your word with love and devotion and come to know Jesus and His Church more fully. Make us saints. We ask this in the name of Jesus. Amen.

OCTOBER 19

The North American
Martyrs (d. 1642–1649)

The eight North American martyrs were Jesuits who brought the Faith to the natives of North America. Saints Jean de Brebeuf, Isaac Jogues, Rene Goupil, Jean de Lalande, Charles Garnier, Anthony Daniel, Gabriel Lalemant, and Noel Chabanel suffered martyrdom in Auriesville, New York, and Quebec, Canada. Their faithful ministry to the Huron Native Americans resulted in conversions and baptisms. But many of the other native people distrusted them, and they were captured, tortured, and killed. They are buried on the sites where their martyrdoms occurred, and their shrines witness to their zeal for God and love of neighbor. These martyrs are the patron saints of North America.

PRAYER

North American martyrs, thank you for willingly giving your lives to bring the Faith to the native peoples of North America. On your feast, pray with us: Loving Father, grant us the virtues of courage and zeal, and give us missionary hearts that desire to share your love with the world. Inspire us through the example of these holy martyrs to faithfully fulfill the work you have given us. Give us the grace to follow your will in everything and zeal to make you known in all parts of the world. Make us saints. Bless the Jesuit order, keeping it faithful to you. We ask this in the name of Jesus. Amen.

OCTOBER 20

Saint Magdalene of Nagasaki (d. 1634)

Saint Magdalene, born into a Christian family in Japan, lost both her parents when they were martyred for their faith. Even so, she willingly assisted the Augustinian friars as a catechist and interpreter and then became a lay member of their order. Her Augustinian spiritual directors were all martyred, and eventually she declared herself a Christian before the authorities. She was tortured and finally killed for clinging to her faith. She is one of the martyrs of Japan.

PRAYER

Saint Magdalene, you held fast to your faith and shared it with others, despite the dangers and the painful loss of so many people you loved. Pray with us on your feast: Merciful Father, inspire us to imitate the martyrs in their love and loyalty to you. Teach us to serve you faithfully, no matter the cost, enduring whatever may come for love of you. Allow us to see and deeply understand that it is a privilege to serve you and to suffer for love of you. Bless and guide all catechists and give them the wisdom to share the Faith. Bless the Augustinian order, keeping it faithful to you. We ask this in the name of Jesus. Amen.

OCTOBER 21

Blessed Karl of Austria (1887–1922)

Blessed Karl was the last emperor of Austria-Hungary, ascending the throne during World War I. He was also a devoted husband and father. He saw his duty clearly and told his wife, Queen Zita, on their marriage day, "Now we must help each other get to heaven." Together, they had eight children and created a beautiful domestic church. A holy Catholic monarch, he was deeply devoted to the Holy Eucharist and Mother Mary, and he had a profound love for the poor. He also participated in the Work of Reparation through Devotion to the Sacred Heart of Jesus. He labored to bring about peace and an end to World War I. Afterward, he was banished with his family and died in poverty when he was only thirty-four. His last words were: "Thy holy will be done. Jesus, Jesus, come! Yes — yes. My Jesus, as you will it — Jesus."

PRAYER

Blessed Karl, pray for us to fulfill the duties of our state in life with generosity and fidelity, as you did, and pray with us: Dear Father, grant us fidelity and dedication in all that we do, fulfilling the duties of our state in life. Help us to keep our eyes fixed on heaven as our goal. Guide us to clearly see your will and faithfully follow it. Bless married couples, and help them to communicate well and to support and assist each other to heaven. Enable parents to teach, and encourage their children to gain virtue and grow in holiness. Make all families holy, and make us saints. We ask this in the name of Jesus. Amen.

OCTOBER 22

Saint John Paul II (1920-2005)

Saint John Paul II, born Karol Wojtyla in Wadowice, Poland, survived the Nazi and Communist occupations of Poland and deeply understood oppression, abuse, trauma, grief, and loss. Gifted in sports, languages, poetry, and theater, he studied for the priesthood in an underground seminary and, after his ordination, went to Rome to pursue doctoral studies in theology. He became an auxiliary bishop of Krakow in 1958 and attended the Second Vatican Council, after which he became a cardinal. Elected pope in 1978 (the first Polish pope), he wrote more, traveled more, and canonized more people than any previous pope. He was instrumental in the fall of communism in Eastern Europe. More than five million people attended his funeral in 2005, so powerful was his witness.

PRAYER

Saint John Paul II, pray for us to love God and the Church as you did, and to give our lives in their service. Pray with us today: Loving Father, give us the virtues we need to live out the call you have for us, especially humility, obedience, and magnanimity. Help us to love you and your Church, and inspire us to put all our talents at the service of the Church. Heal our minds and deliver us from communism and all false ideologies and religions. Make us saints. Bless the pope and all bishops, making them virtuous leaders. We ask this in the name of Jesus. Amen.

OCTOBER 23

Saint John of Capistrano (1385–1456)

Saint John was born in Capistrano, Italy, and he studied law in Perugia after the death of his father. Gifted with great intelligence and talents, he eventually became governor of Perugia. After war and imprisonment, he turned his life completely around and, receiving a dispensation from his marriage, became a Franciscan priest, studying theology with Saint Bernardine of Siena. He reorganized and stabilized the Franciscan order. He preached to great crowds and had a reputation as healer of the sick. With General John Hunyadi of Hungary, he led a crusade against the Turks and died afterward. Saint John of Capistrano is the patron saint of jurists, judges, and military chaplains.

PRAYER

Saint John, you generously used your gifts and talents in positions of leadership in the Church. On your feast day, pray for us and with us: Gracious Father, through the intercession of Saint John, give us the virtues of initiative, diligence, and perseverance. Inspire us to know, protect, and defend our Catholic Faith. Guide us in following the Church's social teaching, and keep us consistent in our prayer and work for the vulnerable. Form us into virtuous leaders and make us saints. Bless the Franciscan order, keeping it faithful to you. We ask this in the name of Jesus. Amen.

OCTOBER 24

Saint Anthony Mary Claret (1807–1870)

Saint Anthony Mary was a weaver from Catalonia, Spain, who followed God's call to become a priest and eventually founder of the Missionary Sons of the Immaculate Heart of Mary (known as the Claretians) and the Apostolic Training Institute of the Immaculate Conception (the Claretian nuns). Appointed archbishop of Santiago, Cuba, he labored for reform, helping poor people to own their own farms and allowing enslaved people to learn the Faith, as well as issuing moral reforms. He faced opposition and was slandered by enemies. Returning to Spain, he became the chaplain for Queen Isabella II, attended Vatican I, and established the Religious Publishing House, publishing two hundred books and pamphlets. He gave missions and retreats throughout Spain on the Eucharist and devotion to Mother Mary. He was known for miracles and prophecy.

PRAYER

Saint Anthony Mary, pray for us to answer God's call and serve the Church with fidelity, as you did. On your feast day, pray with us: Merciful Father, grant us the courage to exercise leadership in the Church and to serve with fidelity. Strengthen our commitment to the Church's teachings on social justice. Bless the country of Cuba and free it from communism. Bring justice for those who have been slandered and falsely accused. Make us saints. Bless all bishops, making them true shepherds and virtuous leaders. Bless the Claretian order, keeping it faithful to you. We ask this in the name of Jesus. Amen.

OCTOBER 25

Blessed Martyrs of the Brothers Hospitallers of Saint John of God (1936–1939)

The Blessed Martyrs of the Brothers Hospitallers of Saint John of God were seventy-one men who were martyred for their Catholic Faith by the revolutionary communist forces during the Spanish Civil War. These brothers, ranging in age from eighteen to seventy-five, came from Spain and Colombia to work with the sick at different places in Spain. They each had different responsibilities. Harassed by the communists and stripped of their clerical outfits, they were finally killed. Pope Saint John Paul II, who beatified them, praised their loyalty to God and witness to the Catholic Faith.

PRAYER

Blessed Martyrs, pray for us to have your courage and commitment to the Faith, even in the face of danger. On your feast day, pray with us: Heavenly Father, give us the virtues we need to remain faithful to you to the end, especially fortitude, and inspire us to live upright and holy lives that witness powerfully to your love. Make us fearless in proclaiming the Gospel and the truths of our faith. Strengthen our desire to do your will. Grant us courage every day to face the spiritual battles that come. Purify our hearts and minds. Confirm us in love and make us saints. We ask this in the name of Jesus. Amen.

Blessed José Gregorio Hernández Cisneros (1864–1919)

Blessed José Gregorio was born into a loving Venezuelan home, of which he later said, "My mother taught me virtue from the cradle, she made me grow in the knowledge of God and gave me charity as a guide." He desired to become a priest but was not able to do so because of ill health. Instead, he became a physician. He attended daily Mass and became a Secular Franciscan. Kind and cheerful, he was highly esteemed for helping others, even those who could not pay him, and he became known as the doctor of the poor. He died after being struck by a car while delivering medicine to one of his patients. He is the first Venezuelan layperson to be beatified, and his relics are in Our Lady of Candelaria Church in Caracas. He is the patron of medical students, diagnosticians, doctors, and medical patients.

PRAYER

Blessed José Gregorio, thank you for your life of service, exemplifying the works of mercy. Pray with us now: Righteous Father, give us deep prayer lives as the foundation of lives of service. Give us zeal and empathy, and help us to consistently perform the spiritual and corporal works of mercy, helping wherever we can to ease the suffering of others. Show us your face in the poor and the vulnerable, especially the preborn. Free those who are enslaved to addictions or suffering from any illness. Make families holy domestic churches, and give mothers the special gift of helping their children to learn their faith and gain virtue. Bless the Franciscan order, keeping it faithful to you. We ask this in the name of Jesus. Amen.

OCTOBER 27

Saint Frumentius (d. c. 380)

Saint Frumentius, along with his brother Saint Aedesius, barely escaped death as they traveled by ship to Abyssinia. When their ship was attacked in the Port of Ethiopia, they were taken captive and brought as slaves to the king of Axum. Later, after they had gained their freedom and risen to positions of trust in the court, Saint Aedesius returned to their native country and became a priest. Saint Frumentius appealed to Saint Athanasius for help converting the Ethiopian nation. Seeing his zeal, Saint Athanasius promptly consecrated him a bishop to carry out the work. Saint Frumentius baptized the new King Ezana, helping the Ethiopian Aksumite nation to become Christian. Tirelessly preaching and working miracles, he was so beloved that the people called him *Abuna* (Our Father). Saint Frumentius is the patron saint of Ethiopia.

PRAYER

Saint Frumentius, you generously shared your gifts and labored for the souls of the people who took you captive. Pray for us to have such generosity, and pray with us today: Loving Father, help us always to follow the saints' examples of love, loyalty, and generosity to you and our neighbor. Guide us to pray for priests and bishops. Teach us how to evangelize others through our witness and our words, in even the most difficult circumstances. Confirm us in love and make us saints. Bless all bishops, making them true shepherds and virtuous leaders. We ask this in the name of Jesus. Amen.

OCTOBER 28

Saints Simon and Jude (d. first century)

Saints Simon the Zealot and Jude Thaddeus answered Jesus' call to follow Him as apostles. Simon had to let the Lord change his expectations, showing him that the Messiah would not be a political liberator of the Jewish people, but a spiritual liberator of the whole world. After Jesus' ascension, Simon preached in Egypt. Jude, the brother of James the Less and Jesus' cousin, preached in Mesopotamia. Later, they both preached the Gospel in Persia and were martyred. Saint Jude wrote the Letter of Jude in the New Testament and is buried in Saint Peter's Basilica. Saint Jude is the patron saint of hopeless causes and desperate situations.

PRAYER

Saints Simon and Jude, your love for Jesus and His Church led you to far-off places and ultimately to martyrdom. On your feast day, pray with us: Gracious Father, give us the virtues of strong faith, zeal, and boldness in proclaiming the Gospel. Grant us the grace to know, uphold, and defend our faith, especially when we are in trials and difficult situations, never giving in to fear. Guide us to find and fulfill our vocations and missions. Make us loyal friends of Jesus who follow Him wherever He leads. Strengthen our desire to do your will. Confirm us in love and make us saints. We ask this in the name of Jesus. Amen.

OCTOBER 29

Blessed Chiara Badano (1971–1990)

Blessed Chiara was a very active young person from Italy who loved singing, dancing, and sports, especially tennis and swimming. She was involved in the Focolare Movement and had a profound experience of Jesus at sixteen that led her to want to be a religious. She noted: "I discovered that Jesus forsaken is the key to unity with God, and I want to choose Him as my only spouse. I want to be ready to welcome Him when He comes. To prefer Him above all else." She proved her love for Jesus after she was diagnosed with a rare and painful form of bone cancer. She prayed, "It's for you, Jesus; if you want it, I want it too." For her burial, she chose a white wedding dress, preparing to go to Jesus, her spouse. She died when she was only nineteen years old, and in 2010 she became the first person in Generation X to be beatified. Blessed Chiara is a patron of athletes.

PRAYER

Blessed Chiara, thank you for showing us how to accept God's will and surrender to Him in everything. Pray with us on your feast day: Gentle Father, give us Blessed Chiara's virtues of acceptance, trust, and surrender. Fill us with your love and life, and help us to bring that to everyone we meet. Bless and heal those who have cancer and their caregivers. Bless the Focolare Movement. We ask this in the name of Jesus. Amen.

OCTOBER 30

Saints Marcellus and Cassian (d. 298)

Saint Marcellus, a Roman soldier who converted to the Christian faith, was no longer able to participate in pagan celebrations and objected when required to do so. He was forced to debate to save his life. Courageously, he upheld the Faith with confidence and eloquence. However, the Romans' closed hearts refused to hear what he so faithfully proclaimed, and he was executed. Seeing this injustice, and deeply moved by his words and example, Saint Cassian, who had been appointed notary to the trial, refused to report on it and was also martyred.

PRAYER
Saints Marcellus and Cassian, you refused to act against your consciences, and you willingly suffered martyrdom as a result. Pray for us to be steadfast in our faith as you were, and pray with us: Merciful Father, grant us the virtues of commitment, strength, and courage. Inspire us to stand fast for our faith in all circumstances, not giving in to fear or going against our consciences, even if we are persecuted for it. Guide us to pray for the conversion of sinners and for those who do not know you. Make us skilled defenders, and give us wisdom and eloquence when sharing our faith. Open the hearts of all people to hear about your love and be converted. Protect those being persecuted for their faith. Bring us peace from our enemies. Make us saints. We ask this in the name of Jesus. Amen.

OCTOBER 31

Saint Wolfgang (924–994)

Saint Wolfgang, born in Swabia, Germany, was very busy as a bishop, preacher, teacher, reformer, and Benedictine monk. He reformed monasteries, convents, and the Diocese of Regensburg, and he worked tirelessly to help the poor. A devoted Benedictine, even after he became a bishop he continued wearing his religious habit and practicing the religious life. Along with Saints Ulrich and Conrad, he was influential in Germany. He tutored, encouraged, and inspired Saint Henry II, who later became the Holy Roman Emperor. Saint Wolfgang is the patron saint of carpenters, woodcarvers, and the city of Regensburg, Germany, and his intercession is invoked against internal bleeding, paralysis, stomach diseases, and strokes.

PRAYER

Saint Wolfgang, you exercised leadership in the Church and served the Lord with great generosity. On your feast, pray for us to be generous in service, and pray with us: Heavenly Father, may we always work diligently to reform ourselves, our families, the Church, and society. Grant us a profound love for everyone, especially the poor and vulnerable. Guide us to perform the works of mercy, and surround us with your mercy. Fill us with joy to encourage and inspire others. Bless all bishops, making them true shepherds and virtuous leaders. Bless the Benedictine order, keeping it faithful to you. We ask this in the name of Jesus. Amen.

NOVEMBER

THE MONTH OF
THE SOULS IN PURGATORY

NOVEMBER 1

All Saints' Day

The feast of All Saints unites us with the communion of saints in heaven. On this holy day of obligation, we go to Mass and thank God for all the heroic people who have gone before us and are now before the Holy Face of Jesus. We also ask them to pray for us, that we might join them when we die. Saint Bernard of Clairvaux said of the saints and their prayers for us: "While we desire to be in their company, we must also earnestly seek to share in their glory. ... Therefore, we should aim at attaining this glory with a wholehearted and prudent desire. That we may rightly hope and strive for such blessedness, we must above all seek the prayers of the saints. Thus, what is beyond our own powers to obtain will be granted through their intercession."

PRAYER
Dear Saints in heaven, pray for us today, that we might follow where you have led, confident in God's grace to make us saints. Pray with us on this feast: Heavenly Father, strengthen in us all the virtues, especially faith, hope, and charity, which is the perfection of all the virtues. Grant us the grace always to strive for the highest, most heroic degree of charity and mercy. Guide us to practice the spiritual and corporal works of mercy. Assist us in finding and fulfilling our vocations and missions. Heal, deliver, convert, and protect us. Guard and protect your Church. Make us saints. We ask this in the name of Jesus. Amen.

NOVEMBER 2

All Souls' Day

The feast of All Souls was first observed by Saint Odilo, Abbot of Cluny. Today the Church prays for the souls in purgatory. Purgatory is part of God's mercy for us. As the *Catechism* teaches: "All who die in God's grace and friendship, but still imperfectly purified, are indeed assured of their eternal salvation; but after death they undergo purification, so as to achieve the holiness necessary to enter the joy of heaven. The Church gives the name *Purgatory* to this final purification of the elect, which is entirely different from the punishment of the damned" (1030–1031). The souls in purgatory are part of the communion of saints, and we on earth can aid them by our intercessory prayers as a spiritual work of mercy. November is dedicated to praying for the Holy Souls. We can gain a plenary indulgence (under the usual conditions) for praying at cemeteries from November 1 to 8.

PRAYER

Jesus reportedly showed Saint Gertrude many souls being released from purgatory when she said the following prayer. Let us join in praying for the holy souls today: Eternal Father, we offer you the most precious blood of your Divine Son, Jesus, in union with all the Masses said throughout the world today, for all the holy souls in purgatory, for sinners everywhere, for sinners in the universal Church, for those in our own home, and in our family. Amen.

NOVEMBER 3

Saint Martin de Porres (1579–1639)

Saint Martin was born illegitimately to Juan de Porres, a Spanish soldier, and Anna Velasquez, a freed Panamanian slave woman, in Lima, Peru. When he was twelve years old, he became apprenticed to a barber, learning this important trade, which included medical healing techniques. At fifteen, he became a lay Dominican brother, spending hours each day in prayer, penance, and helping the sick by founding a hospital and orphanage. He was especially sensitive to the poor because he grew up in poverty. He also cared for slaves and provided spiritual direction. He and Saint Rose of Lima were friends who inspired each other to greater holiness. Likewise, he was friends with Saint John Macias, who lived at another Dominican priory not far away. Martin was spiritually gifted by God in many ways, including levitation, bilocation, and special ways with animals. Saint Martin is the patron saint of race relations and interracial justice.

PRAYER

Saint Martin de Porres, thank you for your witness of God's compassionate love. Pray with us on your feast: Loving Father, help us to grow in humility and charity, that we might always compassionately serve others for love of you. Make us highly sensitive and responsive to the needs of others, especially the poor and vulnerable. Grant us devotion to the Holy Eucharist, and give us a deep desire for penance and sacrifice. Free and heal all who are in slavery and root out any prejudice in our hearts. We ask this in the name of Jesus. Amen.

NOVEMBER 4

Saint Charles Borromeo (1538–1584)

Saint Charles grew up in a castle in Italy, hunting and playing the cello and chess as a boy. A true Catholic reformer, he became bishop of Milan and instituted the reforms of the Council of Trent, helping to write the Catechism, breviary, and missal of the Council. He founded the Oblates of Saint Ambrose (now known as the Oblates of Saint Charles) to help him. Through famine and plague, he served and sacrificed, selling everything, feeding thousands, and caring for the sick. As a leader in the Church, he was inspiring, influential, and effective. He once preached in a sermon: "Stay quiet with God. Do not spend your time in useless chatter … realize that … nothing is more necessary than meditation. We must meditate before, during, and after everything we do. … In this way, all that you do becomes a work of love." Saint Charles is the patron saint of catechists, public libraries, seminaries, boarding schools, the Borromean nursing congregation, the Borromeo societies, Salzburg University, and Lugano and Basel dioceses.

PRAYER

Saint Charles, your leadership in the Church in confusing times continues to guide and inspire us in our own day. Pray for us and with us: Dear Father, help us to use our gifts and talents to effectively build up your Church. Inspire us to pray and meditate daily, and draw us into a deep union with you. Bless all bishops, making them true shepherds and virtuous leaders who guide and inspire us in confusing times like Saint Charles did. Bless the Oblates of Saint Charles, keeping them faithful to you. We ask this in the name of Jesus. Amen.

NOVEMBER 5

Saints Elizabeth and Zechariah (d. first century)

Saint Elizabeth was the first to identify Mary, newly pregnant, as the mother of the savior (see Lk 1:41–42), thus confirming what the angel Gabriel had told Mary at the Annunciation. Elizabeth was a cousin of Mary while her husband, Saint Zechariah, was a priest in the Temple. Saint Gabriel the archangel announced to Zechariah that Elizabeth, though past childbearing years and believed to be barren, would have a miraculous pregnancy. But Zechariah doubted this, and God rendered him unable to speak again until his son, Saint John the Baptist, was born. When Zechariah finally spoke again, his words were a magnificent canticle of praise, which the Church prays every morning in the Liturgy of the Hours.

PRAYER

Saints Elizabeth and Zechariah, in your example, we see God's faithfulness, even in the face of our doubts and fears. Pray with us on your feast: Gracious Father, grant us joy in serving you and gratitude for the gifts you give, even when we do not see them as soon as we would wish. Inspire us to see your faithfulness in the face of doubts and fears, to believe in your miracles, and to hope in your mercy. Grant us the grace to recognize you in the Eucharist, and remove all doubt from our hearts and minds. Make us cling to your promises and trust in your provision. Hear and answer the prayers of those who want children but cannot conceive. We ask this in the name of Jesus. Amen.

NOVEMBER 6

Saint Leonard of Noblac (496–559)

Saint Leonard was a Frankish noble who became a disciple of Saint Remigius (a bishop known as the Apostle to the Franks). Obedient to God's call, he left the courtly life and became a hermit. Later he founded Noblac Abbey, later known as Saint-Leonard Abbey, in Limoges, France. He prayed in silence and solitude and helped his monks to grow in holiness. Imprisoned Crusaders invoked his help for freedom from their Muslim captors. Saint Leonard is the patron saint of blacksmiths, coppersmiths, miners, farmers, grocers, locksmiths, porters, prisoners of war, women in labor, childbirth, horses, and barrel-makers, and his intercession is invoked against burglars and robbers.

PRAYER

Saint Leonard, pray for us to willingly leave all worldly things behind to follow wherever the Lord leads. On your feast day, pray for us and with us: Loving Father, grant us generosity in serving you and our neighbor. Give us a deep desire for prayer. Make us contemplatives in action, serving others through the spiritual and corporal works of mercy. Assist us in doing intentional (not random) acts of kindness. Encourage us to use all our talents and gifts for your service without reserve and willingly leave all worldly things to follow where you lead. Grant us saintly friends who inspire and encourage us, and make us saints. We ask this in the name of Jesus. Amen.

NOVEMBER 7

Saint Peter Wu Guosheng (1768–1814)

Saint Peter Wu, a courageous young man, was not afraid to speak out against injustice and oppression. He knew he could make a difference in the plight of the poor and oppressed, and he did! A faithful husband and entrepreneur, he ran a successful inn in China. Converted by missionaries to the Christian faith, he zealously wished for other Chinese people to come to the Faith. He became a leader among the converts and a catechist for six hundred people. He was arrested, imprisoned, and tortured for his faith. Yet, even then, he still encouraged other prisoners, and wrote to his wife, "Be loyal to the Lord, accept his will." Witnesses say that his last inspiring words were: "Heaven, heaven, my true home! I see my heavenly Mother and my guardian angel coming to take me home." He is one of the thousands of the Martyrs of China.

PRAYER

Saint Peter Wu, thank you for your witness to living out your faith and zealously seeking to draw others to it. Pray with us on your feast day: Righteous Father, help us to imitate all the martyrs in their understanding that love is self-sacrificial and at your service and that of our neighbor. Guide us to see and act out against injustice and oppression. Give us holy friends to help us along the journey. Make us saints. Bless and protect all missionaries and catechists. We ask this in the name of Jesus. Amen.

NOVEMBER 8

Blessed John Duns Scotus (d. 1308)

Blessed John, born in Scotland, became a Franciscan, studying theology at Oxford and the University of Paris. A brilliant theologian, philosopher, and teacher, he used engaging analogies and examples to help people understand complex issues. His explanation of free will, the Blessed Mother's Immaculate Conception, and the Incarnation of Jesus are still referred to by theologians. He taught at Oxford, the University of Paris, and Cologne. Although not as well known as Saint Thomas Aquinas, he was widely respected and is called the Subtle Doctor. He is the father of the Scotist School of Theology.

PRAYER

Blessed John, thank you for using your intellectual gifts to serve the Church and draw souls closer to God. Pray for us to use our gifts for God's glory, and pray with us: Merciful Father, grant us thoughtfulness and eloquence. Inspire us to study our faith with joy and gratitude. Send the Holy Spirit to open our minds and hearts, that we might understand the Church's teachings and help others understand. Grant teachers the grace to be true examples of holiness. Instill in us the confidence and ability to communicate our faith to others. Confirm us in love and make us saints. Bless the Franciscan order, keeping it faithful to you. We ask this in the name of Jesus. Amen.

NOVEMBER 9

Saint Benignus of Armagh (d. 467)

Saint Benignus followed God's call to be Saint Patrick's disciple and help convert Ireland to the Catholic Faith. A native of Ireland and son of Chief Sechnan, he was known as Patrick's psalmist because of his superb singing voice. His gentle soul helped convert people in many other parts of Ireland, including Clare, Kerry, and Connaught. He helped with formulating the Irish Code of Laws, the Psalter of Cashel, and the Book of Rights, and he attended the synod that passed a canon recognizing the See of Peter (the pope) as the final decision-maker in difficult cases. Benignus became bishop of Ireland after Saint Patrick.

PRAYER

Saint Benignus, your gentle, wise leadership helped you carry on Saint Patrick's work of bringing Ireland into the Faith. Pray with us on your feast: Gentle Father, may we always use all our talents and gifts in your service without reserve. Inspire us to listen to your voice and obey your will. Grant us the grace of evangelizing, and guide us to sing for joy at your mercies. Enable us to be loyal, courageous, and faithful friends. Form us into virtuous leaders. Confirm us in love and make us saints. Bless all bishops, making them true shepherds and virtuous leaders. We ask this in the name of Jesus. Amen.

NOVEMBER 10

Saint Leo the Great (d. 461)

Pope Saint Leo exercised incredible leadership in the Church. He negotiated with Attila the Hun and encouraged him not to attack Rome, and later, when the Vandals plundered the city, he convinced them not to burn it. He was influential in convoking the Council of Chalcedon, and his writing and teaching were instrumental for the Council's teaching that Jesus had two natures, one human and one divine. He also helped clarify and strengthen the authority of the pope over the universal Church. Throughout his life, Pope Leo wrote powerful explanations of the Faith that earned him the title Doctor of the Church.

PRAYER

Saint Leo, you provided clarity and leadership in the Church as the western world was in turmoil. On your feast day, pray for the Church and pray with us: Gracious Father, teach us to work faithfully for peace and unity in the Church. Grant us the virtues of wisdom and prudence, and inspire us to pray daily to find and fulfill our vocations and missions. Make us truly holy and self-disciplined. Grant us the grace of determination to restore what has been perverted or destroyed in ourselves, our families, the Church, and the world. Instill in us the gift of hospitality that constantly encourages and uplifts others. Grant us many and holy priests. Bless the pope and all bishops, making them true shepherds and virtuous leaders. We ask this in the name of Jesus. Amen.

NOVEMBER 11

Saint Martin of Tours (316–397)

Saint Martin, a Roman soldier, gave half his cloak to a beggar. Later, Jesus revealed himself to Martin in a dream, wearing the portion of the cloak. Moved, Martin became a Christian and left the army. He became a disciple of Saint Hilary of Poitiers, with whom he founded the first monastic community in Gaul (what is now France). He labored as an exorcist and helped Saint Hilary defend orthodoxy against the Arian heresy. Later made bishop of Tours, he taught and cured his people and destroyed pagan temples. Centuries later, the French Revolutionists attempted to destroy his tomb and thought they succeeded, but Venerable Leo Dupont found it and built a cathedral on the spot. Martin's relics are preserved there today. Saint Martin of Tours is the patron saint of horsemen, tailors, and the impoverished.

PRAYER

Saint Martin, pray for us to respond with generosity to God's call, wherever it takes us, as you did. Pray with us today: Loving Father, make us wise and courageous in accomplishing the work you have given us to do. Inspire us to faithfully perform our duties with care and attention to detail. Form in us a strong and persistent prayer life and give us the gift of contemplation. Inspire us to believe in your miracles and hope in your mercy. Make us saints. Bless all bishops, making them competent administrators and virtuous leaders. We ask this in the name of Jesus. Amen.

NOVEMBER 12

Saint Josaphat (1580–1623)

Saint Josaphat began reading the breviary prayers daily as a child. Raised in the Orthodox church in Poland (not in communion with Rome), he studied theology. Jesuit Father Fabricius gave him instructions, and he came into communion with Rome and entered the Basilian order at the Monastery of the Trinity in Vilna. Attracted by his virtue and holiness, people came to seek his guidance. Later, he was appointed archbishop of Polotsk, Lithuania, where he restored churches and helped reform the clergy by writing Rules and catechisms. Through it all, he fasted, prayed, and worked for the reunion of the Orthodox with Rome. He was martyred, and many miracles occurred. His murderers were converted, and his body was found to be incorrupt five years after his death. Saint Josaphat is the patron saint of the reunion between the Orthodox and Catholic churches.

PRAYER

Saint Josaphat, your tireless work and prayer for unity between the eastern and western churches helped pave the way for dialogue. Pray for unity in the Church, and pray with us now: Merciful Father, inspire us to work for peace and unity between the Catholic and Orthodox churches. Guide us to pray unceasingly until you allow this to happen. Teach us our faith and show us how to be hospitable to others, always hoping to welcome all souls home to your Church. Bless all bishops, and make them wise and virtuous leaders. We ask this in the name of Jesus. Amen.

NOVEMBER 13

Saint Frances Xavier
Cabrini (1850–1917)

Saint Frances Xavier Cabrini, born in Italy, had a deep fear of drowning, yet in obedience to the work God gave her, she crossed the Atlantic Ocean more than thirty times to serve Catholics in America. She founded a religious order, the Missionary Sisters of the Sacred Heart of Jesus, and she and her sisters labored to serve the Italian immigrant community in the United States. She started sixty-seven schools, hospitals, orphanages, and other institutions to serve the poor and vulnerable in America. She became a U.S. citizen and was the first to be canonized. Saint Frances is the patron saint of hospital administrators, immigrants, and impossible causes.

PRAYER
Saint Frances Xavier Cabrini, you served your people with a mother's heart, helping the vulnerable with courage and strength. Pray for us and with us on your feast: Gentle Father, grant us greater trust, determination, and fervor in your service. Inspire us to pray with faith and have a deep trust in your providence and care for us. Grant us the grace to know our vocations and fulfill our missions, faithfully and resolutely carrying out all the work you have given us to do. Teach us how to persist in overcoming any obstacles and trials we may face in completing your work. Make us saints. Bless the Missionary Sisters of the Sacred Heart of Jesus and keep them faithful to you. We ask this in the name of Jesus. Amen.

NOVEMBER 14

Saint Lawrence O'Toole (1128–1180)

Saint Lawrence O'Toole grew up in Dublin, Ireland, the son of a chief. When he was ten years old, he was abducted and held captive for two years by King Dermot Macmurrough of Leinster, who hated his father. He was then given into the care of the bishop of Glendalough, and when he was still a young man, he became abbot of Glendalough monastery. He had a deep prayer life and practiced penance and mortification. Appointed archbishop of Dublin, he proved himself to be a builder and peacemaker, helping negotiate treaties, including the Treaty of Windsor. He built the famous Cathedral of the Holy Trinity (later renamed Christ Church Cathedral) and enacted many reforms. Saint Lawrence O'Toole is the patron saint of Dublin, where a relic of his heart resides in Christ Church Cathedral.

PRAYER

Saint Lawrence, in spite of great difficulties in your childhood, you gave your life to the Lord with generosity and trust. Pray for us to do the same, and pray with us today: Loving Father, heal the wounds of division and grant peace and unity between the Catholic Church and Protestant denominations. Guide us to reform our lives, families, Church, and society. Teach us how to make amends and to practice penance for our sins. Free and heal the kidnapped, enslaved, and unjustly imprisoned, and protect those being persecuted for their faith. Bless all bishops, making them true shepherds and virtuous leaders. We ask this in the name of Jesus. Amen.

NOVEMBER 15

Saint Albert the Great (1206–1280)

Saint Albert, born and raised in Swabia, Germany, entered the Dominican order as a young man, and eventually became a professor at the University of Paris, where he taught and encouraged Saint Thomas Aquinas. He taught philosophy and began the work of showing how Aristotle's human wisdom could be helpful for forming and guiding Catholic thought. Saint Thomas would eventually carry on this great work. He was such a curious, avid learner and committed teacher that he spent twenty years working on a compendium of all knowledge, including topics ranging from natural science and theology to geography and mathematics. A gifted leader, he served as Dominican provincial and bishop of Regensburg, Germany. A Doctor of the Church, he is called Universal Doctor. Saint Albert is the patron saint of scientists, naturalists, philosophers, miners, and Cologne University.

PRAYER

Saint Albert, your love of wisdom led you to marvel at God's creation, and it gave you a deep desire to share what you knew with others. On your feast day, pray for us and with us: Gracious Father, grant us studiousness and a great love for wisdom. Inspire in us a deep love of learning, and help us never to give up seeking to know more about you and our faith. Guide us to study Scripture, the *Catechism*, and the Fathers and Doctors of the Church. Make us loving, compassionate, and encouraging people. Bless all bishops, helping them to be true shepherds and virtuous leaders. Bless the Dominican order, keeping it faithful to you. We ask this in the name of Jesus. Amen.

NOVEMBER 16

Saint Gertrude the Great (1256–1302)

Saint Gertrude entered the Benedictine monastery at Helfta, Germany when she was only five years old. Gifted in languages, literature, and understanding of Scripture, she experienced many visions of Jesus, beginning when she was twenty-six. The Lord taught her the works of reparation through devotion to the Sacred Heart and the Holy Face, saying: "Let the soul who is desirous of advancing in perfection hasten with great alacrity to My Sacred Heart. But he who yearns to make even greater progress and to *mount still higher* on the wings of desire must rise with the swiftness of an eagle and *hover about* My Sacred Face, supported like a seraph on the wings of a magnanimous love." Known as the Herald of Divine Love because of her many books, letters, and prayers, she is the only female saint honored as "the Great." Saint Gertrude is the patron saint of the West Indies.

PRAYER

Saint Gertrude, thank you for telling the world about God's great, merciful love. Pray for us to have greater trust in God, and pray with us today: Merciful Father, give us the same virtues you gave to Saint Gertrude. Inspire us to pray for the Holy Souls in Purgatory and to participate in the works of reparation. Grant the grace of conversion to all who need it. Inspire us to believe in your miracles and hope in your mercy. Bless the Benedictine order, keeping it faithful to you. We ask this in the name of Jesus. Amen.

NOVEMBER 17

Saint Elizabeth of Hungary (1207–1231)

Saint Elizabeth, a Hungarian princess, was so holy when she died at only twenty-three that she was canonized just four years later. Despite being born to nobility, she chose to live a simple life of penance, mortification, and service to the poor, even feeding them at her castle gate. After her husband, King Louis IV, died, his family threw her and her three children out, compounding her grief. She became a Secular Franciscan and founded a hospital for the poor and sick at Marburg. Her spiritual director, Conrad of Marburg, wrote of her: "Apart from those active good works, I declare before God that I have seldom seen a more contemplative woman. When she was coming from private prayer, some religious men and women often saw her face shining marvelously and light coming from her eyes like the rays of the sun." Saint Elizabeth is the patron saint of bakers, Secular Franciscans, and Catholic Charities.

PRAYER

Saint Elizabeth, your love for the poor and vulnerable knew no bounds, and you served them faithfully throughout your life. Pray for us to have that same generosity, and pray with us now: Loving Father, grant us the virtues of compassion and forgiveness. Give us the same generosity and service of the poor that Saint Elizabeth had. Inspire us to pray always and grant us the gift of contemplation. Provide us with wise spiritual directors and guide us to perform the works of mercy. Make us saints. Bless the Franciscan order, keeping it faithful to you. We ask this in the name of Jesus. Amen.

NOVEMBER 18

Saint Rose-Philippine Duchesne (1769–1852)

Saint Rose-Philippine was born in Grenoble, France, and she felt inspired as a child to become a missionary and work among the Native Americans. Entering the Visitation order in her late teens, she suffered through the French Revolution, returning to her home when her religious order was suppressed. Still, she cared for the poor and sick and educated children. Later, she joined the Society of the Sacred Heart with Saint Madeleine Sophie Barat. Her dream to work among Native Americans finally came true in 1818, when she and several sisters were sent to America. Over time, she founded convents in Louisiana and Missouri. She also served for a time in Kansas, assisting the Potawatomi, who called her "Woman-Who-Always-Prays" because she remained still in prayer for so long that objects the children placed on her habit would still be in the same spot hours later.

PRAYER

Saint Rose-Philippine, pray for us to have some of the missionary zeal that you possessed, and pray with us on your feast: Gentle Father, grant us humility and courage, that we might carry out your will without holding anything back. Bless and protect all orphans and people in need, and grant us the grace to be generous to them with our time, talent, and treasure. Help us to find and fulfill our vocations and missions. Conform our thoughts, actions, and lives to Jesus in total surrender to you. Bless the Sisters of the Sacred Heart, keeping them faithful to you. We ask this in the name of Jesus. Amen.

NOVEMBER 19

Saint Nerses the Great (333–373)

Saint Nerses was born in Armenia, and as a young man he married an Armenian princess. After she died, he became a priest, then bishop of the Armenians. Inspired by Saint Basil the Great, he set out to reform the Church in Armenia, founding monasteries, calling synods, and building hospitals. He was exiled for speaking out against King Arshak, who killed his own wife. Later, when he returned to Armenia after Arshak's death, he refused to allow the new ruler, King Pap, into the Church because of his sinful behavior, and he was poisoned for remaining faithful in his role as leader in the Church. His son, Saint Isaac the Great, continued his reforms.

PRAYER

Saint Nerses, you exercised fearless leadership in the Church, even when it meant suffering and danger. Pray for us to be strong leaders, and pray with us on your feast day: Loving Father, give us all the graces we need to imitate the martyrs and become strong leaders in the Faith. May we never deny you, but always hold firm to your promise that you never abandon those who love, live, and die for you. Grant us the grace to live as martyrs of love even if we are never called to give our physical lives. Guide us to be faithful to all the duties of our state in life. Grant us many holy priests. Bless the pope and all bishops, making them true shepherds and virtuous leaders. Make us saints. We ask this in the name of Jesus. Amen.

NOVEMBER 20

Saint Felix of Valois (1127–1212)

As a young adult, Saint Felix gave away everything to live as a hermit in prayer and contemplation. Saint John of Matha, to whom he gave spiritual direction, convinced him to help found an order to ransom Christian captives in the Middle East, North Africa, and Spain. Together, Felix and John traveled to Rome and obtained permission to establish this new order from Pope Innocent III. The pope appointed Saint John the superior general and named it the Order of the Holy Trinity for the Redemption of Captives, known as the Trinitarians. The order spread throughout Europe and the world, carrying on the work of ransoming captives and performing works of mercy. Saint Felix established the motherhouse of the order, the monastery of Cerfroi, and he set up a monastery in Paris attached to the Basilica of Saint Mathurin.

PRAYER

Saint Felix, thank you for your example of obedience to the will of God. Pray for us to follow God's will for our lives, and pray with us: Dear Father, give us the virtues of mercy, compassion, and justice. Inspire us to pray always and give us the gift of contemplation. Make us contemplatives in action. Conform our thoughts, actions, and lives to Jesus in total surrender to you, using all our talents and gifts in your service, without reserve. Fill us with joy. Grant us the courage to assist those who are enslaved, unjustly imprisoned, and abused. Free and heal them and convert their oppressors. Protect all who are being persecuted for their faith. Make us saints. Bless the Trinitarian order, keeping faithful to you. We ask this in the name of Jesus. Amen.

The Presentation of the Blessed Virgin Mary

The Presentation of the Blessed Virgin Mary is a double feast, celebrating both the Church of Saint Mary in Jerusalem and the presentation of Mary in the Temple when she was three years old. According to legend, Mary's parents, Saints Joachim and Anne, were so thankful for the gift of a child after many years of infertility that they promised to dedicate their child to God. Together with Mother Mary's Immaculate Conception and her birth, this feast shows how God's plan for holiness was always operating in her, and it provides encouragement for us to follow her example of surrender to His will.

PRAYER

Mother Mary, pray for us to give ourselves to God fully and with complete trust, as you did. Pray with us on your feast: Gracious Father, on this feast of Mary's presentation in the Temple, we ask you to grant us all her virtues, drawing us closer to yourself each day. Inspire in us the willingness and determination to make the journey of surrender to your will, growing in holiness and becoming the saints you created us to be. May we encourage and help others on their journeys, too. Form us to be empathetic and compassionate, and make us saints. We ask this in the name of Jesus. Amen.

NOVEMBER 22

Saint Cecilia (d. c. third century)

Saint Cecilia, believed to be a Roman patrician raised as a Christian, prayed, fasted, and practiced mortification (wearing a coarse garment under her clothes). She was forced to marry, although she had consecrated herself to God, but her husband, Valerianus, allowed her to remain a virgin after seeing a vision of an angel beside her. He converted and was baptized, and he and his brother, Tiburtius, were beheaded for zealously burying other martyrs. Due to their fortitude during their martyrdom, a Roman official named Maximus was converted, and he was martyred as well. Saint Cecilia continued the corporal work of mercy by burying their bodies, and she was also arrested and martyred by beheading. This is the account we have beginning in the fifth century. Saint Cecilia is the patron saint of music and musicians.

PRAYER

Saint Cecilia, thank you for your witness of faithfulness unto death. Pray for us to courageously hold fast to our faith, and pray with us on your feast day: Gentle Father, give us the virtues of the martyrs, and inspire us to learn our faith as well as possible to be able to live and defend it. Help us to find our vocations and fulfill our missions, and keep us faithful to the duties of our state in life. Remembering that only the pure shall see the face of God, keep us pure and holy. Confirm us in love and make us saints. Bless all musicians, helping them to use their music for your glory. We ask this in the name of Jesus. Amen.

NOVEMBER 23

Blessed Miguel Agustín Pro (1891–1927)

Blessed Miguel was born in Mexico to a pious family. While he was in formation to become a Jesuit priest, the communists took over the Mexican government, banning religion, destroying Church property, and killing priests. Miguel fled the country and was eventually ordained a priest in Belgium. He then returned to Mexico and faithfully served Catholics there, offering the sacraments and instruction in the Faith while remaining in hiding from the government. Finally, he was arrested when someone betrayed his whereabouts and falsely accused him of a plot to kill the communist dictator. He was executed by firing squad, forgiving his executioners. His last words echoed the cries of the other Mexican martyrs: "*Viva Cristo Rey!*" ("Long live Christ the King!")

PRAYER
Blessed Miguel, you were generous and courageous in returning to serve the flock in Mexico despite the dangers. We pray to have that same zeal for the Faith, and we ask you to pray with us today: Righteous Father, make us steadfast and brave, so that we will praise you and serve you faithfully without counting the cost. Bless and comfort all the people around the world who are dying for the Faith. Deliver and protect all who are falsely accused. Keep us patient and steadfast during trials and teach us how to forgive our persecutors. Bless the Jesuit order, keeping it faithful to you. We ask this in the name of Jesus. Amen.

NOVEMBER 24

Saint Andrew Dũng-Lạc (1785–1839) and 116 Companions

Saint Andrew Dũng-Lạc was born in Vietnam to a poor family. When he was still quite young, he became a Christian, a catechist, and later, a priest, even though it was very dangerous at that time in Vietnam. Several times, he was captured and tortured but eventually released. He even changed his name from Dũng to Lạc so as not to be detected. Finally, he was arrested and martyred with another priest, Saint Peter Thi. Pope Saint John Paul II beatified 117 martyrs, of which ninety-six were Vietnamese, eleven were Spanish Dominicans, and ten were French priests of the Paris Foreign Missions Society. These martyrs represent hundreds of thousands of Catholics who died or were imprisoned or exiled in Vietnam between 1630 and 1862.

PRAYER

Saint Andrew Dũng-Lạc and companions, your love for God and His Church led you to give your life. We want to imitate you in your courageous generosity, and we ask you to pray with us: Gracious Father, make us generous, strong, and courageous like the martyrs in our faith, willing to die for love of you if necessary. Grant us the grace to remain steadfast and loyal to you and the Church no matter what. Protect those being persecuted for their faith. Bless the Dominican order and the Paris Mission Society, keeping them faithful to you. We ask this in the name of Jesus. Amen.

NOVEMBER 25

Saint Catherine of Alexandria (d. c. 310)

Saint Catherine was a Christian noblewoman from Alexandria who was arrested because she debated with a Roman citizen about whether the Roman Emperor Maxentius was just or unjust in his persecution of Christians. She was so persuasive in her argument against the persecutions that she converted many listening pagans to Christianity! She successfully persuaded many other pagans to convert to Christianity during her trials, and an angel protected her from a horrible death on a spiked wheel. Finally, she was beheaded. It is said that an angel took her body to Mount Sinai, where Saint Catherine's Monastery was built. Saint Catherine is the patron saint of Christian philosophers, theologians, pupils, teachers, librarians, bakers, barbers, and the Universities of Paris and Valais, and her intercession is invoked against drowning and head and tongue diseases.

PRAYER
Saint Catherine, pray for us to be able to defend the Faith with wisdom and conviction, as you did, no matter what dangers we may face. Pray with us on your feast: Loving Father, grant us wisdom to know you and to make you known. Inspire us to believe in your miracles and hope in your mercy. Guide us to enthusiastically evangelize so all may come to know you. Give us the grace of eloquence in speaking and writing, that we may know, profess, and preach your Gospel. Help us become self-disciplined, living witnesses of your love and faithfulness. Make us saints. We ask this in the name of Jesus. Amen.

NOVEMBER 26

Saint Leonard of Port Maurice (d. 1751)

Saint Leonard was a Franciscan priest from Italy, and his preaching was so effective and popular that he had to deliver sermons outdoors to accommodate the thousands who came to his missions. He promoted devotion to the Sacred Heart of Jesus, the Blessed Sacrament, the Stations of the Cross, and the Immaculate Conception. Before he began this fruitful ministry, he planned to travel as a missionary to China, but he suffered from serious illness for four years that prevented him from leaving Italy. Over the course of his life, he wrote letters and treatises, as well as sermons and devotionals. Saint Leonard is the patron saint of parish missions.

PRAYER

Saint Leonard, your life and mission did not turn out as you planned, yet you remained faithful, and God blessed your labors. Pray for us to be faithful to God's call, even when it doesn't match our plans, and pray with us today: Loving Father, grant us a deep desire to become as holy as you will and make us faithful to your call, even when we don't understand it. Grant us the grace to grow in virtue and remove vice as we strive to detach from the things of this world and attach only to you. Guide and assist retreat masters and leaders of parish missions, and bless all who benefit from their work. Grant us wise spiritual directors. Enable us to be joyful witnesses. Strengthen our desire to do your will, and make us saints. Bless the Franciscan order, keeping it faithful to you. We ask this in the name of Jesus. Amen.

NOVEMBER 27

Saint Maximus of Riez (d. 460)

Saint Maximus had the privilege of having Saints Hilary and Honoratus as friends. He followed God's call to become a monk at Lerins in France, where he eventually became abbot of the monastery. Although he preferred the solitude and contemplative life of the monastery to the active life of a bishop, like Saint Gregory Nazianzen, when he was made Bishop Riez, as a true contemplative in action, he prayed and then faithfully fulfilled his duties.

PRAYER

Saint Maximus, thank you for serving the Church through prayer, leadership, and constant fidelity to God's will. Pray with us today: Gracious Father, grant us the gift of silence to hear your voice and discern your will for our lives. Dispose our hearts to deep intimacy with you. Grant us the gift of contemplation and good works, which are the fruit of prayer. Guide us to faithfully fulfill all our duties, especially when they are difficult. Grant us friends who encourage and support us, and make us saints. Bless all bishops, making them true shepherds and virtuous leaders. We ask this in the name of Jesus. Amen.

NOVEMBER 28

Saint Catherine Labouré (1806–1876)

Saint Catherine's beautiful incorrupt body lies in a glass case beneath the altar of the Chapel of Our Lady of the Miraculous Medal in Paris. When you visit, if you look closely, you can see that her eyes are open! After losing her mother when she was only eight years old, she unselfishly became responsible for her younger brothers and sisters. When she grew up, she entered the Sisters of Charity of Saint Vincent de Paul (Daughters of Charity) to help care for the elderly, sick, and disabled. While she was still a novice, she began to experience visions of Mother Mary, and she obeyed Mary's request to make the Miraculous Medal, with the words, "O Mary, conceived without sin, pray for us who have recourse to thee." Mary promised Catherine, "All who wear [the Miraculous Medal] will receive great graces." Saint Catherine is the patron saint of the elderly, the infirm, and the Miraculous Medal.

PRAYER

Saint Catherine, pray for us to follow God's will always and to grow in devotion to the Blessed Mother, allowing her to lead us to Jesus. Pray with us today: Gracious Father, give us true joy that no one can take away. Thank you for giving us Mary as our mother. Help us to seek her protection always. Grant us the grace to advance rapidly in holiness. Guide us to pray and do works of mercy, and make us saints. Bless the Sisters of Charity of Saint Vincent de Paul, keeping them faithful to you. We ask this in the name of Jesus. Amen.

NOVEMBER 29

Saint Saturninus (d. c. 257)

Saint Saturninus was the first bishop of the area that is now Toulouse, France. He obeyed God's will and converted many people through his excellent preaching and the miracles God performed through him. He could silence demons in the pagan temple as he passed, which enraged the temple priests. They demanded he offer sacrifice, and he steadfastly refused, standing firm in his faith, saying: "I adore only one God, and to Him I am ready to offer a sacrifice of praise. Your gods are devils, and are more delighted with the sacrifice of your souls than with those of your bullocks. How can I fear them who, as you acknowledge, tremble before a Christian?" The pagan priests were enraged, and he was martyred.

PRAYER

Saint Saturninus, your faithfulness and courage silenced demons and turned hearts to God. Pray that we might imitate you, and pray with us: Righteous Father, grant us the virtues of magnanimity, constancy, and obedience. Inspire us through the witness of the martyrs to love you and others in a sacrificial manner. May we evangelize others through our words and the witness of our lives, and may we always remain steadfast in our faith. Send us many and holy priests who help us to live in virtue. Bless all bishops, making them true shepherds and virtuous leaders. We ask this in the name of Jesus. Amen.

NOVEMBER 30

Saint Andrew

Saint Andrew the Apostle introduced his brother, Simon (who became Saint Peter), to Jesus. Andrew had been a fisherman in Galilee and a disciple of Saint John the Baptist, and then he met Jesus. The Gospel of John records: "One of the two who heard John speak and followed Jesus was Andrew, Simon Peter's brother. He first found his own brother Simon and said to him, 'We have found the Messiah' (which means Christ). He brought him to Jesus" (1:40–42). The son of Jonas, Andrew is also recorded in Scripture as finding the boy with the loaves and fishes that Jesus used to feed the five thousand. After Pentecost, Andrew preached in Turkey, Russia, and Greece, and he was martyred around AD 70. Saint Andrew is the patron saint of fishermen, miners, butchers, rope-makers, water carriers, weddings, and many countries, including Russia, Greece, Scotland, and Spain.

PRAYER

Saint Andrew, help us to bring our loved ones to Jesus just as you did, and pray for us to have humility and loyalty like yours. Pray with us on your feast: Gracious Father, make us loyal, obedient, and courageous in our Christian lives that we might bring others to you. Detach us from everything that holds us back from promptly following you. Help us deny our selfish desires and use our talents and gifts in your service, without reserve. Grant us perseverance in prayer for all who have left the Church. Bless and protect all bishops, making them wise shepherds and virtuous leaders. We ask this in the name of Jesus. Amen.

DECEMBER

THE MONTH OF
THE IMMACULATE CONCEPTION

DECEMBER 1

Venerable Leo Dupont (1797–1876)

When Venerable Leo was only fourteen, he suffered an accident to his hand that later prevented him from becoming a priest. He became a lawyer, married, and had a child. After his wife died, he moved to Tours, France, and assisted the Discalced Carmelite nuns, publishing pamphlets about Jesus' appearances to one of their sisters, Sister Marie Pierre, about the work of reparation through devotion to the Holy Face of Jesus. When Archbishop Morlot suppressed public propagation of this devotion, placing an interdict on Sister Marie Pierre's writings, Leo obediently ceased to distribute them. He privately hung a picture of the Holy Face of Jesus in his home, lit a lamp before it, and over time, people received healings of many kinds by praying in front of it. Pope Pius IX called Venerable Leo the greatest miracle worker of modern times. Archbishop Colet, Marlot's successor, lifted the interdict, allowing the devotion to spread, and Pope Leo XIII later established the Archconfraternity of the Holy Face.

PRAYER

Venerable Leo, thank you for your faithfulness in spreading the devotion to Jesus' Holy Face. Pray with us today: Merciful Father, give us contrition for our sins and a deep desire to make reparation for them and those of the whole world. Help us to trust in your mercy, which we see written so clearly in the face of Jesus, and to believe in your power to work miracles. Make us channels of your grace and healing in the world. We ask this in the name of Jesus. Amen.

DECEMBER 2

Blessed John van Ruysbroeck (1293–1381)

Blessed John grew up near Brussels, Belgium, and began to study for the priesthood under his uncle, a priest in Brussels, when he was only eleven years old. After he was ordained, he served for a time as a parish priest at the church of Saint Gudula in Brussels, writing and teaching against heresies and false mysticism that were gaining ground at that time. Later, he helped establish a community of Canons Regular at Groenendaal, and he became prior. He was known for his holiness, intense prayer, contemplation, and ecstasies. An excellent spiritual director, he was sought out by those seeking greater holiness. He was also a great mystical writer, and his writings are considered spiritual classics, including *The Kingdom of the Divine Lovers*, *The Twelve Beguines*, and *A Mirror of Eternal Blessedness*.

PRAYER

Blessed John, your gifts of prayer, spiritual direction, and writing were of great service to the Church. Pray that we might grow in our understanding of divine truth, and pray with us today: Righteous Father, grant us true wisdom and the gift of a consistent prayer life, that we may always know your presence and understand your divine truth. Strengthen our desire to do your will, and give success to our ministries and work for your glory. Grant us wise spiritual directors. Purify our hearts and minds, and make us saints. Bless all priests and religious, keeping them faithful to you. We ask this in the name of Jesus. Amen.

DECEMBER 3

Saint Francis Xavier (1506–1552)

Saint Francis Xavier, a Spanish nobleman, gave up a promising career as a professor at the prestigious University of Paris after making the Spiritual Exercises of Saint Ignatius of Loyola. He helped Saint Ignatius found the Jesuit order and became one of its first priests. Following God's call, he served as a missionary to India, Sri Lanka, Malaysia, and Japan, baptizing and performing miracles (including healings and even raising people from the dead). He died trying to reach China, and his body was taken back to Goa, India. His missions were so successful that he is called Apostle of the East Indies, Apostle of Japan, and the next greatest missionary after Saint Paul. His incorrupt body lies in Goa in the Church of the Good Jesus. Saint Francis Xavier is the patron saint of foreign missions, missionaries, and Japan.

PRAYER

Saint Francis Xavier, thank you for your witness of intense love for God that led you across the globe to share the Good News. On your feast day, pray with us: Gentle Father, grant us the virtues we need to be true missionaries, especially strong faith, burning charity, zeal, and confidence in you. Grant us success in the work you have given us to do, and give us a missionary spirit to share your love with the world. Allow us to be a ministry of presence for others, listening deeply to them, especially the lonely. Bless the Jesuit order, keeping it faithful to you. We ask this in the name of Jesus. Amen.

DECEMBER 4

Saint John Damascene (676–749)

Saint John Damascene, born in Damascus, Syria, is the last of the Greek Fathers. He served for a time in public office in Damascus, which was under Muslim rule. When the Byzantine Emperor Leo the Isaurian began to outlaw veneration of sacred images, John wrote and taught that the veneration of tangible things, such as icons, statues, and medals, helps the spiritual life to grow, since we are physical creatures. His teaching against iconoclasm greatly helped the Church, though he suffered much for it. Retiring from public life, he entered a monastery, and his many writings, including books, hymns, and poems, flowed from his deep prayer life and study. He was named a Doctor of the Church by Pope Leo XIII.

PRAYER

Saint John, even when it led to suffering, you taught the truth with courage and compassion. Pray for us to do the same, and pray with us today: Loving Father, grant us a deep love for the truth and desire to proclaim it, no matter what it may cost us. Grant us respect and veneration for sacred images and teach us to use them correctly to grow more deeply in our prayer life. Teach us to study our faith daily that we may learn the teachings of the Church. Give us obedient minds and hearts and keep us from complaining, even when faced with difficult circumstances. May we share the Faith with wisdom and lead others to you, never causing scandal in our words or actions. We ask this in the name of Jesus. Amen.

DECEMBER 5

Saint Sabas (439–532)

Saint Sabas was such a faithful monk that he was appointed the superior of all the hermits in the Holy Land. Harshly treated as a child by an aunt and uncle, he found solace in the Flavinia monastery where, as a disciple of Saint Euthymius, he worked on self-mastery, growing in all the virtues, and overcoming his passions. He practiced silence and consistent prayer, living the life of a hermit. After some years, as his reputation spread and others joined him, he began founding monasteries for them, including one in Palestine. Opposing the heresy of Monophysitism, he taught the truth that Jesus Christ had two natures, one human and one divine.

PRAYER

Saint Sabas, thank you for helping others to experience God in silence and solitude. Pray with us on your feast day: Dear Father, inspire us to practice silence, mortification, and faithful, consistent, persevering prayer. Grant us the gift of contemplation. Teach us how to overcome our passions and persevere in gaining virtue and self-mastery. Keep us faithful to the duties of our state in life. Never let us justify bad thoughts, words, or actions. Allow us to forgive those who have wronged or abused us without putting ourselves back in harm's way. Assist us in effectively opposing all heresies. Guide all spiritual directors to help those who rely on them. Make us saints. We ask this in the name of Jesus. Amen.

DECEMBER 6

Saint Nicholas of Myra (d. c. 350)

Saint Nicholas, a young boy from present-day Turkey, became a kind, generous, and beloved priest, then bishop. Many stories of his generosity have come down to us — most famously, he is said to have saved three young women from slavery by secretly leaving bags of gold for their dowries in the stockings they hung by the fire. In honor of his feast day, children traditionally leave out their shoes the night before and receive small gifts and treats in them. The inspiration for the popular figure of Santa Claus, he once said, "The giver of every perfect gift has called us to mimic God's giving, by grace, through faith, and this is not of ourselves." Pilgrims flock to Bari, Italy, his burial site. Saint Nicholas is the patron saint of children, sailors in storms, Russia, Greece, Apulia, Sicily, and Lorraine.

PRAYER

Saint Nicholas, pray for us to have generous hearts like yours, and on your feast day pray with us: Gracious Father, make us kind, generous, and aware of the needs of others. May we always be generous with our time, talent, and treasure. Guide us to find and fulfill our vocations and missions, and allow us to put all our gifts and talents at your service. Help us to live the liturgical traditions of the Church throughout the year. Purify our hearts and minds, confirm us in love, and make us saints. Bless all bishops, making them wise shepherds and virtuous leaders. We ask this in the name of Jesus. Amen.

DECEMBER 7

Saint Ambrose (340–397)

Saint Ambrose took his sacred responsibility as bishop so seriously that he never shied away from controversy, even when it meant correcting emperors. Born to a Christian Roman official, he spent his early life involved in politics, serving as consular general of Liguria and Aemilia, Italy, under Emperor Valentinian. While he was living in Milan, the people unanimously voted for him to become bishop of Milan in 374. His life and homilies were so powerful that they attracted Saint Augustine to the Church. In a letter to another bishop he once wrote, "Let no word escape your lips in vain or be uttered without depth of meaning." Ambrose wrote excellent Scripture commentaries, sermons, and hymns, and he is a Doctor of the Church. His relics rest in his basilica in Milan. Saint Ambrose is the patron saint of stone masons, beekeepers, candlemakers, and Milan and Bologna.

PRAYER

Saint Ambrose, thank you for your wisdom and example, which are so inspiring, and your writings, which continue to serve and bless the Church. Pray for us and with us on your feast: Dear Father, grant us wisdom and prudence in living our faith and making it known. Raise up virtuous, skilled Catholic lay leaders to assume positions in political life, and grant success to their efforts to uphold Catholic principles in the secular world. Give us many holy priests. Bless all bishops, making them holy, wise, and competent in administration and pastoral duties. We ask this in the name of Jesus. Amen.

DECEMBER 8

Feast of the Immaculate Conception

The Church teaches that Mary was preserved from original sin from the moment of her conception. The fruits of redemption won by Jesus were applied to her beforehand so she could fittingly bear the Savior of the world. She was free of concupiscence and remained free from sin throughout her life. In his declaration of the dogma of the Immaculate Conception, *Ineffabilis Deus*, Pope Pius IX stated, "We, by the authority of Jesus Christ, Our Lord, of the Blessed Apostles, Peter and Paul and by Our Own, declare, pronounce, and define that the doctrine which holds that the Blessed Virgin Mary, at the first instant of conception, by a singular grace and privilege of the omnipotent God, in consideration of the merits of Jesus Christ, the Savior of mankind, was preserved from all stain of original sin, has been revealed by God, and therefore is to be firmly and constantly believed by all the faithful."

PRAYER

Holy Mother Mary, pray for us to repent of our sins, and pray with us on your feast: Righteous Father, we praise you for preserving Mother Mary from all sin from the moment of her conception in the womb of Saint Anne. Thank you for so fitting and glorious a mother, who inspires us with her purity and intercedes for all our needs. Give us her virtues, especially purity, chastity, modesty, and humility. Help us to repent of all sin and heal from ongoing concupiscence. Guide us to learn and accept all the doctrines of your holy Church. Protect us from all evil and make us saints befitting so beautiful a mother. We ask this in the name of Jesus. Amen.

DECEMBER 9

Saint Juan Diego
Cuauhtlatoatzin (1468–1548)

Saint Juan Diego was a Chichimec peasant man from Mexico who converted to Christianity at fifty years old. Juan faithfully attended Mass, walking many miles. One day on his way to Mass, the Blessed Mother appeared to him and gave him a mission. She asked that he tell Bishop Juan Zumarraga to have a church built in her honor on Tepeyac Hill. Though Juan was initially fearful, Mary confirmed her message with miracles, including the healing of his uncle, the miraculous growth of Castilian roses on the hill in December, and the image of Mary that miraculously appeared inside his tilma. The bishop believed that Mary had truly appeared, and he had the church built as she asked. Soon after the apparitions, eight million Aztec natives converted to Christianity. Juan Diego spent the rest of his days as a hermit near the Basilica of Our Lady of Guadalupe, which still houses his miraculous tilma.

PRAYER

Saint Juan Diego, you were obedient to the Blessed Mother's request, even though you felt unworthy. Pray for us to love Mary and to do as she asks, and pray with us today: Gentle Father, give us confidence in your love and mercy, and help us always to turn to Mother Mary in all our needs, trusting in the power of her prayers and intercession. Inspire us to know our vocations and fulfill our missions. Guide us to faithfully accomplish the work you have given us to the very end. Make us saints. We ask this in the name of Jesus. Amen.

DECEMBER 10

Blessed María Emilia Riquelme y Zayas (1847–1940)

Blessed Maria Emilia, from Granada, Spain, was a talented and generous-hearted young girl who loved to paint, sing, and play piano. A mystical experience of Jesus and Mary when she was seven led her to desire a religious vocation. Her determination to follow her vocation met with her father's disapproval, and she also faced health obstacles. Being unable to enter a convent, but still determined to serve, she prayed at home and assisted at-risk women and seminarians. Others joined her charitable works, and they founded the Congregation of the Missionary Sisters of the Most Blessed Sacrament and Mary Immaculate. She served as superior for forty-four years until her death. She told her sisters: "The Eucharist is the paradise of the earth. Adoration is my hour in heaven, my recreation and spiritual rest." The sisters continue to serve in Spain, Portugal, Colombia, Bolivia, Brazil, Angola, the Philippines, and the United States. When he beatified her in 2019, Pope Francis noted, "The new blessed was an example of fervor in Eucharistic adoration and was generous in her service to those most in need."

PRAYER

Blessed María Emilia, thank you for your example of generous service to those in need. Pray with us on your feast: Gentle Father, give us the virtues of faith, love, and generosity, always looking to help others in need. Help us to be dedicated to prayer and finding and fulfilling our vocations and missions. Give us holy families and make us saints. Bless the Missionary Sisters, keeping them faithful to you. We ask this in the name of Jesus. Amen.

DECEMBER 11

Blesseds Martin of Saint Nicholas and Melchior Sanchez (d. 1632)

Blessed Martin of Saint Nicholas Lumbreras and Blessed Melchior Sanchez, two Spanish Augustinian priests and missionaries, represent many martyrs who died under Japanese ruler Tokugawa Iemitsu. Serving first in Manila, Philippines, these Augustinian priests were called to replace other priests who had been martyred in Nagasaki, Japan, in 1629. They ministered faithfully to the Catholic people of Nagasaki, disguising themselves as merchants so they could secretly minister to the people. Eventually they were caught, and they suffered severe tortures before being martyred for the Faith in 1632. Despite the danger and horrible sufferings, their commitment to bring the Gospel to all nations never wavered.

PRAYER

Blessed Martin and Blessed Melchior, pray for us to have the same missionary fervor and courage that drove you to share the Gospel in dangerous places. Pray with us today: Gracious Father, grant us the same heroic zeal and courage of the martyrs in living our faith and making you known, even in danger or persecution. Inspire us to believe in your miracles and hope in your mercy. Give us the grace to persevere in the Faith throughout our lives, and may we come to enjoy eternity with you in heaven. May we cling tenaciously to our faith and let nothing, even the threat of death, take it from us. Guide and protect all who are persecuted for their faith in you. Bless the Augustinian order, keeping it faithful to you. We ask this in the name of Jesus. Amen.

DECEMBER 12

Our Lady of Guadalupe

The Blessed Mother appeared to Saint Juan Diego on Tepeyac Hill (Mexico City) in 1531. She had the appearance of a native woman, and she asked Juan to go to Bishop Zumarraga to ask that a chapel be built in her honor. She said, "My dearest son, I am the eternal Virgin Mary … and it is my desire that a church be built here in this place for me, where, as your most merciful Mother and that of all your people, I may show my loving clemency and the compassion that I bear to the Indians, and to those who love and seek me." As a sign for the bishop, she filled Juan's tilma with Castilian roses. When he reached the bishop and opened his tilma to show the roses, the bishop fell to his knees, for on the tilma was a beautiful image of Our Lady. Through Mary's intercession, with Saint Juan Diego's help, millions of native Aztecs were converted to Christianity, recognizing Mary as their own mother. The miraculous image remains in the basilica of Our Lady of Guadalupe. She is the patron saint of Mexico.

PRAYER
Mother Mary, you appeared to Saint Juan Diego and told him of your love for his people. Inspire us with greater confidence in your love for us, and pray with us today: Loving Father, grant us the grace of a strong relationship with Mother Mary. Thank you for giving her to us to be our mother. Heal, convert, deliver, and protect us, and make us saints through her intercession. We ask this in the name of Jesus. Amen.

DECEMBER 13

Saint Lucy of Syracuse (d. 304)

Saint Lucy, from a Roman noble family, was only a child when she made a vow of virginity and died a martyr for Jesus during the persecution under Emperor Diocletian. Her name means light, as she was certainly a light of purity in a dark world. While little is known of her story, we know that she was subjected to torture before she was finally killed. Her relics are kept in Venice, Italy, and she is one of the women included in the list of saints invoked in the first Eucharist Prayer. Saint Lucy is the patron saint of the blind and those with eye disorders.

PRAYER

Saint Lucy, pray for us to bear the light of Christ to the world as you did, and pray with us: Dear Father, grant us purity, strength, and fidelity, and make us true Christian witnesses in the world. Inspire us to love you above our lives and not be afraid of living our faith fully, and dying for it if necessary. Conform our thoughts, actions, and lives to Jesus in total surrender to you. Grant parents the grace to help their children form good habits and virtues from an early age. Teach children to trust in you and believe that you honor their prayers. Protect the purity and innocence of all, but especially of children. Allow us to carry the light of Christ into the darkness of the world without fear. We ask this in the name of Jesus. Amen.

DECEMBER 14

Saint John of the Cross (1541–1591)

Saint John of the Cross was a religious, mystic, and reformer, who assisted Saint Teresa of Ávila in reforming the Carmelite order, eventually forming the Discalced Carmelites. Opposed by many in the Carmelite order for trying to bring back the austerity of the original rule, he was persecuted and unjustly imprisoned, yet he always maintained charity. In his teaching and writing, he emphasized the soul's ascent to God through detachment from everything, including worldly desires, passions, and even people. In the end, we must be attached only to God. He described contemplation as "nothing else than a secret and peaceful and loving inflow of God." A Doctor of the Church, known as the Mystical Doctor, he wrote *The Ascent of Mount Carmel, The Dark Night of the Soul,* and *The Spiritual Canticle.* Saint John is the patron saint of mystics.

PRAYER

Saint John of the Cross, you sought God always, no matter the trials you faced, and you taught us how to seek Him in deep prayer. Pray for us and with us today: Gracious Father, make us pious, humble, detached, and self-disciplined. Give us courage to surrender ourselves to you and make us unwavering in our commitment to prayer. Grant us the strength and will to endure the purifications you send us and to receive your gift of contemplation so that we may live in union with you. Allow us to know you so as to make you known. Bless the Discalced Carmelite order, keeping it faithful to you. We ask this in the name of Jesus. Amen.

DECEMBER 15

Saint Paul of Latros (d. 956)

Saint Paul of Latros (also known as Saint Paul the Younger), born in Pergamos in modern-day Turkey, became a monk in Greece along with his brother. Yet he was so eager to grow closer to God that he wanted to become a hermit, committing his whole life to prayer and sacrifice. To fulfill this dream, he moved to Mount Latros in Bithynia in Asia Minor, where he practiced continual prayer and mortification. When others were attracted to his holiness and wished to join him, he established eremitical communities, called lauras, to help them live a disciplined religious life. Later, he moved to a cave on the island of Samos, but again, when men followed him, wishing to live as he did, he set up lauras for them as well, before returning to Latros, where he died.

PRAYER

Saint Paul, you longed to live in complete union with God, yet you never neglected to love and serve those who came to you for spiritual guidance. Pray with us today: Merciful Father, grant us the gifts of contemplation and simplicity of life, and help us to use all our talents and gifts in your service without reserve. Purify our hearts and minds. Strengthen in us the virtues of self-control and charity. In your goodness, teach us how to perform penance for our sins and those of the world. May we always pursue the highest degree of virtue and holiness, with the help of your grace. Make us saints. We ask this in the name of Jesus. Amen.

DECEMBER 16

Saint Adelaide (931–999)

Saint Adelaide was born in France, the daughter of King Rudolph II of Burgundy. Caught in the middle of fierce political rivalries, she was married and widowed young, and was even imprisoned for a time. Holy Roman Emperor Otto the Great of Germany finally came to her rescue and married her, which allowed him to take power in Italy. The Italian and German people loved their empress. After Otto died, their son, Otto II, came to power, but his wife, Theophano, made life difficult for Adelaide. When Otto II also died, Theophano sent Adelaide away. Only after Theophano's sudden death did Adelaide return to court, acting as regent for her grandson Otto III. She generously assisted the poor and founded churches and monasteries. Saint Adelaide is the patron saint of widows, abuse victims, and people in second marriages.

PRAYER

Saint Adelaide, you were a faithful wife, mother, and ruler, but above all, you strove always to be a faithful Christian. Pray for us to be faithful, and pray with us today: Heavenly Father, keep us faithful to the duties of our state in life, remembering that you are with us in the present moment. May we always allow your beauty to shine through us in graciousness, hospitality, and friendship with others. Help us to be generous, and grant us the grace to make amends when we offend and to forgive others who hurt us. Heal all jealousy and give us peace and harmony in our relationships. Make us saints. We ask this in the name of Jesus. Amen.

DECEMBER 17

Saint Begga (d. 693)

Saint Begga came from a family of saints. Blessed Pepin of Landen and Saint Ita were her parents, Saint Gertrude of Nivelles her sister, and Saint Arnulf of Metz, France, was her father-in-law. Her son was Pepin of Heristal of the Carolingian dynasty. She was a faithful and committed wife and mother. After her husband, Ansegilius, died, she built a Benedictine convent in Belgium, where she served as abbess for the rest of her life.

PRAYER

Saint Begga, thank you for your example of following God's call in both a married and then religious vocation. Pray with us today: Gentle Father, help us to pray deeply, carefully discern our vocations, and fulfill our missions. Guide us in understanding what you are asking of us. Assist us in fulfilling all the duties in our state in life. Teach us how to die to ourselves and grow in all virtues every day to do your will. Instill in us the gift of hospitality that constantly encourages and uplifts others. Allow our families to become domestic churches that foster holiness. Make us saints. Bless the Benedictine order, keeping it faithful to you. We ask this in the name of Jesus. Amen.

DECEMBER 18

Saints Rufus and Zosimus (d. c. 107)

Saints Rufus and Zosimus were from Antioch, and they were arrested and brought in chains to Rome in company with Saint Ignatius of Antioch during the persecutions under the Roman Emperor Trajan. Their firm determination to cling to Christ resulted in their martyrdom only a few days before Saint Ignatius. They were killed by the wild beasts in the arena. Their witness in the early Church was so strong that Saint Polycarp exhorted the Philippians to follow their example, saying, "Wherefore I exhort all of you that you obey the word of righteousness, and exercise all patience, which you have seen set forth for you before your eyes, not only in the Blessed Ignatius and Zosimus, and Rufus, but in others that have been among you; and in Paul himself, and the rest of the apostles."

PRAYER

Saints Rufus and Zosimus, pray for us to stand firm in our faith no matter the cost, and pray with us on your feast day: Righteous Father, grant us burning faith, hope, and charity, and make us courageous in living our faith in all circumstances. Inspire us to pray with constancy and always act in loving obedience to you. May we never cease to be your faithful witnesses. We ask this in the name of Jesus. Amen.

DECEMBER 19

Martyrs of Plock (d. 1939–1945)

These 108 martyrs from Poland include bishops, priests, religious, and laypeople who were executed by the Nazis during World War II. Some were killed for their deep Catholic Faith and some for protecting or hiding Jewish people. Hitler wanted to destroy the Catholic Polish nation and exterminate people of the Jewish faith. There are many beautiful stories of religious sisters, such as Sister Klemensa Staszewska, who hid Jewish girls in a convent, or Sisters Ewa Noiszewska and Martha Wolowska, who were shot for protecting Jewish children. Blessed Maria Anna Biernacka, a laywoman, took the place of her pregnant daughter-in-law and was one of ten people killed in retaliation for a German soldier being killed by a resistance fighter. Seventy-eight of these martyrs were killed in the concentration camps at Dachau and Auschwitz.

PRAYER

Martyrs of Plock, thank you for your witness of standing firm in your Catholic Faith and for your solidarity with and protection of oppressed people of the Jewish faith. Pray with us on your feast day: Dear Father, through the intercession of the blessed martyrs of Plock, give us the virtues of loyalty, fraternity, strength, and courage. Inspire us to know, love, and serve you and others for love of you. Guide us to cling to our faith through trial and persecution, being true witnesses to it. Grant us the grace to protect the innocent and vulnerable. Fill us with the Holy Spirit and make us saints. We ask this in the name of Jesus. Amen.

DECEMBER 20

Blessed Peter de la Cadireta (d. 1277)

Blessed Peter, a Dominican priest, continued the work of Saint Dominic, preaching against the Albigensian heresy in his home country of Spain. He had been a companion and student of Saint Raymond of Penyafort, and he became the inquisitor after the two before him were martyred. His powerful and relentless preaching enraged some of those who had succumbed to the heresy and did not want to be converted back to the Catholic Faith. Nevertheless, he continued to try to help them convert, heedless of the danger to himself. Eventually, they acted upon their anger and stoned him to death in Urgell, Spain, in 1277.

PRAYER

Blessed Peter, pray for us to imitate your witness of courage and fidelity to the Catholic Faith, and pray with us on your feast day: Dear Father, give us the virtues of zeal, loyalty, commitment, and courage. Inspire us to truly know our faith so we can effectively help others to understand it when they are confused or misled. Deliver us from false religions and ideologies that cause so much confusion. Open the hearts of those who are confused to be able to hear the truth. Grant power to preachers and evangelists, and protect all who are being persecuted for their faith. Bring us peace from our enemies. Fill us with the gifts and fruits of the Holy Spirit, and make us saints. Bless the Dominican order, keeping it faithful to you. We ask this in the name of Jesus. Amen.

DECEMBER 21

Saint Peter Canisius (1521–1597)

Saint Peter Canisius, born in the Netherlands, studied theology and then, inspired by Saint Peter Faber, became a Jesuit. A true reformer, he was sent to Germany to bring people who had fallen into Protestantism back to the Catholic Faith. He was so effective in helping people understand the Faith and come back to the Church that he is called the second Apostle to Germany. His influential writings include a catechism, called the *Summa Doctrinae Christianae*, which was one of the chief Catholic works of the Catholic Reformation. He advised popes, attended the Council of Trent, and supported Catholic education and the Catholic press. Pope Pius XI proclaimed him a Doctor of the Church in 1925.

PRAYER

Saint Peter, God gave you the gift of wisdom, and you used it to serve the Church and draw people to the Faith. Pray for us and with us on your feast: Loving Father, give us the virtues of faith, hope, and charity. Inspire us to seek the truth, and guide us to learn, understand, and accept our faith, especially through reading Scripture and the *Catechism*. May all children be inspired by their parents and catechetical teachers to love and serve you. Bless and protect catechists, Catholic writers, and the Catholic press, keeping them orthodox, clear, and persuasive. Bless the Jesuit order, keeping it faithful to you. We ask this in the name of Jesus. Amen.

DECEMBER 22

Saint Chaeromon (d. c. 250)

Saint Chaeromon was a faithful Egyptian bishop. As the bishop of Nilopolis during the reign of Roman Emperor Trajanus Decius, he faced danger and persecution for being a Christian leader. Although not directly murdered by the emperor's forces, the elderly bishop and his companions died for their faith while fleeing from the persecution into the desert, and they are honored as martyrs.

PRAYER
Saint Chaeromon, you served the Church faithfully as a shepherd during dangerous times, and we ask you to pray for us, that we may remain faithful to God no matter what may come. Pray with us today: Merciful Father, help us to grow in the virtues of prudence, temperance, fortitude, and justice. Inspire us to imitate the lives of all the saints and conform our thoughts, actions, and lives to Jesus in total surrender to you. Grant us the grace and diligence to be faithful to all the duties of our state in life, not despising lowly tasks, completing all that you give us to do. Form in us, and help us form in children, a beautiful character of integrity and virtue to the highest degree. Bring us peace from enemies and protect all who are persecuted for their faith. Bless all bishops, making them true shepherds and virtuous leaders. We ask this in the name of Jesus. Amen.

DECEMBER 23

Saint John of Kanty (1390–1473)

Saint John (also known as Saint John Cantius) made prayer, penance, and almsgiving his road to holiness. A country boy from Poland, he became a theology professor and completely dedicated himself to his teaching. Due to the jealousy of others, he was ousted for a time from his teaching position, and he served as a parish priest. Later, he was able to return to teaching. After his work was finished for the day, he would spend hours in prayer before the Blessed Sacrament. He led a contemplative, self-sacrificial life and was highly respected for his works of mercy for the poor, to whom he gave everything. Saint John of Kanty is the patron saint of Poland and Lithuania.

PRAYER

Saint John, your generous, humble service to God and the Church are a model for us. Pray for us to love as generously as you did, and pray with us today: Gracious Father, grant us the virtue of generosity and inspire us to persevere in prayer, fasting, and almsgiving. Grant us the gift of contemplation, making us true contemplatives in action. Grant strength, encouragement, and healing to victims of jealousy. Guide teachers and parents to be patient, gentle, encouraging witnesses of authentic Christian love. Make us saints. We ask this in the name of Jesus. Amen.

DECEMBER 24

Saints Irmina (d. 708) and Adela (d. c. 734)

Saints Irmina and Adela were sisters and princesses who both became saints. Their father, the Frankish King Dagobert II, helped Saint Irmina in her grief and loss after her husband-to-be, Count Herman, was murdered. He built a Benedictine abbey for her where she became abbess. Later, she assisted Saint Willibrord with money for his monastery. Saint Adela, too, knew the pain of loss and grief. She was married to a nobleman named Alberic, and after he died, she founded and became abbess of a Benedictine abbey in Germany. She was a student of Saint Boniface.

PRAYER

Saints Irmina and Adela, in your grief and loss, you gave all that you had to God, and He fulfilled your every desire. Pray for us and with us on your feast day: Heavenly Father, grant us the virtues of humility, poverty, and simplicity. Inspire us to truly live our faith in righteousness. Guide us to pray consistently and grant us the gift of contemplation. Make us contemplatives in action. Assist all who are suffering from grief, loss, and trauma, and grant them the help they need. Teach us how to be sensitive to their needs and hear our prayers for them. Make us saints. Bless the Benedictine order, making it faithful to you. We ask this in the name of Jesus. Amen.

DECEMBER 25

The Nativity of the Lord

Jesus Christ, the Son of God, was born in Bethlehem in the poverty of a stable. His arrival went largely unnoticed by the world, but it was announced to poor shepherds in the fields, as we read in the Gospel of Luke:

> And the angel said to them, "Fear not, for behold, I bring you good news of great joy that will be for all the people. For unto you is born this day in the city of David a Savior, who is Christ the Lord. And this will be a sign for you: you will find a baby wrapped in swaddling clothes and lying in a manger." And suddenly there was with the angel a multitude of the heavenly host praising God and saying, "Glory to God in the highest, and on earth peace among those with whom he is pleased!" (2:10–14)

God loves us so much that He sent His only Son to die for our sins. Jesus, obedient even to death, followed His Father's plan perfectly.

PRAYER

Dear Father, through the intercession of the infant Jesus, Mother Mary, and Saint Joseph, give us all virtues and draw us to yourself. Grant us the grace to welcome, rejoice, and savor this feast of your Son's Incarnation. May your angels help us draw nearer to you and become saints. Guide us to live the liturgical traditions of the Church throughout the year. We ask this in the name of Jesus. Amen.

DECEMBER 26

Saint Stephen (d. first century)

Saint Stephen was a deacon chosen to help the apostles with practical matters so they could preach. He was so effective that, to stop him from converting more people to Christianity, his enemies falsely accused him and stoned him to death. We read of his death in the Acts of the Apostles:

> But he, full of the Holy Spirit, gazed into heaven and saw the glory of God, and Jesus standing at the right hand of God. Then they cast him out of the city and stoned him. And the witnesses laid down their garments at the feet of a young man named Saul. And as they were stoning Stephen, he called out, "Lord Jesus, receive my spirit." And falling to his knees he cried out with a loud voice, "Lord, do not hold this sin against them." And when he had said this, he fell asleep. (7:55, 58–60)

Saint Stephen is honored as the first Christian martyr, and he is the patron saint of deacons and bricklayers.

PRAYER
Saint Stephen, thank you for your witness to the Faith and the power of forgiveness. Pray with us on your feast: Gracious Father, give us strength and courage. Inspire us to boldly proclaim and defend your Church. Heal our wounds, and grant us the grace to forgive others and to pray for those who persecute us. Help us to know whom we have offended and to make amends. Protect those being persecuted for their faith. We ask this in the name of Jesus. Amen.

DECEMBER 27

Saint John (first century)

Saint John was an apostle and a close, beloved friend of Jesus — one of the Lord's three closest friends and the one whom Jesus chose to care for His mother. John witnessed the Transfiguration, Jesus' suffering in the Garden of Gethsemane, Jesus' death on the cross (he was the only apostle who stayed at the foot of the cross), and the empty tomb. The son of Zebedee and brother of Saint James, he was the only apostle who did not suffer death by martyrdom. He attended the Council of Jerusalem, and he wrote the Gospel of John, three New Testament epistles, and the Book of Revelation. He is often symbolized by an eagle. Saint John is the patron saint of friendship, love, loyalty, and authors.

PRAYER

Saint John, you were the disciple whom Jesus loved, and you show us what it means to have an intimate friendship with the Lord. Pray for us and with us on your feast: Loving Father, help us to grow in all the virtues, especially charity, loyalty, and compassion. Inspire us to take care of the people and tasks you have entrusted to us. Make us true, sincere, loyal friends who show up for others in prayer and action. Grant unity to the Church throughout the world. We ask this in the name of Jesus. Amen.

DECEMBER 28

Holy Innocents

After the birth of Jesus, King Herod ordered that all male children in Bethlehem two years old and younger be slaughtered because of his paranoia that this newborn king would be competition for his throne. We read in the Gospel of Matthew:

> Then Herod ... became furious, and he sent and killed all the male children in Bethlehem and in all that region who were two years old or under, according to the time that he had ascertained from the wise men. Then was fulfilled what was spoken by the prophet Jeremiah: "A voice was heard in Ramah, weeping and loud lamentation, Rachel weeping for her children; she refused to be comforted, because they are no more." (2:16–18)

Although we do not know how many children were killed, the Holy Innocents are honored as martyrs, and they are the patron saints of babies.

PRAYER

Holy Innocents, your cruel death reminds us of the senselessness of evil, yet we also rejoice knowing that you are in heaven with God. Pray with us: Gentle Father, bless and protect all children, born and preborn. Bless and protect those who do active pro-life work, and heal and convert those who make or promote unjust laws that perpetuate injustice. Comfort and console all parents who have lost their children. We ask this in the name of Jesus. Amen

DECEMBER 29

Saint Thomas Becket (1118–1170)

Saint Thomas's conversion was astonishing. As chancellor of England, he was a friend and advisor to King Henry II. When he became archbishop of Canterbury, he recognized that his first loyalty must be to God. In spite of their friendship, he opposed King Henry's unjust undermining of Church authority. In fear for his life, he left England and fled to France for some years, but eventually he returned, and the struggle for control of the Church began again. One day Henry rashly remarked that someone should take care of "the problem that was Thomas," and some of his knights rushed off to do so, killing Thomas in Canterbury Cathedral. He died for the Catholic Faith and the Church.

PRAYER

Saint Thomas Becket, pray for us to have the courage to remain loyal to God first, even when it means difficulty in our relationships or danger to ourselves. Pray with us today: Righteous Father, fill us with the virtues of justice, commitment, determination, and courage. Inspire us to uphold the truths and doctrines of our Catholic Faith, and help us to stand firm in the face of persecution and suffering. Teach us how to be strong in setting boundaries and fighting abuse and injustice. Confirm us in love and make us saints. Bless all bishops, making them true shepherds and virtuous leaders. We ask this in the name of Jesus. Amen.

DECEMBER 30

Saint Sabinus (d. 303)

Saint Sabinus was a bishop during the time of the persecutions under Roman Emperor Diocletian. He and several companions were arrested and brought before Governor Venustian. Sabinus had his hands cut off before his companions, Saints Experantius, Marcellus, and others, who were then tortured and killed before him. Imprisoned in the dungeon, he cured a blind boy and then healed Governor Venustian himself. As a result, the governor and his whole family converted to Christianity and were martyred for their new faith. Finally, Saint Sabinus himself was martyred.

PRAYER

Saint Sabinus, you gave powerful witness to the love that is stronger than death. Pray with us today: Loving Father, fill us with the Holy Spirit. Guide us to learn our faith and to communicate it effectively to others. Grant us fortitude and compassion, and make us unafraid of suffering for love of you. Instill in us a love for the newly converted. Grant us many and holy priests. Protect all who are being persecuted for their faith. Make us saints. We ask this in the name of Jesus. Amen.

DECEMBER 31

Pope Saint Sylvester I (d. 335)

Pope Saint Sylvester I lived to see the Church freed from the dangers of persecution in the Roman Empire, as Christians enjoyed the newfound freedom afforded by the Edict of Milan. Pope Sylvester worked closely with Emperor Constantine I and was likely involved in the emperor's construction of major churches in Rome, especially Saint John Lateran and Saint Peter's Basilica. Sylvester labored to maintain Church integrity and boundaries. The pope also sent legates to the Council of Nicaea, which dealt with the Arian heresy. His pontificate lasted for twenty-one years.

PRAYER

Saint Sylvester, you governed the Church with wisdom during a period of growth and relative peace. Pray for the Church today, and pray with us on your feast: Heavenly Father, give us the virtues of humility, prudence, and fidelity. Bless your Church and keep her faithful to you in all circumstances. Bless all leaders in the Church and in society. Grant us the grace to work for peace through diplomacy without compromising what is just and true. May we never allow the state to influence how we practice our faith. Preserve religious liberty and freedom, and bless all who are persecuted for their faith in you. Bless the pope and bishops, making them true shepherds and virtuous leaders. We ask this in the name of Jesus. Amen.

Epilogue

I have been praying and am continuing to pray for you to grow closer to the Most Holy Trinity as you learn about and pray with the saints on their feast days. If we pray in power together, we can change the world. We can give each other encouragement that God, the Church, and the saints are with us and helping us. We can begin again (as Saint Francis de Sales loved to say) to bring Christian principles and civilization to bear upon this weary and traumatized world. Let us pray together in unity with all the saints who love us so much and want us to be in heaven with them one day. Let us begin again. God bless you.

Acknowledgments

Thank you to all the saints who have been praying for and with me. What a privilege and awesome education it has been to learn about all of you. I have learned so much and now have so many more new friends and intercessors in heaven. Thanks also to all of you here on earth who prayed for me and helped me finish. I so appreciate Gianna's help with social media, Justin's with house and yard work so I could write, and Mary Beth Hayes' help with preliminary editing. Thank you to all the field testers (a long list) who used the book, praying the prayers and giving me feedback. I could not have done this without all the people who prayed for me, including the Catholic Writer's Guild. I also thank Mary Beth Giltner, my editor, and Rebecca Martin at OSV, who saw how this book could help people to pray and assisted me.

Calendar of Saints

JANUARY

1 Mary, Mother of God
2 Saints Basil the Great and Gregory of Nazianzus
3 Saint Genevieve
4 Saint Elizabeth Ann Seton
5 Saint John Neumann
6 Saint André Bessette
7 Saint Raymond of Peñyafort
8 Saint Severinus of Noricum
9 Saint Epictetus
10 Saint Agatho
11 Saint Theodosius the Cenobiarch
12 Saint Marguerite Bourgeoys
13 Saint Hilary of Poitiers
14 Blessed Odoric of Pordenone
15 Saint Maurus
16 Saint Marcellus I
17 Saint Anthony of the Desert
18 Blessed Juan Barrera Méndez
19 Saint Wulfstan
20 Blessed Cyprian Michael Iwene Tansi
21 Saint Agnes
22 Blessed Laura Vicuña
23 Saint Marianne Cope
24 Saint Francis de Sales
25 Conversion of Saint Paul
26 Saints Timothy and Titus
27 Saint Angela Merici
28 Saint Thomas Aquinas
29 Saint Sabinian of Troyes
30 Saint David Galván-Bermúdez
31 Saint John Bosco

FEBRUARY

1 Blessed Benedict Daswa
2 The Presentation of the Lord (Saints Simeon and Anna)
3 Saint Blaise
4 Saint Isidore of Pelusium
5 Saint Agatha
6 Saint Paul Miki and Companions
7 Saint Mél of Ireland
8 Saint Josephine Bakhita
9 Blessed Anne Catherine Emmerich
10 Saint José Luis Sánchez del Rio
11 Saint Saturninus and Companions
12 Saint Julian the Hospitaller
13 Blessed Jordan of Saxony
14 Saints Cyril and Methodius
15 Saint Claude de la Colombière
16 Saint Gilbert of Sempringham
17 The Seven Holy Founders of the Servite Order
18 Saint Theotonius
19 Saint Lucy Yi Zhenmei
20 Saints Jacinta and Francisco Marto
21 Saint Peter Damian
22 Saint Margaret of Cortona
23 Saint Polycarp
24 Blessed Josefa Naval Girbés
25 Blessed Rani Maria
26 Saint Alexander of Alexandria
27 Saint Gregory of Narek
28 Blessed Daniel Bottier
29 Saint Oswald of Worcester

MARCH

1 Saint David of Wales	16 Saint Dentlin
2 Saint Agnes of Bohemia	17 Saint Patrick
3 Saint Katharine Drexel	18 Saint Cyril of Jerusalem
4 Saint Casimir of Poland	19 Saint Joseph
5 Saint John Joseph of the Cross	20 Saint Jozef Bilczewski
6 Saint Colette	21 Saint Nicholas von Flüe
7 Saints Perpetua, Felicity, and Companions	22 Saint Darerca of Ireland
	23 Saint Turibius de Mogrovejo
8 Saint John of God	24 Saint Oscar Romero
9 Saint Dominic Savio	25 The Annunciation of the Lord
10 Saint John Ogilvie	26 Saint Margaret Clitherow
11 Saint Eulogius of Cordoba	27 Blessed Giuseppe Ambrosoli
12 Blessed Manuel Solórzano	28 Saint Tutilo
13 Blessed Agnellus of Pisa	29 Saint Cyril of Heliopolis
14 Saint Matilda	30 Saint Leonard Murialdo
15 Saint Louise de Marillac	31 Saint Balbina

APRIL

1 Saint Melito	16 Saint Benedict Joseph Labre
2 Saint Francis of Paola	17 Saint Stephen Harding
3 Saint Richard of Chichester	18 Saint Apollonius the Apologist
4 Saint Isidore of Seville	19 Saint Expeditus
5 Saint Vincent Ferrer	20 Saint Agnes of Montepulciano
6 The Martyrs of Persia	21 Saint Anselm
7 Saint John Baptist de la Salle	22 Saint Theodore of Sykeon
8 Saint Julie Billiart	23 Saint George
9 Saint Waldetrudis	24 Saint Fidelis of Sigmaringen
10 Saint Fulbert of Chartres	25 Saint Mark
11 Saint Gemma Galgani of Lucca	26 Saint Stephen of Perm
12 Saint Teresa of the Andes	27 Saint Zita
13 Saint Margaret of Castello	28 Saint Gianna Beretta Molla
14 Saint Lidwina	29 Saint Catherine of Siena
15 Saints Basilissa and Anastasia	30 Saint Pius V

MAY

1 Saint Joseph the Worker
2 Saint Athanasius
3 Saints Philip and James
4 Saint Florian
5 Saint Angelo
6 Blessed Jacinto Vera y Durán
7 Saint Domitian
8 Saint Maria Magdalene o Canossa
9 Blessed Maria del Carmen
   Rendiles Martínez
10 Saint John of Ávila
11 Saint Antonio de Sant'Anna Galvão
12 Venerable Edel Mary Quinn
13 Blessed Imelda Lambertini
14 Saint Matthias
15 Saint Isidore the Farmer
16 Saints Alypius and Possidius

17 Saint Paschal Baylon
18 Saint Eric of Sweden
19 Saint Dunstan
20 Saint Bernardine of Siena
21 Blessed Martyrs of Mexico
22 Saint Rita of Cascia
23 Saint John Baptist de Rossi
24 Blesseds Isidore Ngei Ko Lat
   and Mario Vergara
25 Saint Bede the Venerable
26 Saint Philip Neri
27 Saint Augustine of Canterbury
28 Saint Justus of Urgel
29 Saint Paul VI
30 Saint Joan of Arc
31 The Visitation of Our Lady to
   Saint Elizabeth

JUNE

1 Saint Justin Martyr and
   Companions
2 Saints Marcellinus and Peter
3 Saint Charles Lwanga and
   Companions (Achilleus
   Kiwanuka, Adolphus
   Ludigo-Mkasa)
4 Saint Optatus of Milevis
5 Saint Boniface
6 Saint Norbert
7 Blessed Marie-Thérèse de Soubiran
8 Saint William of York
9 Saint Ephrem
10 Saint Getulius
11 Saint Barnabas
12 Saint Onuphrius
13 Saint Anthony of Padua
14 Venerable María Beatriz del
   Rosario Arroyo y Pidal

15 Saint Vitus
16 Martyrs of Lang Coc, Vietnam
17 Saint Albert Chmielowski
18 Saint Elizabeth of Schönau
19 Venerable Matt Talbot
20 Saint Balthasar de Torres, Saint
   Vincent Kaun, and Blessed
   Francis Pacheco
21 Saint Aloysius Gonzaga
22 Saints John Fisher and Thomas More
23 Saint Alban
24 The Birth of Saint John the Baptist
25 Saint William of Vercelli
26 Saint Josemaría Escrivá
   de Balaguer
27 Saint Cyril of Alexandria
28 Saint Irenaeus
29 Saints Peter and Paul
30 Venerable Pierre Toussaint

JULY

1 Saint Junípero Serra
2 Saints Processus and Martinian
3 Saint Thomas
4 Blessed Pier Giorgio Frassati
5 Saint Anthony Mary Zaccaria
6 Saint Maria Goretti
7 The Ulma Family
8 Saint Withburga
9 Saint Paulina of Brazil
10 Blessed Emmanuel Ruiz and the Martyrs of Damascus
11 Saint Benedict
12 Saints Louis and Zélie Martin
13 Saint Clelia Barbieri
14 Saint Kateri Tekakwitha
15 Saint Bonaventure
16 Saint Marie-Madeleine Postel
17 The Carmelite Nuns of Compiègne
18 Saint Camillus de Lellis (USA)
19 Saint Macrina the Younger
20 Saint Aurelius
21 Saint Lawrence of Brindisi
22 Saint Mary Magdalene
23 Saint John Cassian
24 Saint Sharbel Makhlouf
25 Saint James
26 Saints Joachim and Anne
27 Saint Titus Brandsma
28 Saint Alphonsa of the Immaculate Conception
29 Saint Martha of Bethany
30 Saint Peter Chrysologus
31 Saint Ignatius of Loyola

AUGUST

1 Saint Alphonsus Liguori
2 Saint Peter Julian Eymard
3 Saint Lydia Purpuraria
4 Saint John Marie Vianney
5 Saint Nonna
6 Saints Justus and Pastor
7 Saint Miguel de la Mora
8 Saint Dominic
9 Saint Teresa Benedicta of the Cross
10 Saint Lawrence
11 Saint Clare
12 Saint Euplius
13 Blessed Michael McGivney
14 Saint Maximilian Mary Kolbe
15 Assumption of the Blessed Virgin Mary
16 Saint Stephen of Hungary
17 Blesseds Mary and Caspar Vaz and Blessed Bartholomew Laurel
18 Saint Jane Frances de Chantal
19 Blesseds Joachim Firayama-Diz, Mark Shineiemon, and Bartholomew Monfiore
20 Saint Bernard of Clairvaux
21 Saint Pius X
22 Saint Sigfrid
23 Saint Rose of Lima
24 Saint Bartholomew
25 Saint Louis IX
26 Augustinian Martyrs of Capsa
27 Saint Monica
28 Saint Augustine
29 The Passion of Saint John the Baptist
30 Saint Margaret Ward
31 Saint Raymond Nonnatus

SEPTEMBER

1 Saint Fiacre
2 Saint Solomon Leclerq and
Blesseds Leon Mopinot, Roger
Faverge, and Uldaric Guillaume
3 Pope Saint Gregory the Great
4 Saint Cuthbert
5 Saint Teresa of Calcutta
6 Saints Donatian, Laetus,
and Companions
7 Blessed Frédéric Ozanam
8 The Nativity of the Blessed Virgin Mary
9 Saint Peter Claver
10 Blesseds Anthony, Mary, and
Peter Sanga and Charles Spinola
11 Saint John Gabriel Perboyre
12 Blessed Maria Victoria Fornari Strata
13 Saint John Chrysostom
14 The Exaltation of the Holy Cross

15 Our Lady of Sorrows
16 Saints Cornelius and Cyprian
17 Saint Hildegard of Bingen
18 Saint Joseph of Cupertino
19 Saint Januarius
20 Saints Andrew Kim Taegon, Paul
Chong Hasang, and Companions
21 Saint Matthew
22 Saint Thomas of Villanova
23 Saint Pius of Pietrelcina
24 Our Lady of Mercy
25 Saint Albert of Jerusalem
26 Saints Cosmas and Damian
27 Saint Vincent de Paul
28 Saint Lorenzo Ruiz and Companions
29 Saints Michael, Gabriel, and
Raphael, Archangels
30 Saint Jerome

OCTOBER

1 Saint Thérèse of the Child Jesus
and the Holy Face
2 Holy Guardian Angels
3 Blessed Theodore Anne-Therese
Guerin
4 Saint Francis of Assisi
5 Saint Maria Faustina Kowalska
6 Blessed Marie Rose Durocher
7 Our Lady of the Rosary
8 Saint Reparata
9 Saint John Henry Newman
10 Saint Francis Borgia
11 Saint John XXIII
12 Blessed Carlo Acutis
13 Saint Edward the Confessor
14 Pope Saint Callistus I
15 Saint Teresa of Ávila
16 Saint Margaret Mary Alacoque

17 Saint Ignatius of Antioch
18 Saint Luke
19 The North American Martyrs
20 Saint Magdalene of Nagasaki
21 Blessed Karl of Austria
22 Saint John Paul II
23 Saint John of Capistrano
24 Saint Anthony Mary Claret
25 Blessed Martyrs of the Brothers
Hospitallers of Saint John of God
26 Blessed José Gregorio Hernández
Cisneros
27 Saint Frumentius
28 Saints Simon and Jude
29 Blessed Chiara Badano
30 Saints Marcellus and Cassian
31 Saint Wolfgang

NOVEMBER

1 All Saints' Day
2 All Souls' Day
3 Saint Martin de Porres
4 Saint Charles Borromeo
5 Saints Elizabeth and Zechariah
6 Saint Leonard of Noblac
7 Saint Peter Wu Guosheng
8 Blessed John Duns Scotus
9 Saint Benignus of Benen
10 Saint Leo the Great
11 Saint Martin of Tours
12 Saint Josaphat
13 Saint Frances Xavier Cabrini
14 Saint Lawrence O'Toole
15 Saint Albert the Great
16 Saint Gertrude the Great
17 Saint Elizabeth of Hungary
18 Saint Rose-Philippine Duchesne
19 Saint Nerses the Great
20 Saint Felix of Valois
21 The Presentation of the Blessed Virgin Mary
22 Saint Cecilia
23 Blessed Miguel Agustín Pro
24 Saint Andrew Dũng-Lạc and 116 Companions
25 Saint Catherine of Alexandria
26 Saint Leonard of Port Maurice
27 Saint Maximus of Riez
28 Saint Catherine Labouré
29 Saint Saturninus
30 Saint Andrew

DECEMBER

1 Venerable Leo Dupont
2 Blessed John van Ruysbroeck
3 Saint Francis Xavier
4 Saint John Damascene
5 Saint Sabas
6 Saint Nicholas of Myra
7 Saint Ambrose
8 Feast of the Immaculate Conception
9 Saint Juan Diego Cuauhtlatoatzin
10 Blessed María Emilia Riquelme y Zayas
11 Blesseds Martin of Saint Nicholas and Melchior Sanchez
12 Our Lady of Guadalupe
13 Saint Lucy of Syracuse
14 Saint John of the Cross
15 Saint Paul of Latros
16 Saint Adelaide
17 Saint Begga
18 Saints Rufus and Zosimus
19 Martyrs of Plock
20 Blessed Peter de la Cadireta
21 Saint Peter Canisius
22 Saint Chaeromon
23 Saint John of Kanty
24 Saints Irmina and Adela
25 The Nativity of the Lord
26 Saint Stephen
27 Saint John
28 Holy Innocents
29 Saint Thomas Becket
30 Saint Sabinus
31 Pope Saint Sylvester I

Works Cited

Bunson, Matthew and Margaret. *Encyclopedia of Saints*, 2nd Edition. Huntington, IN: Our Sunday Visitor, 2014.

Butler, Alban. *Butler's Lives of the Saints*. Five-volume set.

—— *Butler's Lives of the Saints, Concise Edition, Revised and Updated*. Edited by Michael Walsh. San Francisco: Harper San Francisco, 1991.

Engelbert, Omer. *The Lives of the Saints*. Translated by Christopher and Anne Fremantle. New York: Barnes and Noble Books, 1994.

Foley, Leonard. *Saint of the Day: Lives, Lessons, and Feasts*, 4th Revised Edition. Edited by Leonard Foley, O.F.M. Revised by Pat McCloskey, O.F.M. Cincinnati, OH: Saint Anthony Messenger Press, 2001.

Gannon, Megan. *Special Saints for Special People: Stories of Saints with Disabilities*. Waterford, CT: Twenty-Third Publications, 2019.

English translation of *The Liturgy of the Hours*. Washington, DC: International Commission on English in the Liturgy Corp., 1974.

O'Malley, Vincent J. *Saints of Africa*. Huntington, IN: Our Sunday Visitor, 2001.

Remery, Michel. *Online with the Saints*. Huntington, IN: Our Sunday Visitor, 2020.

Sisters of Notre Dame of Chardon, Ohio. *Saints and Feast Days: Lives of the Saints with a Calendar and Ways to Celebrate*. Chicago: Loyola Press, 1985.

About the Author

Belinda Terro Mooney is an author, speaker, coach, and instructor. She is mom to seven grown children, whom she homeschooled. She strives to know God so as to make Him known as a Secular Carmelite. Belinda is the author of seven published books (and many upcoming ones). She writes about the saints, the Three Works of Reparation, Catholic history, mental illness, addictions, mental health (including grief), and wellness (including the Therapeutic Lifestyle Changes). She also speaks on these topics. Belinda is a PCCI trained coach working toward ICF certification. She loves to coach Catholic women (especially moms) as well as Catholic authors, coaches, and therapists. She is a Certified Virtuous Leadership Consultant, Licensed Master Social Worker (LMSW), and Licensed Chemical Dependency Counselor (LCDC). As an adjunct professor of human services, she teaches basic counseling skills and addictions courses. When not helping people, Belinda loves praying (at Mass, in adoration, and in intercessory prayer), spending time with family and friends, singing, swimming, jogging, and reading. Connect with her on Instagram and Facebook @belindaterromooney, and at belindaterromooney.com.